Slow Motion

Slow Motion
stories about walking

Andie Miller

JACANA

Grateful acknowledgement is made for permission to reprint excerpts from the following copyrighted works: Selection from *Bloodsong* by Leon de Kock. Copyright © 1997 Leon de Kock. Reprinted with permission of Snailpress.

The title poem from *gone to the edges* by Leon de Kock. Copyright © 2006 Leon de Kock. Reprinted with permission of Protea Book House.

Selections from *Tongues of their Mothers* by Makhosazana Xaba. Copyright © 2008 Makhosazana Xaba. Reprinted with permission of the University of KwaZulu-Natal Press.

The title poem from *These Hands* by Makhosazana Xaba. Copyright © 2005 Makhosazana Xaba. Reprinted with permission of the Timbila Poetry Project.

○ ○ ○

Some of the material in this book first appeared in the following publications: African Writing, Eclectica, Itch, Journal of Commonwealth Literature, LitNet, Mail & Guardian, New Contrast, River Teeth, Spectator, Sunday Independent and Wiser Review.

Slow Motion was approved for the degree Master of Arts (Writing) from the University of the Witwatersrand, Johannesburg.

First published by Jacana Media (Pty) Ltd in 2010

10 Orange Street
Sunnyside
Auckland Park 2092
South Africa
+2711 628 3200
www.jacana.co.za

© Andie Miller, 2010

ISBN 978-1-77009-870-1

Maps by Wendy Job
Cover design by Elsabe Milandri

Set in Ehrhardt 12/16pt
Printed and bound by Ultra Litho (Pty) Limited, Johannesburg
Job No. 001240

See a complete list of Jacana titles at www.jacana.co.za

for everyone who trusted me with their stories

And for Melissa

I'm glad we've
crossed paths.

All best wishes
Andie

Acknowledgements

My thanks to everyone who so generously agreed to talk with me and allow me to translate their stories onto the page. We are frequently warned against writers and journalists, and the trust that I was given was one of the greatest gifts of writing this book.

Then there has been a small group of teachers in the Wits creative writing programme without whom the project would not have become a reality. Michelle Adler, David Bunn and Tim Couzens (the ABC of Travel Writing), who initially opened doors and windows for me. And most importantly Michael Titlestad – who first pointed out to me that I was writing a book – for his hours of coffee and conversation, and showing me what a difference one good teacher can make.

Thanks also to Ivan Vladislavić for always being willing to answer the little questions, even on the way to the airport.

I spent many hours in libraries, which would not have been as pleasant without the help of a couple of extraordinary librarians who went way beyond the call of duty, and challenged the stereotype of the scary librarian. The kindness of Rebecca Eland and Cynthia Ngwenya from Wartenweiler and Norwood libraries made the task so much easier.

Thanks to Maggie Davey, Bridget Impey and the team at Jacana for their unswerving enthusiasm and faith in the project.

Thanks to my editor Priscilla Hall for her meticulous care and attention to detail. I may not always have acted on her advice (any errors are entirely my own), but I always valued her input, which forced me to think.

And finally to my friends and family, who at times were puzzled about how one could write a whole book about walking, but supported me nonetheless.

Contents

The sidewalk is a history book.
– Joni Mitchell

An unhurried sense of time is in itself a form of wealth.
– Bonnie Friedman

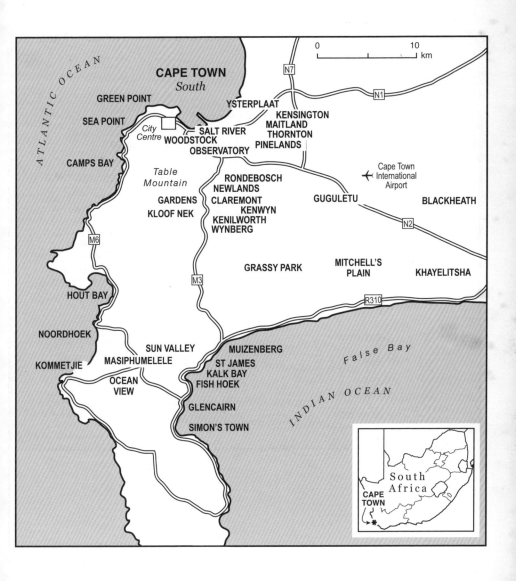

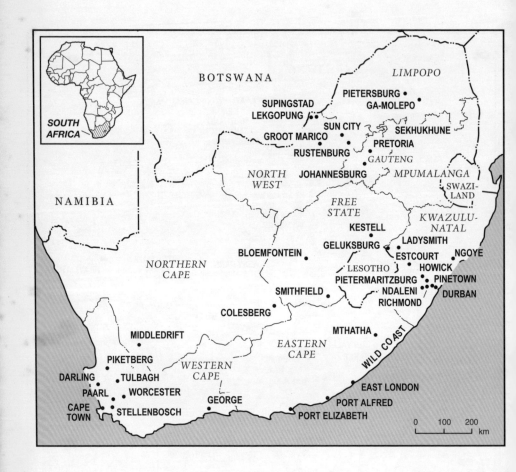

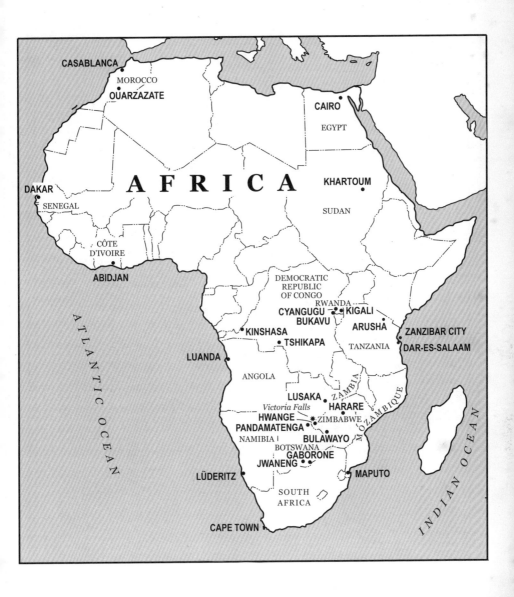

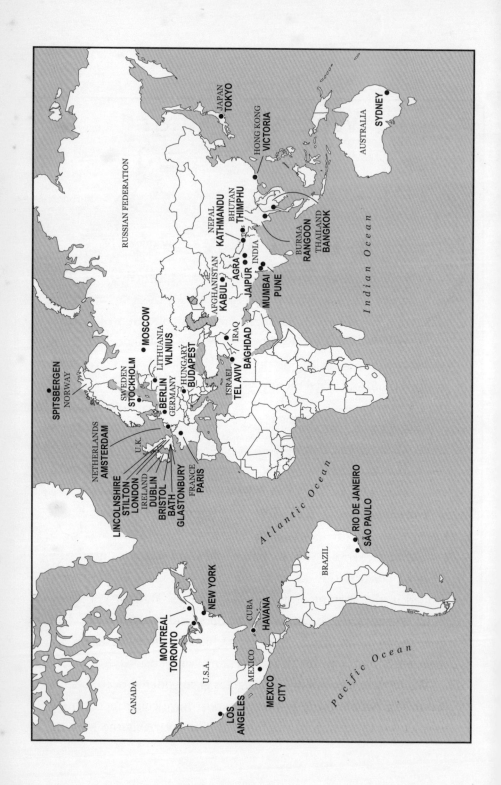

Preface:
Who is Walking?

In 1951 Ray Bradbury wrote his short story 'The Pedestrian'. The story records the last walk of Leonard Mead, the sole remaining pedestrian in AD 2053. Though part of a collection of science fiction stories, it was inspired by Bradbury's experience when out walking in Los Angeles one night with a friend. A police officer stopped them and asked them what they were doing. 'Just walking,' Bradbury replied. 'Well, don't do it again,' said the policeman.

Los Angeles, Bradbury's home, is an extreme case in its autocentricity, but this suspicion of pedestrians is not new. Thomas de Quincey describes – in his account of his 1802 journey from Wales to London – the 'criminal fact of having advanced by base pedestrian methods'. The origins of a vagrant being described as a *tramp* don't require too much speculation.

In South Africa, with its particular history, remnants of the artificial construction of economic access along racial lines are echoed in the current profiles of pedestrians. Walking continues to be considered a practice of the poor and marginalised. And since the majority of the poor remain black, white pedestrians are regarded, if not with suspicion, certainly with curiosity.

While walking at all in Los Angeles is considered perverse, the profiles of people using public transport have come increasingly to resemble those in Johannesburg: almost invariably the working poor, and people of colour. But while in Joburg this reflects South Africa's history, in Los Angeles, with its largely immigrant population on the bus, it highlights America's relationship to the rest of the world, and the massive migrations of people globally, often in search of the American Dream.

At Los Angeles International Airport, with its 23 000 parking spaces, 'the future touches down', writes travel writer Pico Iyer – though many new arrivals don't seem to travel further than the vicinity of the airport and end up working at hotels and gift shops, where their foreign tongues are a valuable asset.

And then there are those who cross the borders in less formal ways.

Over the past few centuries, most of Europe has developed a rich culture of urban walking which is not divided along class lines, as well as decent public transport systems. America, by contrast, has lapsed further and further into autocentricity, apparently taking South Africa with it. It seems as if the rallying cry of 'One man one vote' has alarmingly been replaced with 'One person one car'. The majority of South Africans, it would seem, rich and poor alike, would support Margaret Thatcher's assertion that 'if a man found himself on a bus at the age of twenty-five he knew he had failed in life'.

From the hijackings in Johannesburg to the oil wars initiated by the US (not to mention accidents and everyday pedestrian deaths), Henry Ford's dream seems to be responsible for a lot of violence. Shortly into the twentieth century, Ford stated: 'I will build a motor car for the great multitude ... it will be so low in price that no man making a good salary will be unable to own one.'

In his 1923 autobiography *My Life and Work*, he reflected on the 7882 distinct work operations required to manufacture the Model T. 'Of these, 949 were classified as heavy work requiring strong, able-bodied, and practically physically perfect men; 3338 required men of ordinary physical development and strength.

The remaining 3595 jobs were disclosed as requiring no physical exertion and could be performed by the slightest, weakest sort of men. In fact, most of them could be satisfactorily filled by women or older children.' Of the lightest jobs 'we found that 670 could be filled by legless men, 2637 by one-legged men, 2 by armless men, 715 by one-armed men, and 10 by blind men.'

When people ask me why I don't drive, my answer varies: from economics, to fear of the machinery, to the desire to remain connected to life on the street. All of these are true for me in one way or another. I mistakenly assumed, though, that I was unique in this regard. Most non-drivers, I thought, if not a result of disability or age, either can't afford the car and driving lessons or are simply afraid of it.

So, when I asked a friend who got his licence at almost forty if he had found it a traumatic experience, I was surprised that he said it wasn't really fear that had stopped him from learning to drive sooner. 'I just don't think I'm that kind of person,' he said. It got me wondering what kind of person that is. Or rather, what kind of person is it who chooses *not* to drive? Perhaps there were more of us than I'd imagined.

Further investigation revealed a number of people who walk from choice, and curiously the majority of them seemed to be writers, artists and political activists. It seemed there was a historical link between walking, creativity and protest. I decided to take a closer look at this largely overlooked subculture, and why pedestrianism has been given such a bad name. The essays that follow are the result.

The stories have been written over a period of a few years, and things have inevitably changed in that time. The world has changed as much as individual lives, and so the collection has also become something of a documentary project as many people drive more and walk less.

On 22 August 2009 Ray Bradbury turned eighty-nine. Though

he has taken us to outer space, he has never driven a car. He continues to live, work and walk in Los Angeles.

Andie Miller
Johannesburg
May 2010

Conscientious Objections

A watched kettle takes longer to boil, say the quantum physicists. With this in mind, my housemates and I decided to stick newspaper articles on the kitchen wall for each other to read while we were waiting. It was my week of cut and paste, in July 1988, and this was how I first really became aware of David Bruce.

Of course I had been vaguely conscious of him until that point; his trial had been going on for months. But the idea that anyone would actually be sent to jail for refusing to do national service had not yet become a reality to me. As South African women we faced other threats of violence, but being conscripted into the army was never one of them, and not one I could fully digest.

Turning to the *Weekly Mail* that Friday, what first caught my attention was an article that had originally appeared in the *Village Voice* in New York. It told how Mbongeni Ngema, director of the hit musical *Sarafina!*, was being taken to court by one of his actresses, an American who had stepped in when one of the South African girls became ill. She alleged that he'd hit her with a leather belt. He explained that it was part of his directing process, and his way of keeping order. It was cultural, he said. Outraged, the African-American woman protested that this was unacceptable to her.

Also in the *Mail* that week was an interview with actor John Kani, in which he suggested that, in his opinion, no whites were committed to change.

And then the photograph, on the front page of the *Star* on Tuesday the 26th of July 1988, of David Bruce with a yellow daisy in his lapel. It had been decided. He had been sentenced to six years in jail.

These memories flooded back to me a decade and a half later, after watching John Kani's powerful play *Nothing But the Truth*. And I wondered where it was that the truth was located. It seemed to me somewhere in the subtext, between what we articulate and what we are less sure of. As Kani reminded us, our collective history is a complex and contradictory one.

David, who had since become a friend and work colleague of mine after serving two years in prison (essentially his prescribed two years of military service), had quietly been working at Ceasefire and then at the Centre for the Study of Violence and Reconciliation as a researcher of militarisation and policing issues; with a view to ending the former and transforming the latter. He had also recently acquired a driver's licence.

I had always assumed that he had simply been afraid of driving, so it came as a surprise when he told me he hadn't driven because he just didn't think he was that kind of person

Though he now owns a car, he complains about it eating into his walking time and still seizes any opportunity to travel on foot. On the day of our interview he takes a two–hour stroll over to me.

'Well, the most important thing is being an environmentalist,' he says. 'Nature, and protecting the earth, are very important to me. Cars are just… each individual has got this enormous piece of metal and goes around discharging air pollution simply to get around. It seems like such a selfish thing. But also, there was never a car in my family. I'm the first one in my family to own a car.'

David's late mother's family were refugees from Nazi Germany who came to South Africa in 1939; his father, British, arrived in the country in 1958. David and his brother Eric grew up near the inner city of Johannesburg, in Berea. David now lives one suburb over, in Yeoville, as does his father, and Eric is in England. Their father did try to learn to drive a number of times, but failed. Perhaps, David suggests, this instilled fear in him too about learning to drive. (It makes me think about how no women in my family have ever driven.)

'But also if you grow up in the inner city,' he adds, 'the sense of traffic is very chaotic. It's not like growing up in the suburbs, where you can take the family car around the block. And the idea of learning to drive in that environment is much more frightening.'

My brief spell at driving lessons was with an instructor who insisted on throwing me into the deep end of early morning rush hour Joburg city centre traffic. I suspect this was what finally decided me not to put myself through the ordeal.

'Though I always had a sense that I didn't have the right temperament for it,' he continues. 'My consciousness of the present… You have to be very aware of what's going on around you if you're driving, and in some ways my consciousness seemed quite broken.

'But there's also a sense of real enjoyment and freedom in walking. I can walk from my flat in Yeoville to work in Braamfontein without stopping once. Driving is a completely different experience because you're much more constrained by rules.'

Johannesburg is notorious for its one-way streets. One of them almost cost me my life as a passenger in a near-fatal accident, when a friend drove in the wrong direction. And I've heard a number of moans about the constraints and frustrations caused by urban renewal and building operations in Braamfontein.

'As a driver you need to be very conscious of your visual environment. I don't see things around me all the time. Part of the sensual pleasure of walking is a visual experience; it's the pleasure of being amongst trees.' With approximately six million trees Joburg has the biggest man-made forest in the world, even though rapid development is causing deforestation of the urban environment, and many of the established trees are reaching the end of their life cycle and beginning to decline.

'And the light,' David continues. 'The sense of the natural environment around you. There's an emotional richness to that. But I don't notice the features of the houses that I'm passing.'

He suggests that his visual awareness may be underdeveloped. A result, perhaps, of growing up with a blind mother. Learning to 'stay in the visual' is something he thinks he learned recently on a trip from Joburg to Cape Town, 'after I nearly killed us half a dozen times.

'But there's also an immediacy to walking. Even walking through Hillbrow, I have a sense of being enriched by it. A sense of being on the racial frontier. Not a single other white person in sight. Unless I pass by Look & Listen records at nine o'clock in the morning. Then I see Carlos opening the shop.'

I know what he means. When I read Phaswane's Mpe's novel *Welcome to Our Hillbrow*, it struck me how the streets that Mpe names are the same ones I walked when I first arrived from Cape Town in 1984. And yet they are different streets now. The corner of 'the most notorious Quartz Street' and the 'obscure' Kapteijn, where I lived, is an area I avoid now, skirting around the edges of the suburb, past the police station, up Solitary Lane and over Constitution Hill as I walk. There's a peculiar ambivalence to this experience, of wanting to participate in something new but not knowing one's place in it.

This inevitably leads us to questions of safety. Does David, as a man, feel safer than I do? Has he had any experiences of violence?

In the light of the number of incidents he discloses (and particularly now that he has a car), I am surprised that he is still walking. It seems like an act of passive resistance. 'But I'm not a pacifist,' he emphasises. 'I fight back!'

His first experience of being attacked was in 1991. I become aware throughout the conversation how well he recalls dates. It seems to me that this is David the researcher at work. It's as though many of his choices, which flow against the mainstream, are a process of research, to explore less popular choices in the realm of possibility: a 'What would happen if?' in order to observe alternatives at work, and show that they can be done.

He had recently moved to Gainsborough Mansions, the Herbert Baker building at the top of Nugget Hill, on the border of Hillbrow. 'My friend Karen had just got a new camera, Hillbrow was beginning to develop a certain ambience, and I thought it would make for some quite amazing photographs.' At the bridge above the Windybrow Theatre they were attacked. 'And we'd bought these mielies, so we threw them at the guys. I've got this image in my mind… it's like from *2001: A Space Odyssey*, where that bone goes flying up into the air.' From this point of view, with us laughing in hindsight, a flying mielie-as-weapon seems to be a more interesting urban African image than anything they could have captured on film. That time their attackers ran, and nobody was hurt.

Later that year he was walking across the park next to Abel Road. 'I had two worn-out veldskoens in my bag, and half a cabbage.' (I had been thinking about footwear. As long as I've known him, veldskoens have been David's shoes of choice.) 'And I saw five guys walking in a kind of wall towards me. It was like that image from the John Carpenter movie *Assault on Precinct 13*. The classic street terror image. In those days I had this strategy to scream as loud as I could and then to fight them off.' Which he did, and only after kicking one, and them running off, did he discover that he had been stabbed. But he still had his bag.

'Then I moved to Germiston, just next to the railway station, and I'd catch the last train. The 10.10 train. And walking from the station a guy attacked me, and I shouted at him.'

The last time he was attacked was the second Friday night of January 1999 as he was walking, in the twilight, to his parents for supper. In Berea a man accosted him. The plastic bag with jars of jam that he was carrying fell to the ground and broke. David punched him, and he was stabbed again. This time in the back of

5

his arm, closer to his heart.

At the Joburg Gen (the general hospital, deserted in the post-New Year lull, he speculates), the treatment cost him the money that he had with him. He had the realisation then that if he'd just handed over what he had, there would have been no violence. 'Overwhelmingly in these acts of criminality, the violence comes in where the victims have resisted.'

Now he does little night walking. Since 1999 he's been a practising Buddhist, and occasionally he walks to the Buddhist Centre in Kensington. He remains quite vigilant going through Bertrams. 'But I won't do Hillbrow.'

In *Welcome to Our Hillbrow*, Mpe describes his protagonist Refentše's reaction to his first night in Hillbrow after arriving from a rural village in Limpopo. 'Then you shuddered into wakefulness … A second gun shot rang in Twist Street, and you remembered Tiragolong with greater nostalgia than you ever imagined to be possible. A woman screamed for help. Police sirens went off loudly. You realised a few minutes later, from the fading sounds, that they were going to rescue someone else, elsewhere, and not the nearby screaming soul whose voice continued to ring relentlessly.'

David continues: 'But when I walk at night it's a different kind of walking. It's high-speed walking. And it almost uses an element of stealth. Then you have this experience that you can walk through places and almost have the sense that no one's actually seen you. People are accustomed to a certain kind of rhythm of the environment and so, when people do see you, you enter their space. So *you're* more likely to startle *them*.'

The issue of speed is the one that I'm most interested in, with people who choose to walk. David doesn't seem to feel pressurised by time. Is this accurate?

'No that's not true,' he says. He is very aware how caught up with stress he is when he leaves the front door to walk to work in the mornings. 'A self-imposed anxiety about my employers, and getting to the office on time, and the impression I'm creating when

I arrive late. There's a stress to do with the working day and being productive, so walking to work is always high-speed walking.'

Does he feel that learning to drive has changed his relationship to walking? 'Oh definitely. When I first got a car I suddenly had this feeling that my life had become much more busy and I didn't have any time for walking. The rich variety of things to do that the modern world offers you is much more available to you if you have a car, so you can go to Cinema Nouveau five nights of the week if you like. And you can go to the opening of this little exhibition at that little gallery, and you can make little dinner arrangements. Whatever takes your fancy. So driving also requires learning the skill of choosing. When you have fewer choices, choices are made for you. Before I had a car I had to follow set routes.

'And then there's also this issue of buying things. With a car you can go out and get things that you can bring back to your home. You can purchase big things. And this is the model being exported to the developing world. But it's unsustainable, this lifestyle that we take for granted.'

Does he consider himself a Marxist? 'No. Of course as a student almost everyone was once a Marxist, but by 1987 I was no longer a Marxist. It seemed to me a materialist philosophy that didn't really understand human beings.'

Now that he's driving, he also misses his interaction with taxi drivers. 'Everyone always seems to exclaim in shock and horror when I tell them what a taxi costs, but now I spend more than I've ever spent in a month on taxis, on car insurance. Especially since I've lost my no claim bonus.'

In February this year David had his first car accident. 'They don't really teach you when you're learning to drive about speed and dirt roads,' he says wryly. 'All the tests are on tarred roads. But gravel roads are a different story. I was on my way to Mountain Sanctuary Park and I had some idea that one could get out there fairly easily in about two hours. When I hit the dirt roads there was a sign that said *Road in bad condition – drive at own risk*, but towards the end I was racing because I was worried that I wouldn't get there before the gates closed at half past six. And my car spun out of control.' He was unhurt, but the car was beyond repair.

The most painful part of the process for him was the 'schlep' of the paperwork; of 'having to deal with the administrative side'. He was without a car from February to July, 'and it was actually quite nice,' he says. But now he's back in the driver's seat. 'Driving is about taking yours and other people's lives in your hands.'

The complexities and contradictions implicit in decision making are not new to David. Speaking of his choice to go to jail instead of to the army, he talks about the 'bizarre and peculiar heroic act' that people witnessed. 'But there was also a type of madness associated with it.' In 1999 he was diagnosed with bipolar (manic-depressive) disorder. And he was, he recognises now, in a bipolar episode at the time.

A manic phase involves heightened mental activity and lucidity, which gave him a very clear understanding of the situation. Questions of morality and principle were at stake, particularly with his family's history. 'In many ways it was an act of warfare,' he says. 'With all of the armed propaganda that was going on at the time... there was political potential. I saw all its dimensions, and being manic enabled me, as a usually introverted person, to make the decision.

'I was deeply affected by fear, and I wouldn't have been able to deal with physical assault. I didn't have the kind of temperament, the mental coolness, required for going underground. There were people going on trial all the time for various things, and being sent down for extended periods of time, and the government was able to portray them as terrorists. Armed struggle increased a kind of polarisation. But there were different potentialities here. It was one way of fighting the war, while being loyal to the soldiers on both sides. Of doing no harm.'

He adds soberly: 'I think that violence is what men are emotionally and physically programmed for. And when you're fighting a war, protection is achieved through vanquishing the enemy. If I had been forced to, I would have been a committed soldier.'

More recently, however, the war that either unites or divides us is the war on crime. And walking in the streets of Johannesburg is now, for David, a way of doing no harm. A way of trusting, despite fear, that humanity will prevail rather than savagery. And a way of crossing battle lines, when excessive consumerism itself appears to have become an almost violent act, particularly in relation to men and their cars.

As a driver, he has now become aware of the sense that pedestrians have to scurry out of the way of cars. 'I've had people driving virtually over my toes. But pedestrians can't afford to get into confrontations with cars. And when you're driving, you suddenly have that sense of power when people have to scurry around in front of you. Particularly the elderly. It's a type of tyranny.'

The gender dimension of not being able to drive had become an issue for him too. 'In a couple of relationships that I was involved in there was an enormous discomfort on my part. I was continuously being driven around by women. There's a sort of judgement of you by society, or sense that you're stupid if you don't buy into accepted lifestyles, that was challenging my masculinity. As if you can't be a real man if you don't drive.' And perhaps, it occurs to me, a similar perception by some if you won't carry a gun.

'The one thing I've always found incredibly difficult about walking is, I've always felt so visible. Not to fellow pedestrians, but to the gaze of the people in the cars. And I felt a sense of increasing marginalisation. So, getting a licence was a moment of liberation, but I really would have preferred not to buy into the whole materialism thing.'

For the past few years, as a Buddhist, he has been engaged in daily yoga and meditation. And while his sense of identification with it grows and diminishes in intensity ('I've never completely abandoned my Jewish identity'), it is, he believes, what has enabled him to keep balanced. He has never taken medication for his bipolar disorder.

'And walking?' I ask.

'Oh I'm sure the walking helps,' he smiles.

It's been three hours since he arrived on foot, armed only with pawpaws as a gift for me. But now the light has begun to fade and I suggest that we call a taxi for him. 'That's probably a good idea,' he agrees.

As he waves goodbye, we can smell the approach of a welcome Johannesburg thunderstorm.

Border Crossings

I was standing on Hollywood Boulevard, waiting for a bus. I know, it sounds like the beginning of a bad joke. But it isn't, believe me. If you've ever caught a bus in Los Angeles you'll know that it's tedious. It seems *Who Framed Roger Rabbit?* was closer to the truth than many people would care to admit, and General Motors crippled one of the best public transport systems in the world in the 1940s in order to sell more of their vehicles. GM was found guilty in 1949 of 'conspiring to monopolize sales of buses and supplies to companies owned by National City Lines', and fined five thousand dollars. But the damage was done.

As Judge Doom says in *Roger Rabbit*: 'I see a place where people get on and off the freeway. On and off, off and on all day, all night! Soon, where Toon Town once stood will be a string of gas stations, inexpensive motels, restaurants that serve rapidly prepared food. Tyre salons, automobile dealerships and wonderful, wonderful billboards reaching as far as the eye can see! My god, it'll be beautiful!'

As a non-driver, I found LA the only place in the world where walking felt pathological. Walking down Sunset Boulevard one evening to the Comedy Store, I had that familiar feeling of discomfort I experienced on my first walk down Quartz Street in Hillbrow in 1984. 'Well you know, about sixty-four hookers work this street,' my friend Elzabé had said (I don't know where she

11

got that figure). A sign at an entrance off Sunset Boulevard reads *Pedestrians not allowed*. Planners in the Sixties had declared that 'the pedestrian remains the largest single obstacle to free movement', and now, according to the National Highway Capacity Manual, pedestrians are endured as a 'traffic interruption'. Apparently the only walking seen as normal here was the Walk of the Stars, on Hollywood Boulevard, where tourists read the names of celebrities as they hopefully walked in their footsteps.

'Autopia' is the only one of Disneyland's original rides that remains, dating back to their opening day on the 17th of July 1955. But while each new freeway in LA promised to solve the growing traffic problem, gridlock became the order of the day, and Disneyland is probably the only place where Autopia still exists. There, however, not only pedestrians but all humans have been disposed of. In the new version of the ride, a giant video screen plays 'animated scenes of cars discussing life's challenges while providing insights into the world as they see it ... billboards along the highway advertise directly to the vehicle'. As visitors circle the tower building, shaped like a giant piston, windows provide glimpses into a three-dimensional model city inhabited exclusively by animated talking cars. This paved the way for the feature film of *Cars*, where Paul Newman, along with all the other actors, has been relegated to the soundtrack.

Anyway... I was standing waiting for the bus, with my best friend and guardian of my sanity: my walkman. The radio in LA was pretty good. So I switched on and heard: 'There were things I said to my son as he grew into manhood. You want your laundry fast, take it to that Chink on the corner. When you go to buy that car, don't let 'em try to Jew you down. I don't want you to take any shit from that man you work for. You're not his nigger. I did not view these things as a mark on him. They were just a necessary evil of living in a hard world ...

'This morning I went to his house to borrow his mower. Had it in the basement all winter, dad. Haven't brought it up, yet. You'll see it down there. In the basement, where I had never been, were all the things my son had learned from me. There were weapons. There were explosives. There were maps outlining a proposed White Homeland. There were newspapers: *The Spotlight, The Thunderbolt, The Torch, The Way, The Aryan Nations Newsletter.* There was a picture of Adolf Hitler. And beside it, also in a place of honor, was a picture of me.'

It was a play called *God's Country*, on at the ACT Theatre in Seattle. Must contact the playwright, I thought, sounds like a play we should do in South Africa.

The bus arrived.

After the Great Depression in the 1930s, and World War II, Americans were thankful for the birth of the suburbs, which enabled working class people to own their own homes. Government insisted on racially segregated developments, however, and the Federal Housing Authority Underwriting Manual stated that 'if a neighborhood is to retain stability, it is necessary that properties shall continue to be occupied by the same social and racial classes'. After 1950 this was outlawed by the Supreme Court, but divisions were already established, and the 'white fright' of the post–civil-rights period caused more people to flee to the suburbs, to 'places empty of anyone else's memories and rich with potential'. Now everything was spread out and far away, and public transport was poor. And thus the sprawl began. Individual car ownership, which had become affordable to the majority, became the aspiration. It is said that, in a poll during the war, 87 per cent of Americans stated the first thing they wanted after it ended was a new car.

Anita Bryant, after being crowned second runner-up to Miss America in 1959, performed in Flint, Michigan – home to one of General Motors' biggest manufacturing plants – carrying a giant sparkplug and singing 'You'll never walk alone'. There are five hundred bus routes in LA, but the majority of Angeleños pride themselves on never having caught a bus, which they see as only for those who are too poor to afford a car. According to Anthony, the gangster in *Crash*, 'they put them great big windows on the sides of buses' for one reason only: 'to humiliate the people of colour who are reduced to ridin' on 'em'.

I'm without the walkman today, and catching the bus with my friend Carol, a playwright with whom I'm staying in LA. It is a sweaty, humid day, but on Hollywood Boulevard, outside a theatre advertising Live Nude Show, Peep Show and Adult Book Store, we encounter a pile of snow. Where did it come from? This is Hollywood.

I am shocked to discover how rundown Hollywood is. It reminds me of Hillbrow. 'But of course Hollywood is no longer a place,' says Carol. 'It's a concept. When you write for Hollywood, you're simply writing for a market. Where the movie gets made is irrelevant.'

Finally the bus arrives. 'You notice everyone's in their own movie,' she continues. There's an old woman in a shiny green outfit – including tinsel – looking like an out-take from the Emerald City scene in *The Wizard of Oz*. And an old man in soiled pyjamas. 'I suspect he checked himself out of a hospital,' she says. I imagine how scary it must be to be old and poor in this city.

Carol explains how Reagan cut social programmes when he was governor of California. And we're now in the run up to the Bush *vs* Dukakis election. A bumper sticker reads: 'A Dukakis in the hand is better than a Quayle in the Bush.' But this doesn't seem to stop them just a few months later. It seems Dukakis is too short, Greek, and his wife has a problem with prescription drugs, if the 'debates' are anything to go by.

We visit an exhibition of Hollywood as it was in the Fifties, and even I feel nostalgic.

On the walk home, the Steven Cohen print I'm wearing prompts conversation with some strangers watering their garden under the H O L L Y W O O D sign. Turns out the woman is South African too (from Pietermaritzburg) and we have some acquaintances in common.

Steven Dietz, the playwright, returns my call. The publicist of the theatre has given him my number. He sounds cagey: 'Where would the play be staged?' I've no idea, I tell him. I haven't thought that far. 'Tell me about your country,' he says. I send him three articles: a piece on director Mbongeni Ngema hitting the cast of his play *Sarafina!* with a belt to discipline them; an interview with actors John Kani and Winston Ntshona, suggesting no whites are committed to change; and a piece on David Bruce, sentenced to two years in prison for refusing to do military service. I don't know why I brought them to the States. It seemed like a good idea while I was packing.

He sends me a copy of the play.

My friend Phillippa – a native Johannesburger, but working and playing in LA for a while – always on the lookout for the odd and eccentric, takes me on some adventures. First stop, 3 a.m. to an old movie theatre in downtown LA. She has befriended the elderly Latino caretaker, so he lets us in to look around the empty theatre, which she has seen before. The ghosts of the past are almost visible. We imagine what it must have been like in this vast expanse of foyer, now with worn carpets, when the stars frequented it in their furs. Now the theatre screens Charles Bronson and Clint Eastwood movies with Spanish subtitles for the local youth. There's graffiti scratched on the back of the seats. Its history has no meaning for those using it.

The next day is Sunday, and we visit the Superet Light Church. Its entrance is lit up by an eleven-foot purple neon heart of Christ. A brochure declares: 'Dr. Trust gives lectures of the Atom Aura Light Science every Tuesday at 8 p.m. at 2512 West Third Street. (Los Angeles, California). All religions are welcome; and is free to all to hear and see facts on the screen.'

This visit is Phillippa's first too. Unfortunately they will not let us in with bare arms, so we sit in an antechamber and listen to the service of Dr JC (Josephine) Trust over a loudspeaker. We discover later that it was a recording: 'Mother Trust' has been dead for decades. All of her followers appear to be Latino.

Their brochure states: 'Dr. Josephine C. Trust, S.A.A.S. is the only Founder of this Superet Science, the Superet Light Doctrine and also the Superet Brotherhood with the P.O.P.M. Club – being the only Chartered Superet Atoms Aura Scientist of the Superet Science in the world, which started in 1925 with the Charter and the Name, Superet, Copyright.'

The POPM, or Prince of Peace Movement, 'is a non-sectarian Club of Peace composed of all denominations, religions, nations and colors – rich or poor – united in one thought: to create peace'. Colour, it appears, is central to their philosophy, which examines 'invisible spectrums and the spiritual significance' of favourite colours. Later, in 1992, the Superet Light church building was declared a Historic Cultural Monument (No. 555) by the Los Angeles City Council.

September 1990

Steven Dietz arrives on my doorstep in Yeoville. He is in Johannesburg for the opening of his play, which is being staged by the Performing Arts Council of the Transvaal, at the Windybrow Theatre, at the top of Nugget Hill in Hillbrow. He appears surprised as I open the door. Since we have never seen each other during our communication, it seems he thought I was black. He writes later: 'Though I wanted to think I was different, I remembered boarding my plane in Frankfurt to fly to Johannesburg. And, as I watched each white person get on board, something in the back of my mind that I am not proud of pointed at them, one by one, and said "Racist, racist, racist."'

'Your trip,' a friend had told him, 'will be about one thing and one thing only: confronting your own whiteness.'

October 2005

It's been half a century since Rosa Parks (who died in her sleep on 24 October at the age of ninety-two) 'stood up by sitting down' in one of the seats reserved for white passengers on a bus in Montgomery, Alabama. As the Neville Brothers sing, because of her, 'we don't ride on the back of the bus no more'. These days in LA, local historian and essayist DJ Waldie observes, the bus is 'an unstable, third-world country on wheels'. A middle-aged not-quite-middle-class white male, he is in the minority, and something of a curiosity. He uses the bus because, though he can drive, his eyes won't allow him to.

Information about bus routes, times and stops he describes as 'mostly folklore'. Some of this information you could learn 'if you spoke Tagalog or Khmer', or at least Spanish. Since he appears both competent and harmless, he is often asked for assistance, but anything he has to offer – relying on the official version – could also be a myth.

There is a map. But the map is never the territory. And like LA's fragmentary stories – believed to intersect at certain points – one is often left with nothing but white space. 'If you're smart and you must ride the bus,' Waldie says, 'the word of mouth of beauticians and factory hands will make bearable your powerlessness.' Allow ten minutes for transfers, say officials; but travellers know half an hour would be safer. The bus is not for the impatient, or the incontinent: there are rarely public toilets along the way.

He tells his stories, says Waldie, because of a 'longing for a sense of place'. And this sense of place is most real to him in the 'brown city' – in the words of memoirist Richard Rodriguez – that lives in the shadows of the glamour and wealth.

LA is a city where many go to be discovered, but as many go to get lost. Addressing the drivers cocooned inside the gridlock on the freeway, Waldie writes: 'Public transit is almost invisible to you … You won't ever see the civil gesture of the tall, young black man toward the old white man whose leg he must brush aside to pass down the aisle of the packed bus, a light double tap with the side of the young man's hand on the old man's shoulder and a low word of excuse answered with a nod and a word, and the old man's mild face half turned to the young man's.'

'It's the sense of touch,' says Don Cheadle in *Crash*. 'In any real city, you walk, you know? You brush past people, people bump into you. In LA, nobody touches you. We're always behind this metal and glass. I think we miss that touch so much, that we crash into each other, just so we can feel something.'

Of the future of LA literature, Waldie predicts: 'The standard for the excellence of our stories won't have been set in the Iowa Writers' Workshop, but by women talking at a hearth baking *chapati* and men whispering in Spanish before slipping between strands of barbed wire across any border south of here.'

Hillbrow, too, is finally a Third World country; no longer reserved for whites or sheltered from the rest of Africa north of its borders. I walk around the outskirts rather than through the middle of it, when I can. The late Phaswane Mpe's novel *Welcome to Our Hillbrow*, it has been said, 'shows the complexity of blackness in a context in which race is no longer a defining factor and even ethnicity has been overtaken by the large movement of non-South Africans into Hillbrow'. Now the questions about race seem as unclear as the answers.

These days the buses in Joburg still run, but they are erratic, so I prefer to use the less formal minibus taxis, the Zola Budds, which zip by every few minutes; named after South Africa's little barefoot runner of the Eighties, now most famous for accidentally tripping Mary Decker at the 1984 Olympics in Los Angeles. Usually I am the only white passenger, just one among the carless masses moving from A to B. Despite precarious driving, I put my trust in this foreign country where I do not understand the languages, the lyrics of the songs or the news on the radio. Nobody asks me for directions. It's the one time when I'm forced to confront my whiteness.

Speeding towards Paris

It was the first spring of the new millennium. I was doing an internship in London, and felt burnt out from just a couple of months on the London streets, which seemed populated by a tightly packed frenzy of people racing to Who-knows-where-dot-com. I tried to step aside and let those who were in more of a hurry than me pass, but there was nowhere to step aside to. I was met with glares and curses. Nothing to do but keep on moving.

'I apprehended for the first time those particular illusions of mobility which power American business. Time was money. Motion was progress,' said essayist and cultural commentator Joan Didion in the 1970s.

Back in 2000, a giant billboard for a computer company, Breathe. com, towered over me in the gloom of the Underground each morning: 'One big rush – does that describe your life? Sometimes it's a great feeling, but when it's not and life gets too much: Relax. Just Breathe. Breathe brings you sophisticated technology which is easy to control, to help you get the most from whatever you are doing, whether you're at your desk or on the move.' A picture of a fish with an oxygen tank on its back dominated the ad. This was particularly ironic in light of the recent dot-com boom and freefall of a few weeks earlier. And there we were thinking for one brief moment that this miraculous invention, the Internet, was going to save the world and make us all rich.

I decided to take a few days off and visit an old friend in Paris. Three hours on the Eurostar, the high-speed train that travels under the English Channel through the Channel Tunnel, and I would catch up with Paris, which is an hour ahead of London, arriving four hours later. It was twelve years since I'd been there.

The day I left, a colleague sent me an email about a call for submissions for a journal called *M/C* (Media Culture), and said: 'You should contribute something to this.' It was for their 'speed' issue. 'Speed,' it read, 'is a drug: it gets us up, gets us going, gets us going somewhere, but where and why remain unanswered questions. Speed is one of the defining metaphors of contemporary life in advanced capitalist economies: the speed of the stock market, the speed of technological change.' I had nothing else to do while sitting still for hours on the train, so I spent the journey pondering these questions and what I might write.

'Urbanist and militant' French philosopher Paul Virilio – author of books like *Speed and Politics* and *The Information Bomb* – came to mind as I was hastening towards his home. Virilio coined the term Dromology for the study of speed, and has defined it as 'the social, political and military logic of systematic movement accelerated to a vanishing point at which territory, as traditionally conceived, is replaced by a government of nothing but time'. We must beware the approaching 'dictatorship of speed,' he warns.

I had visions of time warps and tumbling down rabbit holes as we travelled through the tunnel, and arrived with my mind racing, feeling exhausted, and not prepared for a sharp change in perspective.

Paris was home to the *flâneurs*, those nineteenth-century bourgeois bohemian gentlemen of independent means and leisure who would 'promenade without purpose' and go 'botanising on the asphalt', where the trendiest pastime, legend would have it, was to take your tortoise for a walk. But the golden days of *flâneurie*, alas, are gone. Strolling has been replaced by browsing, generally done online.

Charles Baudelaire, the most famous *flâneur*, scented 'a chance rhyme in every corner'. But Baudelaire's 'cosy, dirty, mysterious' Paris of winding streets in which the *flâneur* could lose himself with ease was bulldozed by Baron Haussmann, commissioned by Napoleon Bonaparte's nephew in 1853 to modernise the city. The 'labyrinthine medieval Paris of the romantics' was destroyed, as Edmund White puts it, 'by one of the most massive urban renewal plans known to history', and replaced by a city of broad, strictly linear streets, unbroken façades, roundabouts radiating avenues, uniform city lighting, uniform street furniture, a complex, modern sewer system and public transportation (horse-drawn omnibuses eventually replaced by the métro and motor-powered buses)'. The real reason for the new broad boulevards was to obstruct barricade building, and according to one more cynical suggestion there were also 'hopes to flush out the hidden haunts of low-life where bohemia had once gathered and barricaded'.

In 1857 photographer Eugène Atget was born near Bordeaux. By the end of the nineteenth century – at the same time that motion pictures were being born in California, which 'has no past – no past, at least, that it is willing to remember', Atget, 'penniless but driven', was obsessively photographing every corner of Paris, determined to document it before it disappeared.

Yet it was in Paris that the first commercial exhibition of moving pictures occurred, and *le cinéma* began. On the 28th of December 1895, at Salon Indien in the basement of the Grand Café on Boulevard de Capucines, while the wealthy and fashionable dined upstairs, the Lumière (Light) family introduced their new invention, the Cinématographe, to the public and screened ten of their films to an audience of thirty-three. The press, though invited, failed to show. The price of entrance was one franc. Inventor son Louis continued to assert to his shrewd businessman father Antoine that it was 'an invention without any commercial future'.

The screening included their first film, *La Sortie des Usines*

Lumière à Lyon–Montplaisir (*Workers Leaving the Lumière Factory*), but the film that caused a stir was *L'arrivée d'un train à La Ciotat*. It was a minute long, and the cast was made up of members of the Lumière family and employees from their photographic supplies factory. 'It showed a school-of-Monet style train arriving at a station' and, according to popular legend (depending on which version you hear), 'at the sight of the train steaming ever closer to the screen, a number of the … audience ducked behind their seats' or 'fled the café in terror, fearing being run over by the "approaching" train'.

In the year of documentary photographer Atget's birth, Karl Marx had begun drafting his *Foundations of the Critique of Political Economy*, in which he predicted that the contradictions of capital would spur on the annihilation of space by time. He wrote: 'While capital … must strive to tear down every barrier … to exchange and conquer the whole earth for its markets, it strives on the other side to annihilate this space with time.'

Herman Charles Bosman said of Paris in 1936, 'A lot of people complain that Paris is not what it used to be. They say that the old carefree life of the artist and the poet are no more. They blame all sorts of conditions for it. They say it is the fault of the machine age, or of the rise of materialism, or of the tax on opium.

'For that matter, people say the same thing about Chelsea. They say that many of Chelsea's best artists have been driven south of the river into Battersea, or they have been driven west into Hammersmith, or in a northerly direction into Hampstead … But if the best artists have been driven out of Chelsea, the worst ones have remained. And they will always be there, no doubt, introducing unwonted splashes of colour into the sombre King's Road when they walk abroad; leaving behind, when they move from one set of furnished apartments to another, weird stacks of paintings in lieu of rent.'

And he concludes: 'So, too, it is with Paris. The Paris that Villon knew is still there. The Paris of Baudelaire and Verlaine

… It lives on, that wayward spirit animating the visionary and the past, arraying the half-god in sudden jewels and startling sublimities, and then putting him again in the gutter, to wonder vaguely, without splendour and without laughter.'

'In the cracks,' says White, 'are those little forgotten places that appeal to the *flâneur*, the traces left by people living in the margins'. According to White, the most interesting parts of Paris now are 'Bellville and Barbès, the teeming *quartiers* where Arabs and Asians and blacks live and blend their respective cultures into hybrids'.

When I arrived in Paris, my friend and I, with different needs and having too many years between us now, were prickly with each other. Seeing things from different directions, our history was not enough to revive our friendship. These few months had been my first time out of South Africa in twelve years, and I guarded them selfishly as my time out, wanting to talk of other things. But she had been gone for thirteen years, having left to get away from inequalities and the burden of being privileged, and to find the space to be an artist, and wanted to know how things were back home.

Relying solely on the weight of my own body to transport me, I felt drained by the heat, wandering aimlessly, my tired sore feet and the price of water. We didn't have the economic luxury of nineteenth-century gentlemen to stroll from café to café and sip coffee while watching the world go by.

'I wish you could stay for longer,' she said with regret. Perhaps then we would have unravelled our differences and become reacquainted. But a few days was all I could afford. I had to get back to work. Time was money – someone else's.

The night before I left, after eating dinner at McDonalds (the cheapest place available), we snuck guiltily through the foyer of a fancy restaurant to use the toilets and admire the marble and the view. 'Well, at least you can go out safely at night,' I said. 'To do what?' she replied. And I realised the sad irony that – apart from the independently wealthy – those who can afford what Paris has to offer probably seldom have the time, rushing from one thing to another. As Baudelaire observed: 'for businessmen … the fantastic reality of life becomes strangely blunted.' And then again, as someone once said to me: 'There's nothing worse than being poor in a rich country.'

Slow Walk to Freedom

I suppose by the law of averages it was my time. I was mugged again today. Though technically I'm not quite sure: just as I assume rape means penetration, I always get the feeling mugged means there has to be actual – rather than just the threat of – violence involved. Is this accurate, or just South African perversity?

The first time I was attacked was December 1996, Hillbrow, Sunday 7 p.m. Preparing to go on holiday, I had been doing last-minute work that weekend. My friend David had too, and so on the Saturday evening we walked home together from the Centre for the Study of Violence and Reconciliation in Braamfontein where we worked, to Yeoville, through Hillbrow.

When we reached the park on the border of Hillbrow and Berea (most memorable at one time for the pigeon lady, who could be seen on any given day covered in the pigeons she was feeding), we debated whether it would be more sensible to walk through it or around it, and we decided that open streets were more conducive to safety than being fenced in. 'What would you have to lose now if you were mugged?' David asked.

'Oh, not much, just my life,' I replied, thinking about the tedium of replacing my ID book and bank card. But we reached our shared corner safely that evening, wished each other happy holidays and went our separate ways.

Perhaps because of that, a false sense of security, or invincibility, denial, foolishness, I reasoned that the biggest thing I had to fear was my own lack of trust, and decided not to call a taxi the following evening, and walked home on my own. Stopping off at the Hare Krishna restaurant for a take-away, I continued on around the park. By the time I realised the three men were converging on me, it was too late. 'We want money,' the one with the knife threatened. Mid-thirties, perhaps younger, prematurely aged. His accomplices holding me from behind, I didn't see more than their shapes. But his face was close to mine, as he broke the chain with the labradorite crystal (*helps one remain calm within chaos*) around my neck, and I screamed rebelliously at his knife at my throat. They scattered, and I continued home with my curry, effectively shaken (*can't walk alone after dark any more*, I thought), thinking about the month of paid leave ahead of me and how the man with the dangerously desperate face now etched into my memory had in all likelihood never been and would never go on a holiday. (Was I being naïve?) I felt entangled in rage, and guilt, and a dark sadness.

But that was a long time ago and had faded into a distant memory now, as I was confronted again with a knife in my ribs: 'Give me your bag. Don't scream. Just cooperate, and we won't hurt you.' Muggers seem to have become almost polite, and more educated, since my last encounter. And much younger. (But they still swarm, in threes.) Sixteen? Eighteen? It was hard to tell: disturbingly young.

Of course I couldn't be sure if he would stab me or not, but this time I wasn't taking any chances. Last time my rage and pride got the better of me and I was determined to be heard. This time I was sandwiched between the boys and the suburban wall with a German shepherd behind it (*must remember to walk closer to the road*), screaming louder than I ever could. It's a pity dogs don't protect you when you're on the outside.

I had been happy this afternoon. I was walking home from a visit to the dentist, where thankfully she had managed to desensitise a tooth and avoid having to pull it. Just a few blocks from the dentist in Glenhazel, I encountered something unusual for the northern suburbs of Johannesburg, an elderly white lady walking down the road very slowly – looking vulnerable but self-assured – with an umbrella, as though on an outing. I don't often encounter any other white pedestrians. Walking in Johannesburg seems to be a pastime of the poor or eccentric.

'Do you know where I can buy chocolate?' she asked. 'I don't live here. I am staying with friends. I am alone there now – they can't baby-sit me all day long – but I suddenly have a craving for chocolate.' How delightful, I thought. An elderly woman, willing to step out into an unknown neighbourhood and go on a little adventure all on her own.

'Do you know the Balfour Park Shopping Centre?' I asked.

'That's a long way away.'

'No, just five or ten minutes. Do you want to walk with me?' So we walked and talked.

'People don't walk here,' she said.

'No,' I replied. 'I think it's partly a class thing.' (I didn't mention safety. Was that irresponsible of me?) 'But also the public transport is poor.' I recalled similar frustrations with public transport in Los Angeles years ago. Coincidentally, she had lived there too for a few years. We compared notes on the incredulous stares we got when out walking in the streets of LA.

'Are you from Israel?' I recognised the accent. Perhaps this accounted for her bravery. The rules change from one volatile city to another, but I expect the pragmatism of getting on with your life is the same.

Inevitably our talk turned to Israel. She was originally from Lebanon, and her family before that was from Russia. 'Is it safe to catch the buses in Israel?' I wondered. I remembered that my Israeli friend Anat had told me this is one of the first ports of call for suicide bombers. 'You become vigilant,' said my walking companion. 'Why is he wearing a jacket on a hot day like this? You notice. That's how someone was stopped recently.'

We commented on the beauty of the purple rain falling from the jacarandas on the street. 'It's such a beautiful city. I hope it doesn't go the way of the rest of Africa.' Of course I should have known the conversation was going to veer in this direction, but I decided to sidestep some of these uneven and rocky bits. She was from another time and place, and I am trying to open myself to conversation with people who don't think quite like I do.

She told me the cousins she was staying with in South Africa say, 'The government is only interested in feathering its own nest'.

'But isn't this true of most governments?' I wondered. 'Isn't this true of George Bush?'

'How is it true of George Bush?' She was clearly confused. 'He only wants freedom for everyone. Look how good he has been to Israel. He just wants to put an end to terrorism.'

'He also wants control of oil in the Middle East,' I said.

In response to her 'Look at the rest of Africa,' I tried to explain how it is in the West's interest to help put African dictators in power and keep them there. How Patrice Lumumba in the Congo, to name but one example, would have been different if he wasn't assassinated. But there's only so much you can cover in fifteen minutes (we were walking slowly).

The closer we got to the shopping centre, the more it dawned on me that she would have to make this walk back on her own. It occurred to me that she could be mugged and I would never know it. I recalled Lily Tomlin's character in Robert Altman's *Short Cuts*, who knocks over a child. She helps him up and he walks away. But she never knows that he goes into a coma later on. Do I remember correctly that he never wakes up from it? I don't read the newspapers. There could be a story about an elderly Israeli woman on holiday mugged and killed near Balfour Park Shopping Centre, and I would be none the wiser.

As we said goodbye, all she said was: 'You have been very patient with me.'

It is rare that I pray. But that was one of those moments. I prayed that she would get her chocolate and wander home slowly and safely, with nothing more than her sweet tooth satisfied, and a tale of her adventure in the streets of Johannesburg. Quite selfishly, I had seen someone that I might become in her, and longed for the freedom to do it. But in the process, perhaps I had put her – and myself – at risk.

Never for one moment did I dream, as I waved goodbye, just how close that risk was. I doubled my pace and crossed the street, and there they were waiting for me. Even then I was more concerned with being startled by the aggressive suburban dogs. They bark ferociously every time, and every time I am taken by surprise. It called to mind something someone once said, in a diversity workshop I was once part of, about dogs in the suburbs only barking at black people. It's a myth. It didn't cross my mind that there were three young men in different parts of the road, or that I should be wary of them.

So what did they take from me? A beautiful bag made in Nepal (in all likelihood by workers under appalling conditions). An umbrella that folded down to just the right size. Sunglasses, new, in a purple case that I bought in London. Lip balm and a hand mirror. A short story by Ivan Vladislavić, 'The Box', half read. (The prime minister had just been let out of the bird cage where he was being held captive, and he was about to give a speech. I wonder what he had to say.) A little bag of inspirational cards and a crystal that my friend Sophia sent me from Glastonbury. Keys and cards that gave me access to my home, the recreation centre, the university, and frequent flier mileage for escapism at the movies. Then, of course, there was what they really wanted: a purse with a R180. Or was it R80? I had a feeling I might have spent the R100. Thank goodness not my bank card. And thank god not my phone book! Was it really worth the effort to them, I wonder?

'I was not emboldened to leave the station until the sun was shining on everyone equally,' says Paul Theroux of his arrival at dawn at Park Station in Johannesburg, in his *Dark Star Safari*. A soldier trapped with Theroux in a highway robbery on his travels offers him these words of comfort: 'They do not want your life, *bwana*. They want your shoes.'

I had the sense that if I cooperated, I would not be harmed; a disturbing indictment of our society, where cooperation has become an almost acceptable requirement from one's attacker rather than the cooperation of citizens with one other. The saddest thing was that these boys did not seem to need my shoes, or my bag. They were well dressed and well spoken. They seemed like nothing more than spoiled brats, for whom a good hiding years ago, rather than a jail sentence now, would have made a difference. It called to mind Scott Peck: 'Maybe we should condemn a little more and understand a little less.'

But I remind myself that the compassion I aim to cultivate is mostly for me, in order to keep *me* human.

What those boys stole more than anything was not from me; it was my trust given to the others also just walking peacefully down a quiet street filled with jacarandas and bougainvillea on a beautiful spring day. The sun was shining on us, and the dogs were barking at us, all equally in that street. It's such a shame they couldn't see that.

For now, it's back to the busy roads and exhaust fumes for me, and walking wide circles around people again for a while. But I'll be walking.

Finding the Balance

1.

'Have you ever thought of moving to somewhere like Bloemfontein?' Gary asks. He's not being ironic. He left the country in
1985 and is trying to think of a place that may not have changed
very much. He is back for one of many lightning visits, and we
are sitting in the winter sunshine at a pavement café in tree-lined
Parkview, catching up, and inevitably discussing the stresses of
living with crime in Johannesburg, and my mugging last year.

He is here to rehearse a play that he's written, with his friend
Neil. They will perform it in London in a few months. But they've
had to juggle both their schedules to find a time and place to
rehearse. Johannesburg, July 2003 it is.

Gary didn't leave South Africa voluntarily. Like so many young
white South African men at the time, he had the choice of fighting
a war that he didn't believe in, going to jail, or leaving the country.
Since his parents were British and he had a British passport,
Europe seemed the logical choice. Careerwise, as an international
media consultant, he has never looked back, but he still has mixed
feelings about his homeland.

'Well, at least you're safe,' I say.

'Safe from what?' he asks. 'Do you know what the temperature
is now in Europe?'

Just then Sue walks by. I haven't seen Sue in half a dozen years, since she moved from Yeoville from the block of flats that we shared. 'Where are you living now?' I ask her.

'Up the road,' she says. 'But we're moving soon. To the Free State.' Gary and I both laugh. She looks at us quizzically.

2.

My earlier memories of Sue call to mind the injunction from Chris-in-the-morning, the manic philosopher–DJ, to pilot Maggie in the TV series *Northern Exposure*: 'You'd better slow down, or you'll catch yourself coming the other way.' Sue appeared to be someone on a mission. With a place to go, and her head down, it wasn't easy to distract her from her path. She seems to have changed. 'Well, in those days it didn't seem important,' she says. 'The whiteys in Yeoville didn't really care if you greeted them or not. But now it's different.' In the course of walking in the suburbs of Johannesburg now, apart from the few remaining 'villages' like Parkview and Melville and Norwood, it is rare to encounter other white pedestrians. Greeting, in a formerly racially divided society, is a simple act of building bridges. As a colleague of mine once put it: 'When we greet, it means we are at peace.'

'When I lived in Cape Town years ago,' Sue continues, 'I used to be more guarded. I used to think that people wanted something from me when they greeted me. That they wanted money or something. But things have changed.'

It's funny that, at a time when many white South Africans feel overwhelmed by a growing economic underclass (largely pedestrian) and are suffering from compassion fatigue and probably more likely to be wary of being solicited for money on the streets, she seems almost oblivious to this. But she is a massage and polarity therapist by profession, and addressing imbalances is her aim.

There are some who would argue that the entire act of walking is a balancing act. British anthropologist John Napier wrote that during walking 'the body, step by step, teeters on the edge of catastrophe … because only the rhythmic forward movement of first one leg and then the other keeps [man] from falling flat on his face'.

For Sue, the speed of her movement has less to do with a need to get places fast and more to do with her own internal rhythm. She feels, she says, 'like a hummingbird', and sitting still is hard. 'The only time I'm comfortable being still is when I'm with a client. Then my focus is completely on the client. Otherwise I need to keep moving or doing something. Slowing down makes me feel like an elephant.'

'There is a secret bond between slowness and memory, between speed and forgetting,' wrote Milan Kundera. 'The degree of slowness is directly proportional to the intensity of memory.' And an elephant, they say, never forgets.

Though she does drive, and it would be faster, Sue often chooses to walk 'from one side of Johannesburg to the other. It's so versatile,' she says. 'You can multi-task. I can think. And I find things!' The streets for her are a place for gathering overlooked treasures. This may also explain why she is so often looking down when she walks.

Working part-time at Congo Joe craft shop to supplement her income, she has been walking from Parkview to Killarney, a 45-minute hike. But it's proving a bit much in the summer heat. 'I arrive at work all hot and sweaty.' So Steve, her partner, 'has been very kind. He's been taking me and fetching me. Parking is such a nightmare at the Killarney shopping mall!' Parking problems and expenses are a complaint I hear over and over from drivers.

'I do have a sense of anxiety about having my car stolen. But the thing with Killarney… Well, I have this thing about chaos, and Killarney is the epitome of chaos. It's full of elderly people. And people don't stop their cars close enough to the ticket box when they're leaving, so someone has to come out of the cubicle and punch it for them because they've stopped too far away, so they hold up the traffic. And when they're coming in, they get just past the boom and stop and wait there for a parking place near the entrance. So nobody can get past. Nobody can get in, and nobody can get out. It can take you twenty minutes just to get out of the car park. It winds me up like nothing else.'

Is she ever afraid for her safety when she walks around Johannesburg? 'No. Maybe because I've never been attacked. But I'm not afraid of other people. My fears are of my own demons... Of getting old, and slow, and being useless to anyone. But I can usually walk the fear off.'

On Sundays she and Steve walk to the Rosebank Market. 'And that's great. We don't have to find parking or worry about the car. We watch all the building developments along the way. We're always harassing security guards to let us in to see. It's great to see what people are doing to their houses. I get ideas. And building rubble! I *love* building rubble. There are always interesting things lying in the street that you can bring home.'

We are walking round her garden and she is showing me some of the things she has found. 'Look at this beautiful old window that I got in the street outside the library. It must have been in the storeroom there. I'm going to use it in my house in the Free State. And I found, just now, this pile of beautiful old pressed-steel ceiling squares. I'll make something out of them. I don't know what yet.'

I look closely at the colourful mobile hanging in a tree nearby, that she's made from bits and pieces she's found. Plastic bags cut into strips; a milk carton; a snuff lid; chip packets; a hair curler; a scoop for baby's milk formula; the lid of a Vim canister, already conveniently punched with holes to thread the string through; and a child's abandoned slip-slop.

Mobiles, said Jean-Paul Sartre, 'have no meaning, make you think of nothing but themselves ... A general destiny of movement is sketched for them, and then they are left to work it out for themselves.'

'When I'm making something like that,' says Sue, 'I'm

completely absorbed. It's one of the few times I can sit for hours without budging. Because my senses are completely engaged. And occasionally when I'm watching a movie.'

'Which movie?' I ask her. 'Off the top of your head.'

Babette's Feast, she says immediately, recalling the 1988 film of Karen Blixen's short story. It shows Babette preparing a magnificent, sumptuous meal; a wonderfully sensual film about cooking.

'Oh look at this,' she leads me to a knobkierie planted in the garden. "My maid was a bit horrified. She said to me: "You don't know who it belonged to!" But I like it. Just feel that,' she says fingering the top of it. 'Imagine how much handling and walking it took to make such a smooth surface.

'Sometimes we go out walking just for pleasure, for exercise, and I say to Stephen, "Let's not come home until we find something!" And we find amazing things. We knock on people's doors as well, when they've got things outside their houses, and ask them if we can have them. So it's nice… And sometimes we just knock on people's doors and ask them what colour paint they've used, and then they'll say: "Well, come in." And then we'll get to see their house. And then we also sometimes on Sundays go and see show-houses.

'This was our big find,' she says with satisfaction, lifting a plastic sheet off a high pile next to a wall of the house. 'About sixty square metres of parquet flooring. Somebody pulled all the parquet out of their house and threw it on the pavement. So we asked the security guard if we could have it. "Sure," he said, "just give me small change." We did trip after trip of full-to-the-roof bakkie loads. Hundred-year-old Rhodesian teak going to the dump, for the price of a Coke!

'My maid gave me these. All her grandfather's old enamel pots with holes in them. And I put plants in them. I'm interested in the transformation of old things into new things, and what you can really make with them. The mouldy old beauty of things that people have discarded.'

The pots are standing on a lovely old dresser on the stoep, and the dresser, too, has a story. 'That was one of the times we knocked on a door. All this stuff was standing on the pavement, and it turned out their granny had just died and they'd come from somewhere up country to sort things out. They were only too happy for us to take it away.

'Steve and I are quite a good match, because I've got the ideas, and I want to do it, for free, and I want to do it quick. But Stephen's technical, and he can do it slowly and properly – so, if it wasn't for him, everything in the house would be put up with a glue gun, masking tape and a stapler.

'If Steve sees a hole in the wall and it worries him, he'll scrape it all down, fill it with Polyfilla, repaint it, and then it will disappear for him. I can fill it with toothpaste and I'll never think about it again. And if and when it falls down, which might not be in my lifetime, then I'll deal with it.'

Steve is a photographer by profession. 'His last exhibition was working with Polaroid lifts, emulsions… You take a certain kind of Polaroid, then you put it under water and the image floats off into a kind of jelly, a tight little ball. Then you have to take a wet piece of paper, hand-made paper, put it underneath and catch it, and slowly open it up. Of course, it'll never be completely square again, but you try and get it as close to what it used to look like. The exhibition was called *Striving for Imperfection*,' she laughs.

'If he was renovating the house, in his lifetime he'd do one door perfectly. It would be the most perfectly stripped and sanded door in the universe. I would do everything badly but quickly. My feeling is, even if we were going to be here for the rest of our lives it's good enough for me. The next person's going to bash the house down and turn it into something else, so what's the point?'

3.

Early next year Sue and Steve will be moving to Smithfield, which according to journalist Charmaine Naidoo is 'the Free State's best-kept secret'. Only an hour from Bloemfontein, and yet until about seven years ago it had become a virtual ghost town. But two men passing through on the N6, and looking for a new place to settle, drove in and began resuscitating the town.

'Frans and Julius,' says Sue. 'Frans is a fine artist, and Julius is a lawyer. They had been living as part of the artists' colony in the Sabie area and had done very well with their restaurant and art gallery there. But they'd sold their business and were looking for a new challenge. They bought a row of semi-detached cottages in the main road, and the magistrate's house. At that stage a house hadn't been sold in Smithfield for years, so the locals were delighted. Though they were a bit wary of the *Engelse mense* in the beginning!

'Anyway they opened a bed and breakfast, and a restaurant. And all their friends started coming to town. People would come for a night and end up staying the weekend. They're very sociable; fabulous cooks, and great raconteurs. And they started a pottery project too, training people from the area. And then word of mouth spread, and other artists and creative people started buying there.'

I'm beginning to have visions of Cicely, Alaska, the little town featured in *Northern Exposure*. But without the radio station and the manic DJ. And a lot hotter.

'Oh, it can get very cold in Smithfield,' Sue says. Sometimes in winter it goes as low as minus twelve degrees, it snows there; and in summer it gets to thirty-five. It's actually remarkable that anyone wants to live there.

'But now that there are more and more toll roads, and the national road goes through there and more people are taking that route...' *Halfway to Anywhere in South Africa*, proclaims the ad for the Pula Guesthouse.

'We'd been holidaying in the Eastern Cape for a few years and we always drove past there, and then one year we drove in. I can't say it was love at first sight. It's an awkward little town, but it's got little pockets of charm and the people are delightful, and it grew on us. And the joke around town was that you could buy a house on your credit card without even going into budget.'

Now, it seems, you can escape the congestion and traffic of big cities to remote places accessible only by highways and cars. As architecture critic Martin Pawley says in praise of the car: The modern man and woman have 'learned to live in the country. Today country life is entirely possible with a car.'

Were Sue and Steve wanting to move from Joburg? 'No,' she says. 'But, you know, the opportunity presented itself, and I wanted to do it while we still have a choice. We're both almost fifty now, and we both freelance, and neither of us has a pension. I didn't want us to get to where we have no choices and, god forbid, can't even afford our rates and taxes. I've seen it with a lot of people around here.'

Earlier this year, Sue started a campaign to have Parkview's electricity converted to the prepaid system, which is 'cheaper, and more manageable. Particularly if you have tenants.' She didn't get the required number of signatures, but in the course of the campaign she heard numerous stories from pensioners who were 'too scared to even put the heater on in winter. It was heartbreaking. I don't want to end up like that. At least this way we can rent out this house for a few years and get a small income while we find our feet in Smithfield, and eventually sell it.'

Her mobile flutters in the September breeze, almost a mirage from the stoep where we're sitting, and I wonder silently if, in the vast distances that we now cover in a globalised world, and in order to find affordable housing, small country towns have become the new suburbs; and with all the Pam Golding estate agents' signs popping up all over the country, how long Smithfield will remain the Free State's best kept secret.

So what does she plan to do in Smithfield? 'Well, I want to continue with the healing work. But I also want to start a community project. It might be possible to get a government grant. There are a few projects there, the pottery project and a knitting project, that have got grants.

'There's a woman called Betty West, a Zimbabwean woman, she had a knitting project in Zimbabwe that employed thousands of rural women. The most exquisite knitting and crocheting. Anyway, she's left Zimbabwe and gone to Smithfield, and has been given a government grant to start a knitting project for all the little towns around there – Bethulie, Rouxville… But the funny thing is she's working in cotton, and it's sheep country. So I'm thinking definitely something with wool. My inclination is to make felt. Felt clothing. Felt making is very labour intensive but not very skilled. So it's perfect for the area. It could provide jobs for a lot of people.

'And of course we'll be working on the house. It's almost falling down at this point (and there are bats in the ceiling!). It'll take time, but time is one thing we'll have. Who knows, maybe I'll even learn to sit around and drink tea. It's a common pastime there.

'It's fitting that I'm moving to the area, because my father's family were originally from there. *Boere-Jode* from Colesberg in the Northern Cape; in the sheep industry. And my grandfather's brother was a stockbroker. Literally, with stock: an auctioneer of sheep. Everyone from the farms around the area used to take their sheep for auction to Colesberg. It was the big centre. And it had the nearest *shul*, so on Jewish holidays all the Jews from the area would go there. And that was where my father was born. When he matriculated he couldn't leave the countryside fast enough, he didn't want to be a country boy, and he settled in Cape Town.

'But people want to visit small towns now, where their children can walk to the café and ride their bicycles. They can't do that here,' she says with a sweep of her hand, 'stuck behind high walls.

'And the locals are loving it. There's this really old man, Oom Jurie, he's in his early eighties. He was the mayor before. Now he's in his bakkie, and he's become an estate agent. He's got this formidable bunch of keys, he's got keys to everyone's houses.' (I imagine the bunch of keys she's describing looks like the average householder's keys in the suburbs of Johannesburg.) 'You can phone him in winter and tell him you're coming, and he'll get your

40

house ready for you.'

This reminds me of Jurie Steyn, the postmaster in Herman Charles Bosman's Groot Marico stories, who was thought by the locals to be steaming open their mail. No doubt there is an Oom Jurie in every small town.

'And we had a man running down the street to greet us when we arrived the one day,' Sue continues, 'who said, "I saw your car. My name is Sedi, and I work in the municipality. I've been dealing with your accounts. I'm looking forward to you moving here."'

In his 1945 essay 'Rebuilding Europe's Cities', Bosman wrote: 'The difference between the city and the farm is, alas, age old. The city has gutters.' While myths about big bad Joburg – which 'flourished on vandalising and extinguishing its own past', as Stephen Gray put it – proliferated among Bosman's characters in his Marico stories, the truly mythical Marico 'hovered on the fringes of [his Joburg readers'] world, as a fantastic remoteness'. Bosman chronicled the migration from the rural to the urban. Now it seems to be time for chronicling the move back to the country. I can see Sue sitting on a stoep, not unlike this one, telling stories. Though how long it will remain 'the country' is a big question.

It is time for me to leave and Sue walks with me to the library, where I'm to meet my taxi driver. On the way we see a star shining up at us from between a pile of new bricks. She reaches down and pulls it out. 'You see!' she laughs. It's a completely silver Christmas tree, made of barbed wire, tinsel, candleholders and tin stars. 'Oh, I can definitely do something with this.'

In the Footsteps of Bosman and Dickens, via Hillbrow

'Kaffirs? (said Oom Schalk Lourens). Yes, I know them. And they're all the same. I fear the Almighty, and respect his works, but I could never understand why he made the Kaffir and the rinderpest. The Hottentot is a little bit better. The Hottentot will only steal the biltong hanging out on the line to dry. He won't steal the line as well. That is where the Kaffir is different. Still, sometimes you come across a good kaffir, who is faithful and upright and a true Christian and who doesn't let the wild dogs catch the sheep. I always think it isn't right to kill that kind of kaffir.'

This is Phaswane Mpe, author of *Welcome to Our Hillbrow*, quoting from memory the beginning of 'Makapan's Caves', the first Herman Charles Bosman story he read as a teenager and one that remains a favourite. I am a little shocked. I can hardly bring myself to say the K-word out loud, let alone repeat it over and over, and I was never at the receiving end of apartheid's brutality.

'I don't think words in themselves are bad,' says Phaswane. 'I'm more interested in how those words get used. We need to distinguish between insults and ironies.'

I have a feeling Phaswane would like Sixties American comedian Lenny Bruce, who said: 'Satire is tragedy plus time. You give it enough time, the public, the reviewers will allow you to satirise it.'

For the majority of South Africans, though, there has not been enough time, and just a few years ago a schoolteacher was dismissed when parents accused him of setting a 'racist' exam paper based on Bosman's story 'Unto Dust'.

But Phaswane is able to laugh. He laughs a lot.

'I think it may have something to do with my experience of apartheid,' he says. 'I didn't experience it in the same way, for example, that people in Soweto experienced it. I was living in a rural village, Ga-Molepo, about fifty kilometres to the southeast of Pietersburg, in the Northern Province (what is now Limpopo). And most of the terrible things I heard on the radio rather than actually coming into direct contact with them. Apart from Bantu education, I experienced it indirectly. Part of what that did for me, I think, is that I never developed bitterness. I just thought about it as something that we needed to do away with, and move on.'

A teacher who introduced Phaswane to Bosman has been one of the most positive influences in his life. She is the Catholic nun, Sister Mary Anne Tobin, to whom *Welcome to Our Hillbrow* is dedicated.

'Our school library wasn't very well stocked, so my introduction to literature was really through Enid Blyton, particularly the *Famous Five* series. I read almost everything in that series. I liked George, and Timmy the dog. I also had a dog that I was very close to. I could relate to the characters on an emotional level.

'Then I read *Alice's Adventures in Wonderland*, and I found it a great book. I keep on going back to it. I loved the magical nature of the characters, which spoke to my enjoyment of folk tales and, on another level, its subversive humour. Mary Anne moved me away from Enid Blyton when she introduced me to Herman Charles Bosman. And from there I moved on to Charles Dickens.'

It was the opening passage of *Great Expectations* that captured his imagination: 'My father's family name being Pirrip, and my Christian name Philip, my infant tongue could make of both names nothing longer or more explicit than Pip. So, I called myself Pip, and came to be called Pip.'

'I don't know exactly what it was,' says Phaswane. 'I suppose part of it is just the confidence of the child. Knowing what he cannot do, but being able to improvise and feeling that he's doing it well. Achieving great success at something that seems so small.'

In 1988, at the age of seventeen, during the school holidays Phaswane visited Johannesburg for the first time. 'I never got to Hillbrow that year. There were bomb scares in town, and my brother and cousin wouldn't hear of me going there. So it was a very dull three weeks I spent in Highlands North, where I was staying with my brother. I was very bored. There wasn't much that was exciting in the street. People were very quiet, and I'm not a great fan of shopping centres. I didn't know at the time that I could use the library.'

The following year Phaswane moved to Joburg to attend Wits University, and though *Welcome to Our Hillbrow* is not autobiographical, the walk the novel's hero Refentše makes – from Vickers Place to the campus in Braamfontein – is the walk Phaswane made daily as an undergraduate when he lived in Hillbrow. These days he lives in Braamfontein, and doesn't have far to go to get to campus while he does his doctorate, but he is still committed to walking. 'I think I'm a great walker partly because I had to walk; there was just no other way out. And so walking became both a necessity and a pastime. If there's a distance that I can walk I prefer to walk. I want to see the world around me. It's how I find my stories,' he says.

'The thing that strikes me about walking is that, no matter how often you travel one route, you always observe something new every time. It might be a very small detail, which at the time perhaps doesn't matter. After a couple of days, a couple of weeks, months, perhaps even years, it just comes back to you, and during the course of time it has become so significant, without you making an effort to make it significant.

'At one time on my walks through Hillbrow there was something like a dog kennel outside the city shelter. And then they moved it. Now that corner of Kotze and Hospital Streets is sort of changed for me. When something changes, that's been part of your consciousness, it's as though you're walking a slightly different route, now that the familiar landmark is no longer there.

'I'm very bad with dates. If I write something, I tell a story. As long as I know I got the sequence right, I don't care very much about the exact time. I want to concentrate more on the meaning of place for me. I tend to use incidents and events to locate myself in terms of time. You never know at what point an event or an incident will become significant in your own life. And it's mostly only in hindsight – with the exception of the things you have planned for, and if you don't achieve them, they become significant because of your failure!' he laughs as an afterthought.

'But place, of course, has a lot to do, not just with the landmarks but with the people who are in that place. And your experience of meeting those people. The social interaction. Your experience of those interactions. When I began writing the book I initially thought I was just doing a portrait of Hillbrow. And I realised as I started working on the map that actually I can't have a map with no one to move around in it. That's how I ended up putting Refentše into the map.'

Refentše was a character from Phaswane's earlier short stories. In one of them, 'Occasion for Brooding', Refentše had committed suicide, so Phaswane decided to 'resurrect' him by having the book's narrator in dialogue with the deceased. His use of the word resurrect and his friendship with Sister Mary Anne make me wonder if he's religious.

'There are things about Christianity I don't agree with,' he says. 'One of my biggest problems is the idea of original sin. I just can't accept that I'm born a sinner, so I'm not Christian. I became aware as I was growing up that increasingly I was going to church because I wanted to meet my friends there, and I realised I could make arrangements to meet them after church. And then at some point I decided there's no God, but I've sort of changed my mind. Now I'm not sure. Either way it doesn't actually bother me.

I believe in the power of the ancestors. I subscribe to elements of Christianity and elements of traditional belief; I think they both have their own limitations. Maybe I'm just an opportunist,' he laughs. 'I like the Bible as a collection of stories, though. I think it's great.

'In one of his essays, on why black South Africans shouldn't really care about being called 'Kaffir', Bosman points out that the word actually means unbeliever; it was only at a later stage that it began to accumulate these political meanings, so we should be thankful for not being associated with conservative Christianity.

'I think what I particularly like about Bosman is the way he captures the complexity of the rural mentality. The prejudices and gems of wisdom.' This mentality, that feeds so much on second- and third-hand stories, often mythology, is something Phaswane explores at length in *Welcome to Our Hillbrow*.

When I ask him how he deals with issues of safety while walking in the inner city, he reminds me that, like Refentše, he had been warned often about the dangers before he left home, and while Hillbrow is not quite the menacing monster he'd been told to expect, he too has had his share of violent experiences. 'I've had several,' he says, as though this is completely normal. And then proceeds to list a number of incidents, all cellphone-related.

There's a line in *Skin Deep*, a recent play at the Market Theatre, where one of the young women asks if a potential lover has the three Cs: a car, a cellphone, and a credit card. This is what will make him successful in her eyes. Though probably, to muggers, cash is still king.

'When they took my first cellphone, they had guns,' Phaswane continues. 'That was in the daylight. The second time they had knives. But my third cellphone was quite an interesting case. I actually felt I wasn't safe, so I decided to catch a cab. The driver called someone over, and I thought he was just saying goodbye to his friend. I had the door open, and was about to get in when this guy, the taxi driver's friend, took out a knife and robbed me and the driver just kept quiet. In the end I didn't get into the car, I went back to drink where I'd left my friends at my drinking hole.

'If I'm carrying a lot of money, I'll carry it in a book. For some reason criminals don't like books,' he laughs. 'There was one day, I had just come back from Germany, where I received a stipend, so I ended up not having to use my own money. I had about a thousand euros. I carried it inside *The Tin Drum* by Günter Grass, which I was reading at the time, and walked quite safely to deposit it in the bank.'

If not conventionally religious, he is fatalistic. 'I walk through Hillbrow at any time of the day or night,' he says. 'If it's your turn, it's your turn.' Perhaps this is influenced by coming from a rural area, where nature can be more of a threat than one's fellow man. One of the biggest dangers in the wide open space, while walking, is lightning. 'Shortly after I wrote my first short story, 'Brooding Clouds', a story about witchcraft and lightning,' he says, 'my mother got struck by lightning. She wasn't fatally injured, but nevertheless I started feeling guilty, and I put the story in my briefcase for a while before it was published.'

On the question of owning a car, Phaswane says he has no need. 'I've been teaching at the university, so I don't have far to travel. And if I need to travel a long distance for any reason I catch a cab. But when I do travel long distances, it's usually to far off places, where I use a plane.'

In 1997 he spent nine months in Oxford doing a diploma in publishing studies. He didn't realise that this was the home of Lewis Carroll, author of the *Alice in Wonderland* that he so loved, but a friend, knowing his love of Dickens, invited him to visit London for a few days. 'I went to see the Old Curiosity Shop. I didn't recognise anything in London from Dickens's work, not in a physical sense anyway, but I did have some sort of emotional response, which worked wonders for me, because I didn't actually like London. It's too congested and too busy for my liking. Hillbrow is congested,' he adds, 'but there's a lot of social life in

Hillbrow. I didn't feel that in London. There's a lot of busyness, but...,' he trails off, hinting at a loneliness in the London crowd that is very different from Africa.

Bosman once related a story of meeting a South African on a bench in Hyde Park who 'told me the funniest Afrikaans story I have ever heard. It was about a predikant and the district drunkard. Afterwards, I thought much about the man. I wondered how long he had been there, sitting on that park bench, in childlike faith that some day a stranger would come past who would know about the veld and who would listen to his story.' And then he continued in his usual irreverent fashion: 'It's queer how London always seems to lead the world in art and literature ... Here I have to come all the way to London, to Hyde Park, to hear the world's best Afrikaans story.'

Bosman's years abroad, it is said, 'seemed to offer less of the stimulus of a fresh environment than a re-affirmation of love for his old one'. Though Phaswane has travelled a fair amount, I get the impression the same may be true for him.

Back home, Phaswane realises that he may at some point be forced to learn to drive. 'I've not had a strong motivation to do it. But I may one day end up working far from Braamfontein, and then it will become unavoidable. Public transport in South Africa, if you are under time constraints,' he concedes, 'can be a problem.

'The only people who have responded with a sense of surprise when I tell them I don't drive have been my students. "We thought you were successful," they say. But from very early on I defined success in my own terms, by the kind of things I *do*, rather than what I don't do. That's another thing I got from Mary Anne. If I had followed what others have told me constitutes success, I'd probably have stopped teaching much earlier and done something that made a lot more money.'

Commenting on his doctoral thesis, on representations of sexuality in post-apartheid literature, he says: 'I particularly like K Sello Duiker's novel *The Quiet Violence of Dreams*, because it deals with issues of black homosexuality, black identity and masculinity, but he does it in a way that takes homosexuality for granted, in a context where many people argue that homosexuality is a white man's disease. I like the honesty with which he treats the issues.'

Throughout our conversation, his 2-year-old daughter Reneilwe has been peacefully sleeping in his lap. She stirs, and our attention is brought back to the room; to the sun fading outside his office window. It is time to get the little girl home. He gathers her things together, picks up his cellphone, and prepares for their walk, ready for any stories they might encounter on the way.

This interview took place shortly before Phaswane's sudden death on the 12th of December 2004.

Tragically, K Sello Duiker – whom Phaswane mentions in the interview – committed suicide just a month later.

A Cappella

It was midnight. The room was dark and smoky when four voices burst out on stage, in perfect synch, from Bach to Led Zeppelin, teasing, captivating, and proving George Milaras wrong. He was the owner of the Black Sun cabaret venue in Berea, who had said (Greek accent): 'No tits, no arse – it'll never work. Just a bunch of people singing around a microphone and telling silly jokes. But, OK, you wanna make fools of yourselves, I'll give you the midnight slot for the next two weeks.' And so, Not the Midnight Mass was born. After the performance they passed around a hat for collection.

That was 1988. Since then the voices from that night have scattered. After twelve years in New York, dramatic mezzo Natalie Gamsu now lives and sings in Sydney. (George Milaras is there too.) The unmistakable bass, Alan Glass, the only one who remains in Joburg, is a businessman and can be heard on the occasional TV commercial. But Not the Midnight Mass, after many incarnations with brother and sister Graham and Christine Weir at its core, is still going strong, now delighting a new generation in Cape Town, where they both live, and Graham is a dedicated walker.

He lives in a beautiful old building, Victoria Court, which was saved from demolition at the last minute by a petition and is home to a number of artists. Situated at the top of now trendy Long Street, right next door to the Long Street Baths, it is in one of the most pedestrian friendly areas of Cape Town.

'Often if I'm working on a song, or writing a story, I take a walk,' he says, 'and it comes to me while I'm going along. Ideas formulate then. I use walking as a time to meditate, and realign my body. If I'm in the mountains, I chant as I walk. Buddhist chants. They give me a rhythm. Or if I'm around here, in the city, I just meditate on the walking. It motors me along. Seeing the left, the right, the left, the right… Putting my feet down squarely on the ground. It carries me along. To me it's a constructive time, an unwinding time, which I find very different when you drive a car. Then you're constantly edgy.

'I'm a streetwise walker, so I walk with my antennae up. I'm not scared. There *are* gangs in the city, particularly street kid gangs, but I've never been harassed when I walk. My mother was mugged at twelve o'clock on a Saturday afternoon walking in the city centre,' he adds. 'But generally I don't feel at all unsafe from gangs and people. I walk fairly often in the city centre and don't feel any threat. I feel more threat from motorists, actually,' he laughs.

'My particular gripe is that more and more, when people come to a red robot in their cars, instead of coming to a full stop and engaging the handbrake they start edging forward. Eventually the whole car is over the pedestrian line and the next car is already edging its way forward, and you have to work your way round these cars. Here in town, because the laws aren't enforced (it's a sixty-kilometre zone), people drive along Orange Street and Long Street sometimes at a hundred and twenty kilometres an hour, so it makes it hard for pedestrians to judge. If you're in Orange Street, for instance, and you're halfway along and you want to cross, and you look along and see a car coming, if people are keeping to the speed limit you'd be able to get across, but you're often uncertain because people are coming at you at ridiculous speeds. Motorists constantly treat pedestrians like vermin they can bump out of the way. It's unbelievable. People resent having to slow down.'

Los Angeles writer and pedestrian DJ Waldie describes the

combat zone between drivers and pedestrians: 'Traffic safety trainers suggest that pedestrians stare at drivers ... The theory is that human beings are quick to sense when someone is staring at them – a common primate threat behavior – and a driver who's stared at will react unconsciously as if the pedestrian is real. My belief that staring actually works is my only protection.'

But sometimes that is not enough. 'One Saturday night recently, it was bedlam here in Long Street,' says Graham. 'At about 9.30 p.m. I was crossing over Orange to Long with the pedestrian light green in my favour, and a man roared around the corner right at me. I stopped dead still. So did he – a foot from me. I pointed to the green man with deft articulate gesticulations, and went on my way. I decided to cross at Lola's Café. I looked towards the oncoming traffic and the way was clear, so I stepped into the road – and felt something bash into my hip. A reversing car lifted me onto its boot, but not before I had gouged a mark on it, banging till he stopped!'

Though Graham doesn't own a car at the moment, he does drive, and knows about life on both sides of the windscreen. He likens it to someone who's worked as a waiter: 'Then you know what it's like when you eat at a restaurant. But I don't think the majority of people in this town ever set foot on the pavements. Most of them, the only place they walk is in the shopping malls.'

When his car – which he had for a year and a half, his first in fifteen years – began to develop problems and started to become more trouble than it was worth, 'I knew it was going to cost me money I didn't have, so I decided to get rid of it. A lot of people are buying flats in the city centre, and in Long Street you don't have a place to park. You don't get residence permits or anything like that. Some people park at the church across the street, but a lot of people don't get space to park. For me it became such a hassle because the City Council brought in these bylaws where, between eight and five o'clock if your money's run out in the parking meter they clamp your wheels and tow your car away, so I'd have to get up at seven o'clock before rush hour starts and go and move my car to Orange Street, where there are no parking meters. And then I'd have to be back at about seven at night, before the revelry started outside in Long Street, so it actually became a nuisance having a car.

'The only reason I'd have a car now would be to get out of town at weekends, to Tulbagh or Piketberg, where I have friends with farms. It's difficult sometimes, when time is short and I have to go somewhere like Constantia that's not on the railway line, and the minibus stops about a half hour's walk from where I have to get to. But during the day things are mostly accessible by public transport.

'When I go to yoga at five o'clock in the evening, I walk through the Gardens, down Adderley Street to get a minibus to Sea Point, and that's wonderful. There are lots of people out and lots of things to see, squirrels, office workers going home, tourists in the summer.'

He zooms in closer: 'As an actor, I find I'm always imitating people's walks. Watching people walk is a fascinating indication of where they're at mentally, and where they hold their tension. When a person carries all their tension in their chest for example, and therefore their left shoulder is hunched, and therefore the right foot moves further forward than the left… Some people hold their tension in their groin, and push their groin forward. People with short hamstrings tend to stoop forward, and walk looking at the ground.'

A walk then, like a laugh, or one's handwriting, becomes a signature, making our mark across space.

'If your chin is parallel with the ground,' he continues, 'you can take in the whole universe, and therefore you're going to have a state of mind where your chest is filling, but the minute you get depressed, everything starts collapsing, and you start seeing the world like a horse with blinkers on. The more vivacious and outgoing someone is, the more of the world they see.'

'I'm often late for things because I stop to watch people, and how they interact,' he says. 'Particularly *bergies*. I find their way of walking fascinating. And old people. There's a chap who lives at the old age home, in about his late seventies. He's suddenly started using a stick. He's always in his suit, and he's a pub crawler. His last port of call is the Labia cinema next door, where he has a glass of red wine. Sometimes on a Sunday afternoon I see him wandering around by himself. One thing I will say about when I first came to Cape Town, I was quite amazed at how many more old people I saw in the streets. It's lovely seeing old people out for a walk.

'And the people who live on the streets, you get to know about them and their lives. There's a wonderful lady who lives in the park at the moment. She always calls me Freddy. Her name is Sylvia. She'll tell you stories about her life. "For a small fee,"' he laughs. As someone who earns his living as an entertainer, Graham is happy to support her.

'She says, "Come talk to me, come talk to me…,"' he mimics, in a high-pitched voice. 'I can never remember any of her stories, but they're very amusing at the time. I think it's more her personality and her way of talking that's interesting. She'll say weird things, like she'll point to the guy who's with her, a white guy, and say: "Shame, he's mixed race you know." It would seem that Sylvia herself, in old South African race classification terms, is 'coloured'.

'You also pay more attention to detail when you walk. Every time I walk out here I see something new. I often get transfixed. The buildings in Cape Town are so beautiful. Particularly in Long Street, many of the buildings are national monuments, and around the older areas of town. The detail in the architecture is quite amazing. So I often walk around like a tourist, spending my time looking up at the buildings.

'I could only live in the country or the city centre. I could never live in suburbia. To me there's nothing more depressing than having to get in the car to go to the shop. Here I can walk to any number of restaurants or coffee bars. I can walk to an art gallery around the corner, or the Labia cinema within a few blocks, or the Gardens, or Greenmarket Square.

'The one place I avoid is the Waterfront. There's no way to walk there without going over a massive highway. If you go down Buitengracht Street there's a five-lane highway. All around the International Conference Centre, that whole area where all the big hotels are, is in amongst highways. It's absurd. So there's a massive divide between the tourist area and the city centre. In a way, actually I think it's a good thing,' it seems to just occur to him, 'because it's kept the false trappings of the Waterfront away from the charm of the city.

'It's a bit like walking in Sandton,' he says, referring to the Joburg suburb that has replaced the city centre as its central business district and is known globally for playing host to the 2002 World Summit on Sustainable Development. WSSD 2002 became known simply as 'Sandton', as the summit before it was 'Rio'.

It's fair to speculate that many of the delegates of WSSD rarely left the area. On the few occasions I get to Sandton (not easily accessible by public transport, though the Gautrain should change that), I always have the feeling there should be signs up saying *You are now leaving Sandton*. Its residents seem content to work, play and shop within its confines. There is little reason to leave and to be confronted by the harsher economic realities that lie just outside its borders.

'I spent a week in Sandton last year when we went up with Midnight Mass,' says Graham, 'and I felt stuck there. It was very depressing. You couldn't walk anywhere. There are no pavements really. The only place to go is Sandton City, which is horrible,' he adds, referring to Joburg's largest shopping centre. 'All the office buildings have tinted windows, and they're all set back in the road behind hedges and security fences and awful architecture. So there's a bleak pavement and nothing to see when you're walking there, except the cars, until you get to the shopping centre.'

When you get to Nelson Mandela Square, alongside Sandton

City, there is the six-metre bronze statue of Nelson Mandela to see and be photographed underneath.

Lost one day in Sandton City (not so named for nothing), I asked a shop assistant the way back to Sandton Square. 'Which hotel are you staying at?' he asked, assuming I must be a tourist. Why else would I be lost? Finally, coming out into the street in front of the conveniently situated Michelangelo Hotel, a porter in colonial top hat and tails greeted me: 'Good day, Ma'am.' A sign less of old South African racial deference, it would appear (he, too, seemed to think I was a tourist – why else would I be on foot?) than the growing global class system.

British sociologist Paul Gilroy commented when he was in South Africa on the renaming of the former Sandton Square to Nelson Mandela Square: 'People are trying to invest the experiences of shopping with the moral gravity that it should never hold and should never be asked to bear … To try to infuse that with the iconic heroic figure of Mandela seems a good symptom of where the critique of capitalism goes at a time when it is impossible to articulate it.

'I think it is shocking, but interesting, that they think of it as a brand asset, that they think they can borrow that life to build their brand. And if you think also that these private spaces are placeless, it could be anywhere in the world, and they cater largely for a shopping clientele which is also not affected, which is floating. It's about trying to tell these people they are in South Africa, when they just as well might not be.'

'I get the impression in Johannesburg people think you must be poor if you're walking,' Graham continues, 'whereas in Cape Town I don't think that's the case. In the city centre, Sea Point, Observatory, people walk all the time. Also, I suppose, because of the beach. But walking as recreation is one of the greatest things. It's wonderful exercise. You're getting fit, and getting fresh air and stimulation, and seeing things.'

Like so many of the avid walkers I talk to, Graham rarely

watches TV. He doesn't own a set. As early as 1951 Ray Bradbury predicted that television would be the death of walking. In Bradbury's short story 'The Pedestrian', Leonard Mead, the last remaining pedestrian in 2053, whispers to the flickering shadows behind the curtains of the houses that he walks by: 'What's up tonight on Channel 4, Channel 7, Channel 9? Where are the cowboys rushing, and do I see the United States Cavalry over the next hill to the rescue?'

At the time Bradbury wrote this story, Bhutan, the isolated little kingdom in the Himalayas, shrouded in mystery and known to the outside world as Shangri-la, did not yet have paper currency. By 1999 they became the last country on earth to get television, and by 2002, along with their first crime wave, walking was becoming a thing of the past too. Says Sangay Ngedup, minister for health and education: 'We used to think nothing of walking three days to see our in-laws. Now we can't even be bothered to walk to the end of Norzin Lam high street.'

'To me one of the most terrifying things about the modern age,' Graham picks up, 'is the way that people seem scared of silence. My nephew used to watch the cartoon channel: %&*@ $%#!.' He imitates *Road Runner* sound effects. 'You eventually want to throw yourself off the building. In the gym they've got these big screens, and music blaring. Any exercise you're doing, you should be aware of what your body's doing. So if you've got headphones on, sure you're getting fit, but you're not in touch with your body.

'It's amazing, if you go onto the beach and look around, you see how many people are talking on their phones at any one time. And at restaurants, or even just on the pavement. In another time, they would have been relaxing, but now they're all caught up in that. Even at urinals I see people talking on the phone next to me. It's totally mad.'

In his article 'Remember the Sabbath', encouraging people to take one day (any day) off a week from buying and selling, technology writer Douglas Rushkoff describes a TV commercial 'in which a young executive conducts a business meeting over a cellular phone – while standing at a urinal. When it comes time to zip up, he cradles his cellphone on his shoulder and goes on talking. But then the phone slips out from under his chin, and tumbles – splash – you guess where. The answer to this dilemma, according to the ad, is a new "hands-free" cellular phone service.' Rushkoff concludes with a compromise: 'Is a whole day too much to ask? Okay ... Just promise not to take the telephone into the bathroom.'

'Younger actors had cellphones long before I did,' Graham continues. 'I caught up late. But when people want you to do a voice over, they want to get hold of you *now*. If you don't keep up you lose work. The young actors even shoot clips of themselves on CD. They're very sussed in that regard. When they're not, they're considered out to lunch.'

Admitting that he has no television (and no wife), Bradbury's pedestrian is taken off by the police to the Psychiatric Center for Research on Regressive Tendencies.

Returning our attention to Cape Town, Graham reflects: 'I think they can slow everything down, and they should. They should make Long Street into a pedestrian mall. There is talk of it. Clean out the cars and make the entire city centre into pedestrian walkways. Vehicles can come in before nine o'clock in the morning, make their deliveries and then get out, the way they do at St George's Mall. Look at St George's Mall, the whole place changes. People are relaxed, they're not bumping into each other. There's less commotion and friction because people aren't pushing each other off the pavement to get down the street. If they did that and introduced cycles and rickshaws, it would make much more sense than all of this jostling for space.

'They can keep Buitengracht and those streets on the perimeters of the city centre as car-ways. I think it would help a lot if we had all-night trains, and the trains were secure. Also that would cut down on drunk drivers. People could catch a train to the city centre and walk to Long Street and come and *jol*, then get a rickshaw back to the station if they don't want to walk.

'To me rickshaws make a lot of sense, because, first of all, with the unemployment rate we have in this country… People say it would be exploitation of poor people. But at least it's something they could do. It would employ hundreds of people and be better for the environment. And everyone would slow down a pace.'

Talk of rickshaws recalls his time in India. 'Everyone hoots all the time, and the trucks and the buses push the cars out the way, and the cars push the tuk-tuks out the way, and the tuk-tuks push the bicycles out the way, and the bicycles push the pedestrians out the way, and the pedestrians push the animals out the way. And the animals all end up in the middle of the road. There's a thin concrete island that runs down the centre of the road, and a long line of cows, dogs and chickens lie along it sleeping, unperturbed by the mayhem. But on Independence Day, I couldn't believe how quiet it was. I took a walk along the beachfront in Mumbai, and hardly a car was moving. The city was so pleasant suddenly. There was time and space to look at the architecture.'

Of course in India, as someone once pointed out to me, hooting is not an aggressive act. It is saying, 'Watch out, I'm coming' rather than 'Fuck off out of my way', as it generally is in South Africa. In a country where weapons are common, cars in South Africa are used as weapons too, in incidents of road rage. 'I'm sure the average person who chooses to walk,' says Graham, 'is less likely to have a gun, or a weapon of any kind.'

There is a neglected and growing underclass on Long Street, though, amidst the backpacker hostels and trendy nightspots. 'There's no doubt about the fact that the street kids are dangerous. As much to themselves and each other as to anyone else. I saw one of them stab someone to death outside the 7-Eleven a few years ago. I didn't know that's what they were doing at the time. It was early evening and the guy was waiting at the gate. I thought they were just pulling at his jersey. They were only about seven or eight years old. And the next morning in the paper I read that they'd murdered someone, and I confirmed that it was him. And another time they stabbed someone at the garage on the corner, in the spine, and paralysed him. They get out of their heads on glue, and then they're quite fearless.'

Tourists are often the worst hit. 'Tourists tend to stop and talk to them, which residents don't. And the minute you stop and talk to one, they surround you in a flock. Also tourists are often walking around with big bags and hats that spell "Tourist". And they're stupid enough to open their bags to hand over a coin, and then that's it. So the kids pretty much know who to attack.'

In the end, though, Graham is pragmatic. 'Ultimately, hopefully, it's about... One has a choice to live life fearfully or to live life joyfully, and someone can come and mess up your life by stabbing you in the spine, but maybe no one will, and you've gone through your whole life worrying that you might be stabbed or you might be attacked. Or you can walk, and you see things and enjoy life, and until such time as something goes wrong... It's a choice, and the more people choose fear, the more fearful the society becomes, and the more people choose freedom, the more free the society becomes. And I think walking is one of those things that most symbolises that feeling. If you choose not to be part of the fearful mindset...'

Our conversation is interrupted by the phone ringing: a friend has arrived to fetch Graham for rehearsal.

Outside in the sunshine, as I say a quick hello to his friend Bo, waiting in the car, we muse on the inevitable contradiction, that it is liberating to not own a car, but it's always a blessing having friends who do.

Moving Across the Page

Half a lifetime ago when he was just nineteen Damon Galgut's first novel, *A Sinless Season*, was published. He describes it now as 'not a book I'm very proud of' and 'too way back in the mists for me to dredge up', but even then he touched on his recurring theme of walking. 'He preferred to be alone and in motion,' he wrote, 'not allowing his body to solidify into the restrictions of companionship or stillness.'

More recently, his story 'The Follower' begins: 'He is intensely happy, which is possible for him when he is walking and alone.'

'I spend at least a portion of every day walking,' he tells me. 'There's a certain security and comfort associated with it, I guess. It started in mid-adolescence when things were quite unpleasant at home, and I think it was a way of escaping, but that impulse has never entirely left me. I'm always very restless if I sit in the same place for too long.' Now, as a writer, 'the impulse to get away from home is sort of grafted onto the impulse to think about what I'm doing at home, in other words, the work. So the two are really inseparable.

'It's about the rhythm of the walk. There's something about the rhythm of walking that's deeply satisfying. It's partly to do with the fact that you can do it without having to think about it. I mean, one can't drive a car without thinking about it. Your mind has to stay on what you're doing, whereas with walking you can actually do it automatically, with an unconscious part of your mind, which sets the rest of my mind free to work in a very particular way. So that's very often what I do if I'm stuck. I'll create a mission to go down to the shops to get something I don't really need, but I persuade myself I do, to get away from sitting still.'

Funnily enough, he is unfamiliar with Virginia Woolf's wonderful essay 'Street Haunting', in which she describes this dilemma. For her the solution was a pencil. 'No one perhaps has ever felt passionately towards a lead pencil,' she wrote. 'But there are circumstances in which it can become supremely desirable to possess one; moments when we are set upon having an object, an excuse for walking half across London between tea and dinner … So when the desire comes upon us to go street rambling the pencil does for a pretext, and getting up we say: "Really I must buy a pencil," as if under cover of this excuse we could indulge safely in the greatest pleasure of town life in winter – rambling the streets of London.' A justification seems necessary when simply walking for its own sake is seen to be doing nothing.

And then sometimes she finds that suddenly the fog that has been gathering while sitting still for too long clears, like the time when 'one day walking round Tavistock Square I made up, as I sometimes make up my books, *To the Lighthouse*; in a great, apparently involuntary rush'.

German writer Robert Walser, in his novella *The Walk*, elaborates when pleading for a reduction in taxes. '"Permit me to inform you," I said frankly and freely to the tax man … "that I enjoy, as a poor writer and pen-pusher or *homme de letters*, a very dubious income." … The superintendent or inspector of taxes said: "But you're always to be seen out for a walk!"

"Walk," was my answer, "I definitely must, to invigorate myself and to maintain contact with the living world, without perceiving which I could not write the half of one more single word, or produce the tiniest poem in verse or prose. Without walking, I would be dead, and my profession, which I love passionately, would be destroyed. Also, without walking and gathering reports, I would not be able to render one single further report, or the tiniest of essays, let alone a real long story. Without walking, I would not be able to make any observations or studies at all … On a lovely and far-wandering walk a thousand usable and useful thoughts occur to me. Shut in at home, I would miserably decay and dry up.'"

Rebecca Solnit, in her chapter on labyrinths in *Wanderlust*, compares writing to walking. 'I have often wished,' she muses, 'that my sentences could be written out as a single line running into the distance so that it would be clear that a sentence is likewise a road and reading is traveling (I did the math once and found the text of one of my books would be four miles long were it rolled out as a single line of words instead of being set in rows on pages, rolled up like thread on a spool).'

Along with criticism of idleness when out walking, comes suspicion of the walker, wariness of the stranger entering or passing through, in the words of Thomas de Quincey, 'by base pedestrian methods'. In Olive Schreiner's *The Story of an African Farm*, described as 'a strange coming and going of feet', when Bonaparte Blenkins arrives the Dutch woman says: 'I'll have no tramps sleeping on my farm. If he'd had money wouldn't he have bought a horse? Men who walk,' she reasons, are nothing but 'thieves, liars, murderers, Rome's priests, seducers'.

In De Quincey's day innkeepers developed a shrewd way of evaluating potential guests. 'Four wax-lights carried before me by obedient mutes, these were but ordinary honours,' he noted, 'meant (as old experience had instructed me) for the first engineering step towards effecting a lodgment upon the stranger's purse. In fact the wax-lights are used by innkeepers, both abroad and at home, to "try the range of their guns." If the stranger submits quietly, as a good anti-pedestrian ought surely to do, and fires no counter gun by way of protest, then he is recognised at once as passively within range, and amenable to orders. I have always looked upon this fine of five or seven shillings (for wax that you do not absolutely need) as a sort of inaugural honorarium entrance-money; what in jails used to be known as smart money, proclaiming me to be a man *comme il faut*; and no toll in this world of tolls do I pay so cheerfully.'

Damon, in his novel *The Quarry*, conjures up the pedestrian stranger appearing on 'the road unspooling through that landscape of grass in which nothing moves except what you dream up in it … I started with an image of a man on a road,' he says. 'I had no idea who he was, where he was coming from, where he was going.' Only that 'he was a man with a past'.

More unexpected, perhaps, is suspicion from those you're walking away from. 'When he first started walking he was twelve or thirteen years old,' Damon writes in 'The Follower', 'he walked aimlessly for hours through the quiet suburban streets, he liked feeling that he was inside everything but also outside it at the same time. But when he took to walking at night it caused consternation and alarm, his mother started questioning him, where do you go to, you can tell me …

'She takes his arm and looks into his eyes, searching for lies or drugs, what does she see there. Soon afterwards he goes out walking again. He goes through the cool dark, with lighted windows in the distance, dogs barking far off, scents of flowers heavy on the air, he is everywhere and nowhere, he is what his senses tell him, he is nobody.

'Years later, when he has left home, he continues to walk. By now it's probably himself he's escaping. It's something that he needs to do and he goes out a few times a day. Other people, those who don't walk themselves, are still suspicious of him, more than once he is asked that same question, where do you go to, you can tell me, where do you go.'

As a child Damon had cancer and was bedridden for a long period of time. When he finally began to recover and was allowed to leave the bed, the mother in his autobiographical novella *Small*

Circle of Beings tells us: 'I must teach him to use his feet. An infant once more, he staggers and reels on thin white legs.' And later, when he is an adolescent: 'I still think of him as weak and soft. His body has lain on too many beds, under too many sheets, to lie down on mountains now.' I wonder if perhaps it was having this simple but precious act of independence, that most of us take for granted, snatched away from him for a time, that compels him to walk. 'I haven't thought about that in terms of the obsession with walking,' he considers. 'Maybe there is such a connection, but it's a deeply unconscious one. It's possible, I guess. Most of the people I know see little point in walking just purely for enjoyment. It's a foreign idea to them.'

'By contrast,' he continues in 'The Follower', 'he's learned to recognize other walkers in the street, a weird and various tribe of nomads, driven by different motives and intentions, some looking for a room, some trying to escape the room they have. Their faces and clothes and histories don't match, but there is something common to them all, something hard to define but it has to do with the way they carry themselves, the intensity of purpose as they move.'

It is this that he recognises in Reiner, whose follower he reluctantly becomes. 'As he comes to the crest of a hill' while walking in Greece 'he becomes aware of another figure far away … When they draw even they stop.' They conduct a conversation 'with a curious formality, the width of the road between them,' like a blank page, 'and yet there is something in the way they relate that is not quite intimate, but familiar. As if they have met somewhere before, long ago.' But this is a mirage; no two walkers are alike.

Later, in Africa, Reiner wants more detailed maps: 'Then we can plan every part of the walk.'

The way Damon's novels have taken shape gives us a clue as to how he prefers to walk. 'I didn't know the whole arc of the journey from beginning to end, but I did know points along the way, and the exploration for me lay in joining the dots. There's the same sense governing the unfolding of a plot as there is that governs a certain kind of journey, in the sense that you might begin your journey without knowing where you were going to, and without knowing exactly which choice you would make if you came to a place where the road forked. There are infinite numbers of ways you can go. Or perhaps they're not infinite, but they feel infinite. And the choice you make at a particular fork will determine where your road's going to take you and to what further choices.'

Unlike Damon, Reiner has no curiosity about people. 'Even here in South Africa, where he had never been, Reiner has no interest in what is happening around him, when he goes on his long walks through the streets' of Cape Town 'he has a pair of earplugs that he pushes into his ears, he doesn't want external noises to intrude.' And when he returns from the library 'it turns out he hasn't found out about the history of the country at all. Instead he's researched the climate, the terrain and topography, everything coded into numbers.' And yet he is contradictory. Even when Damon 'leaves his flat on the most mundane errand Reiner is always with him. He is worn down by the constant presence.'

Though Damon says he has little faith in the human race as a whole, and his writing is often described as bleak, he is fascinated and moved by relationships between individuals. 'I always find myself on slightly uncertain ground when this question of bleakness comes up,' he says quite undefensively, considering the question, 'because I have to recognise it as part of... it's clearly present in the work because nearly everybody comments on it in some shape or form, but it doesn't feel like bleakness to me because it just is intrinsically part of how I see things. In a way I'm trying to understand something that's maybe more apparent to other people than it is to me. I have to acknowledge that my view of the world, of the way the world works, of the way human interactions work, is very often out of step with the general view. People have a lot more optimism about their own lives, and about human life in general than maybe I do. But what other people see as bleakness or cynicism, I really do see as a form of realism. It really is just how I see things to be. I don't think my temperament is so unnaturally weighted that I'm distorting the way I see.'

At the same time his writing displays compassion and intimacy. And at times in our conversation I find myself uncomfortably wondering which of my idiosyncrasies he might be observing for use in his fiction later. 'I think people manage to connect in quite extraordinary ways, actually,' he says. 'That there are moments of, for want of a better word, real meaning that happen between people.'

In his story 'Lovers', a son goes in search of his remote, deceased father, and discovers an old love that his father never acted on. In her confusion, the old woman mistakes him for the father. 'I could think of little other than this soft, appalling caress,' says the man. But at the same time 'her body did not seem old in the blue dark…. I did pause a moment to think before I performed this final act of kindness allowed me in my life. But it was more than that. There was a kind of love in it, and a passion too. It gave her peace, and him. Perhaps it also gave me peace.'

In Edgar Allan Poe's 'The Man of the Crowd', a convalescent, with the heightened senses that come from a long illness, sits in a coffee house and observes the passing crowd: 'It seemed that, in my then peculiar mental state, I could frequently read, even in that brief interval of a glance, the history of long years,' he says. But in the end he concludes: 'It was well said of a certain German book that … it does not permit itself to be read.' Likewise, there are people we would not want to really know. And Reiner was better left to finish his walk on his own.

Reflecting on the need to walk, Damon says, 'I suppose there's a certain melancholy associated with it, too. Walking features a lot in the long, lonely midnight walks through strange cities in the writing of WG Sebald' (referring to one of his favourite authors). The title character in Sebald's *Austerlitz* recalls, 'How secure have I felt seated at the desk in my house in the dark night, just watching the tip of my pencil in the lamplight following its shadow, as if of its own accord and with perfect fidelity, while that shadow moved regularly from left to right, line by line, over the ruled paper.... But I soon realised that the shadows were falling over me ... I found writing such hard going that it often took me a whole day to compose a single sentence.' Accelerating towards a mental breakdown, he begins to echo the remedy used by Dickens more than a century earlier, and goes on 'nocturnal wanderings through London, to escape the insomnia which increasingly tormented me. For over a year,' said Austerlitz, 'I would leave my house as darkness fell, walking on and on ... It is a fact that you can traverse this vast city almost from end to end on foot in a single night ... and once you are used to walking alone and meeting only a few nocturnal spectres on your way, you soon begin to wonder why, apparently because of some agreement concluded long ago, Londoners of all ages lie in their beds in those countless buildings in Greenwich, Bayswater or Kensington, under a safe roof, as they suppose, while really they are only stretched out with their faces turned to the earth in fear, like travellers of the past resting on their way through the desert.'

On his 'Night Walks' Dickens explores the experience of 'houselessness'. And both Dickens and Austerlitz are preoccupied with 'Bedlam ... the hospital for the insane and other destitute persons'. 'I had a fancy in my head which could best be pursued within sight of its walls and dome,' wrote Dickens: 'Are not the sane and the insane equal at night as the sane lie a dreaming? Are not all of us outside this hospital who dream, more or less in the condition of those inside it? ... Do we not nightly jumble events and personages and times and places, as these do daily? Are we not sometimes troubled by our own sleeping inconsistencies, and do we not vexedly try to account for them and excuse them, just as these do sometimes in respect of their waking delusions?'

Austerlitz is troubled by 'where the dead were buried once the churchyards of London could hold no more. When space becomes too cramped the dead, like the living, move out into less densely populated districts where they can rest at a decent distance from each other. But more and more keep coming, a never-ending succession of them … At Broad Street station, built in 1865 on the site of the former burial grounds and bleachfields, excavations during the demolition work of 1984 brought to light over four hundred skeletons underneath a taxi rank. I went there quite often at the time, said Austerlitz, partly because of my interest in architectural history and partly for other reasons which I could not explain even to myself, and I took photographs of the remains of the dead.'

'And indeed in those houseless night walks,' wrote Dickens, 'it was a solemn consideration what enormous hosts of dead belong to one old great city, and how, if they were raised while the living slept, there would not be the space of a pin's point in all the streets and ways for the living to come out into. Not only that, but the vast armies of dead would overflow the hills and valleys beyond the city, and would stretch away all round it, God knows how far.'

And yet at that time of night, in South African cities, perhaps a lone pedestrian would welcome the dead, for as Ivan Vladislavić wistfully observes, a 'stranger, passing fearfully through the streets, whether in search of someone with open hands of whom he might ask directions or merely of someone to avoid in the pursuit of solitude, finds no one at all.'

Robert Louis Stevenson warned against walking companions. 'A walking tour,' he wrote, 'should be gone upon alone, because freedom is of the essence; because you should be able to stop and go on, and follow this way or that, as the freak takes you; and because you must have your own pace, and neither trot alongside a champion walker, nor mince in time with a girl.' When he found himself in the company of a four-legged 'lady friend' in his *Travels with a Donkey in the Cévennes*, he decided: 'Let her go at her own pace, and let me patiently follow' – though 'what that pace was, there is no word mean enough to describe; it was something as much slower than a walk as a walk is slower than a run; it kept me hanging on each foot for an incredible length of time; in five minutes it exhausted the spirit and set up a fever in all the muscles of the leg. And yet I had to keep close at hand and measure my advance exactly upon hers; for if I dropped a few yards into the rear, or went on a few yards ahead, Modestine' as he had christened her 'came instantly to a halt and began to browse.'

He had bought her for sixty-five francs and a glass of brandy and 'sold her, saddle and all, for five-and-thirty. The pecuniary gain is not obvious, but I had bought freedom into the bargain.' Nevertheless, when they had to part after twelve days, he found himself weeping.

Happily, Damon tells me that not all his shared walks have been disastrous. One of his best memories is when he and his friend Graham Weir 'met up in India, and four of us went hiking up in the Himalayas, and that was fabulous. It was fantastic.

'Nepal is covered by paths that have been made by walking. Primarily because the terrain is so impenetrable that they haven't been able to put roads through anywhere. So people still rely on walking, simply because they have no other choice. So all the mountain villages and little settlements are connected by footpaths, and you're just walking on that network of paths, and there's something very simple and lovely about it. Nothing connects you to a landscape more intimately than walking through it. We had a wonderful time, walking from village to village. And wherever you happened to land up that particular day is where you'd settle down. There's always an inn, with people willing to take you in. We did that for about two weeks.

'Though I guess for some of the locals, who were carrying the most unbelievable loads up to their villages, the walk was not nearly as spiritually uplifting an experience as it was for us,' he adds on reflection.

Travel is one of his great passions, particularly to India, where he keeps returning. It's hard to say what attracts him to it, he says, 'because it's actually a dreadful place in lots of ways. I hate speaking in clichés and I'm scared I'll lapse into cliché if I start talking about it. It's the sensual experience, I guess, of being there. Because India's a full-on assault on your senses. Absolutely in your face, you can't escape it at all, and it's an assault on every sense that you have, I mean the smell… sight… The noise levels are very hard to deal with, especially for me, I like silence. It's colours, it's textures, it's tastes, it's sounds. It's a complete invasion. And in many respects that's a positive experience. A lot of it is very, very inspiring, very stimulating. It kind of throws the familiar world on its head and turns it inside out.

'But obviously in many ways the invasion of your senses is not a welcome one. Some of the sights are really overwhelmingly unpleasant. A lot of what you see will never leave you. It just jangles you up in the most painful kind of way. But even that in the long term I think is beneficial. I don't believe in staying inside comfortable boundaries; especially if you want to be writing about the world, you have to continually shake up your perception of the world and see it in a different kind of way. So India is a very reliable way of doing that.

'Although, in the end everything becomes familiar,' he adds. 'Even pain and poverty become familiar. I think people get used to anything, which is one of our limitations, because it's only when you see something as strange that you're willing to change it. When you see something as normal you see no reason to alter it,' he says, touching indirectly on what outsiders often observe about South Africans' responses to crime. As he puts it in *Small Circle of Beings*: 'That is our affliction, if you like. There is nothing in the world, nothing at all, which we cannot, in the end, come to accept.'

As if unconsciously illustrating the point, he mentions that he has been lucky in his experiences of crime, because they were only 'near muggings. On both occasions I've become aware of people sneaking up behind me, but I used the oldest and safest avoidance tactic – I ran like hell, and got away!' In both cases it was in the belt between the Cape Town city centre and Green Point, where he lives. 'In the early evening, twilight time.

'A lot of the time when I'm walking I'm not very present in the real world,' he says. 'But at particular times of the day and in particular areas my awareness would revert, as a natural safety measure, to the world around me. You can sense when you're more vulnerable than at other times. Like walking to yoga,' about which he is also passionate, 'it's through Sea Point. And on the surface of it, Main Road Sea Point is probably not the most savoury area, but it's been absolutely fine. One of my familiar sights then is seeing the workers who have finished for the day hurrying to catch their taxi or train. So there's a certain kind of intent loping that's going on in the street. If I had to walk on that Main Road just a few hours later, when it's getting dark, all my senses would be tuned very differently. But it's also what you put out,' he reflects.

'The guy who lives downstairs, two nights ago I had to take him to Somerset Hospital because he was walking home and got stabbed. I don't think he was trying to resist. But he was seen as trying to resist. He was trying to get his wallet out of his pocket to give to them.' In this instance the car that Damon recently ambivalently acquired proved to be useful.

'It's my mother's 17-year-old Honda,' he says. 'I've acquired a car, if only to fill up the parking space that I've also come by recently. I'm using it for the kind of journeys that I wouldn't be able to walk, particularly at night, because walking at night is not always a viable option. And for long-distance journeys. And that's about it, actually. So nothing's really changed. I still walk to yoga every day. I still walk to town.'

This is the third car he's owned in his life, but it's been about ten years since he's owned one. 'I don't enjoy the experience of driving,' he says. 'I find it extremely unnatural. I constantly have a shift in my head where I see myself from a distance, and I see what I'm doing, and it seems quite bizarre. You're sitting on a seat with a little circle in front of you, with your feet on little pedals, and according to how you're depressing the pedals you're going faster or slower, and according to how you turn the circle you're adjusting your direction. It's a very strange activity.

'One of the satisfying things about walking as a mode of travel is that your input and effort are directly proportionate to the distance that you cover, so for me that's a real journey. There's a direct correspondence between the energy, the amount of time that you're taking, and the surface of the earth that you're covering. All the modern forms of transport, from the motor car through to the aeroplane, are unnatural, in the sense that you get in, into an enclosed space, and in a disproportionately short period of time you can go right around the world, and step out.' You can also avoid seeing what you find unpleasant. As the child says in Flannery O'Connor's story 'A Good Man is Hard to Find': 'Let's go through Georgia fast so we won't have to look at it much.'

'The shock of that has been culturally absorbed into the normality of our present lives,' Damon continues, 'but there's actually nothing normal about it. I love to travel, but I take days to recover and accept that I've arrived somewhere, or that I've left where I was.

'I long in a nostalgic way – as though I've ever done it, and I haven't – for the days of ship travel. It strikes me as a satisfying way to travel because you're physically present in the space that you're crossing. It doesn't cut you off from the distance, or the space, or the time. On a train you also go through every stage of the journey.'

Thoreau, commenting on the new railroad between Boston and Fitchburg, not far from the famous Walden Pond where he lived, was of the opinion that walking would remain the fastest and most efficient way to get anywhere. Someone suggested to him: '"I wonder that you do not lay up money; you love to travel; you might take the cars and go to Fitchburg today and see the country." But I am wiser than that,' he wrote. 'I have learned that the swiftest traveller is he that goes afoot. I say to my friend, Suppose we try who will get there first. The distance is thirty miles; the fare ninety cents.... Well, I start now on foot, and get there before night ... You will in the meanwhile have earned your fare, and arrive there some time tomorrow, or possibly this evening, if you are lucky enough to get a job in season. Instead of going to Fitchburg, you will be working here the greater part of the day.'

Rebecca Solnit believes that thought moves best at three miles an hour, and 'the surprises, liberations, and clarifications of travel can sometimes be garnered by going around the block as well as going around the world'. And when the threads of restlessness and anxiety, or the intimidation of being confronted by a blank page, have been untangled and one is pleasantly tired, it is good to return to one's room. Michael Ventura reminds us that it's the only talent you really need as a writer – 'the talent of the room'. Without it 'your other talents are worthless. Writing is something you do alone in a room ... How long can you stay in that room?'

When Virginia Woolf returns home from her 'Street Haunting' adventure, she concludes: 'It is comforting to feel the old possessions, the old prejudices, fold us round; and the self, which has been blown about at so many street corners, which has battered like a moth at the flame of so many inaccessible lanterns, sheltered and enclosed... And here – let us examine it tenderly, let us touch it with reverence – is the only spoil we have retrieved from all the treasures of the city, a lead pencil.'

Seeing by Ear

She recognises me as usual. If I hadn't been told I'd never have guessed there's anything wrong with Sarina's sight. 'Well, I have peripheral vision,' she explains. 'But it means that I don't see beyond the periphery, so I don't have depth of picture. In essence I see two of you, but I'm able to piece you into one picture. I can see what you look like, it's just hard for me to keep you in my area of focus. It's not like having one eye... The message to my brain is a double message, basically, so I'm not always sure how far things are.'

Remarkably, she only became aware of this when she was twenty-four years old and went for a driving test. 'I couldn't judge the distance when I was trying to park,' she says. 'I couldn't see the curb, I kept on crashing into it. If they had picked it up in the first five or six years of my life they could have done something about it, but because they didn't notice it when I was younger, you get what's called neural compensation – when your eyes physically are not what they should be, your brain overcompensates. So basically I see double all the time, I just don't know it.'

There is no name for her condition because 'I'm a bit of a freak case. I have three conditions in one that don't usually happen together. Basically it's an ectopia', a displaced organ, 'so what it means is that your eyeballs are like wheels on an axle, and my axle isn't straight, so my eyes don't turn properly. My eyes move in the right direction but can't keep still, and when they shift my spectrum of vision shifts.'

As she points out, it's shocking that she ever got a learner's licence. 'The only reason I got into the car was because when I went to do the eye test the guy wasn't concentrating. He kept saying to me "A1" and I'd say "B", and he'd say "*A1!*" and I'd say "C", and he'd say "Okay." I was saying what I was seeing, which wasn't correct, and he kept prompting me till I got it right!'

Not being able to drive, Sarina has walked all her life, which also has its challenges. 'Well, I use my ears,' she says. 'My ears are probably much sharper than most. So my hearing tells me how far a car is. I use my ears to judge when I cross. But I do use robots. I've learned to discipline myself to use robots and not to jaywalk. If I'm listening I can hear, more or less, but when I see the car and hear it at the same time the two don't correlate. It always seems much closer than it really is.' And even without this challenge, traffic lights stay green for pedestrians for precisely four seconds – little more than an invitation to cross, during which time drivers turning into the street, who also have right of way, rarely wait for those on foot. By the time pedestrians have a chance to cross the light is invariably red again. The only safety, it seems, is in numbers. When pedestrians cross in a crowd, drivers are a little less pushy.

Apart from the threat of being hit by metal at high speed, South African streets also have human predators for pedestrians to contend with. Given her limited vision, I wonder how safe she feels. 'Well, I don't know if anyone feels safe in the streets, really… But my ears are actually very good. In fact, a few months ago when I was almost attacked from behind, I heard them before I saw them.' In an environment where it would be useful to have eyes in the back of one's head, Sarina says that's not far from the truth with her: 'My back was to them, but my vision is very wide, so I could actually see before I turned.'

Originally from Glenhazel in Johannesburg, she has lived

in Cape Town for sixteen years, 'and I would say that I've only felt unsafe here in the last four years. In the last two or three dramatically. But up until then it's never really been a problem. I've walked at night and never been scared. These days there are always people on top of you, they're always hovering around you, you never know where a hand's coming from. I find it very nerve-racking. Now I prefer not to walk with a bag, I just walk with a key in my hand if I have to.

'Generally I've always lived around the City Bowl. I lived in Green Point at one stage. Obviously there are some areas that are more dicey, there are a lot of alleyways and they're darker, and they're not frequented often by people. But I would say that here in Gardens, particularly, it's quite bad. I live in a cul-de-sac in Hof Street near the Mount Nelson Hotel, where the bowling green is, and I've been caught there about three times in the last year. I don't feel safe to walk like I used to. I'm not a calm walker like I used to be.' This area, with its upmarket hotel and numerous guesthouses and backpacker lodges in the vicinity, is probably targeted particularly because there are likely to be tourists around. As the owner of Fields health shop, at the top of Kloof Street, this is Sarina's daily walk to and from work.

'During the last year I've been mugged three times on my way from work. At peak hour, five or six o'clock, when there are people in the street, so you've got to be very astute. You've got to look around you, and I think the best is not to carry a cellphone. And to look very stern and like you're together. You can't get caught unawares – speaking on cellphones is the worst thing to do. My phone rang and then two minutes later… I'm on my eighth cellphone in about two years!

'Now I try not to have stuff on me, and I also try not to look half asleep, because I'm small and I didn't look up when I walked. I used to look down on the ground with my head right down, but after occupational therapy I've learned to look up and use my feet to feel the ground. I've learned now to stand up more straight.'

I assume her attackers have been armed. 'Mostly knives,' she says. 'Though one guy threatened me with a cigarette lighter. I told him, "You've got to be kidding me!" What's he going to do, burn my head off? I mean it was ridiculous. I couldn't believe it.' And presumably she didn't argue, but simply handed things over? 'Ja,' she says, though on second thoughts, 'I didn't even have a chance to hand things over, they just grab. Once he pushed me against the wall, and my bag got hooked onto a branch so he couldn't get access to my bag, but I was talking on my telephone, so he just pulled it out of my hand. And another time he just came straight for me with a knife, and I just handed it over. I mean it was only a cellphone. I just feel constantly that I'm always looking around, at shadows, because there's always somebody behind you, always someone under your feet, asking you, distracting you, and the other one's grabbing on the other side. It's very tiring.'

She does enjoy the city, though. 'I think what's nice about walking in Cape Town is that you see a lot of beautiful things. There's always the mountain in your view, and there's the sea in your view, and it's a very pretty place to walk. The buildings are beautiful in town. It's also good for exercise – lots of hills. I walk to Camps Bay over the Nek on a Sunday and meet friends there for coffee, and then to my dad in Mouille Point, and all in all it's two hours of walking and it's very pleasant. I don't have as much time as I used to, the business traps me quite a lot, but when I have the time I do that.'

I try to imagine how the environment appears to her. 'It's very sensory,' she says. 'I see the changes in light. I'm sensitive to… It's more image… I'm very aware of cloud formations, the way the light hits the clouds, and the different colours, pink light and yellow light.'

I wonder if she's noticed an increase in traffic over the years. 'Oh, definitely,' she says. 'I think public transport is so bad here, when you're not mobile it's a nightmare. It's not like overseas where there are networks. A journey that'll take about an hour overseas will probably take about three hours here.

'Some of my family is Israeli, so I've lived in Israel quite a bit. I remember walking less in Israel because the public transport is so good. The main advantage about being here is that I walk more, so I get more exercise, which for me is quite important because when you're visually impaired your motor muscle development gets a bit impaired as well. If you're reluctant to walk because you can't see, you don't use all the muscles in your body, because you walk very tentatively. So the walking's actually good for me, because it forces me to be proactive. It makes me participate more in things, so in some ways it's probably a good thing.

'But it's not so accessible. The streets aren't really pedestrian streets. It's not conducive to walking. I choose routes where I know the pavements are properly paved and they're smooth. And I like the forest walks, Newlands and Kirstenbosch, but you can't really do that any more either. I can't do most of the walks that I used to do on my own any more.'

She prefers not to walk with others, she explains, 'because people get a bit neurotic with me. One time I went with people I knew, and one girl twisted her ankle because she was so busy watching me that she fell into a hole herself!' she laughs. 'So I get into a bit of a huff. I used to be a good hiker. I used to do lots of nature walks, but I lost my confidence. But recently I've changed. I never used to walk up mountains or do walks that I don't know the routes of. I didn't do that for about five, six years. And then recently, in the last year, I've forced myself to go on new routes.

'I got a stick, and now I just push the stick in front of me and I can feel the change of levels. If I was disciplined I'd use my stick more, but I'm also reluctant to do that because I don't want to get into a whole blind syndrome either. So I do a bit of both. I try to stick to routes that I know, and I'm also trying to get out a bit more, or go with someone who's not going to get too hysterical. I think it is uncomfortable for people because they're not quite sure how I feel. It's not something that most people can grasp or understand, so they don't know how much I see and how much I don't. And I feel bad about it, because you don't want to be an imposition, you want them to enjoy their walk and not be worrying where you're putting your foot!

'I also got into running. I run up to about fifteen kilometres, and I have one route so I know exactly where everything is.'

On the subject of poor public transport, I wonder if she feels confident enough to catch the train. 'Not now, because it also doesn't feel safe any more. There's chaos, and times are erratic. They never leave when they're supposed to, I don't know why they bother to have timetables. They change platforms... I think it's appalling. The public transport is pathetic, it's actually nonexistent, and I think that's why the roads are becoming so congested.

'I stayed in London for about three weeks with my cousin, and she was amazed. It's so much more friendly there if you're visually impaired, because everything talks to you.' I recall the famous *Mind the gap* warning passengers about the gap between the platform and the train at some Underground stations. 'In the beginning I was like, my god, my cousin must have a red-alert eye,' she laughs. '"If you see that girl just tell her where she is... You in the corner who can't see!" I was flabbergasted.'

But, despite the pleasure of usable public transport in London, she was astounded by people's resistance to walking there. 'It's interesting, because a lot of behaviour's learned and becomes a habit, and I find a lot of the time people don't walk even if it's just five minutes away. They'll catch a Tube from one stop to the next even when it's a beautiful walk. I once asked somebody where a Tube station was and she was horrified, and it was about ten minutes away. But I think it's nice to know that if you're in a rush and you want to go from here to the suburbs there's a bus, and you don't have to walk into town, get a train to a central bus station, and then get a bus to where you need to go. The nice thing about overseas is you've got the choice to use it when you need to.

'The interesting thing about the system in London was that

the Tube maps were a bit too small and hard for me to read, but I used the bus route map for the Underground. I worked out how the stations are linked, and the bus is networked parallel to the stations. I worked it out without really knowing… It was my first time in London since I was a child, and I found it the easiest experience because it all uses logic, in the way the stations and the streets and the buses intersect. And it's a pleasure, even if you can't see that well, because then you do have a choice.

'Even in Israel, you go to the central bus station and everything's on computer. You just press a little button and the bus number will come out, and how many routes, and what time it will arrive at what street. It's fantastic. That's how it should be, because not everybody can afford to drive, or wants to drive, or can drive, and walking here is not so practical always. The suburbs are quite far apart, the streets are far apart. Things aren't on top of each other.'

As these things happen, at this point in our conversation someone interrupts us as we sit in the courtyard of Sarina's shop, and asks her: 'I wonder if you can tell me where the library is?'

'About three blocks up,' she says.

'So I should take my car,' the woman decides.

Before she opened the shop, says Sarina, 'I started studying natural medicine, through the London School of Phytotherapy. But by that time my eyes weren't so good, I couldn't get through that volume of stuff, so I didn't finish. I was working in another health store, and then I decided to open my own store.'

I wonder if her condition ever gets her down. 'No,' she says, 'I know my limits, and I know it's disenabled me to do certain things that I'd love to have done. But I often think that you can make something a problem, or you don't have to. That's why I'm reluctant to use all the aids, a dog, and a stick, because I think once you get into that syndrome you do less.

'It took me a while to accept what I couldn't do, I mean I walked into a few cars,' she says matter-of-factly, 'because I wasn't really accepting that I couldn't use my judgement to cross the street.

81

And now I've learned. I've disciplined myself and I've promised my family I will only cross at the robots. But I'm not sad about it. I feel that I'm blessed with so many things I can do, and I'm still able to have a beautiful life. I don't feel upset about. I feel limited, but I find my own way of doing what I can.

'Now I listen to more music, and it's interesting because I'm finding that the very things I was doing a lot of, that were putting a strain on my eyes and giving me migraines, like watching a lot of junk on TV and a lot of videos, they aren't things that really nurture me as a person or make me grow. Sometimes now I'll just lie in Kirstenbosch and listen to the birds and relax, smell the flowers, so there are a lot of sensory things that are amazing that I probably wouldn't notice if my eyes were stronger. My other senses are very acute, so I can hardly complain.'

I mention to Sarina that over the past few years a number of restaurants have opened around the world where sighted customers can experience eating in a whole new way. From the time they enter the restaurant, they are guided through their gastronomic experience by blind waiters, as the dining room is completely dark. There is often a set menu, so they don't know in advance what they'll be eating. This is one of the few times when the power shifts, and sighted people are dependent on the blind. The innovation has also resulted in job creation for a largely marginalised group of people. 'The chef's aren't blind, I hope!' she laughs, and adds more soberly: 'That's amazing. But I doubt it would work in Cape Town.' Though Cape Town has become a popular tourist destination, it's largely seasonal, and upmarket restaurants remain fairly empty for several months of the year.

'And the whole social structure for the visually impaired,' she says, 'there's nothing here. There's only one guide-dog association, and it's in Johannesburg. So if you want a dog you have to go to Joburg and stay at the school for about a month with your dog, your puppy, and they train you. There's one association for the blind, and if you want a stick you go on a course, and that's about it. When I see my cousin who's completely blind, the stuff that she has, in Boston, it's just unbelievable. There they don't separate the blind kids from the other kids. They're in the class, in a normal school, they've got their Braille books, they listen to the class, and that's it.' It is Richard Nixon, not usually remembered for being progressive, who Americans have to thank for this. He signed into law the Vocational and Rehabilitation Act of 1973, which later became the Americans with Disabilities Act. This allowed children with disabilities to be mainstreamed into public schools.

I imagine if I was blind it would be reading that I'd miss. 'I listen to books,' she says, 'and they're starting to bring out some nice ones a bit more now, because with people's busy schedules they like to listen in their cars. So audio books are starting to become more popular. I hear some lovely books on tape. But I'm quite a simple person,' she adds, 'I don't need much. I need peace more than anything else.'

Shortly after I chatted with Sarina she moved to Israel.

Filling the Spaces

'Thirty-seven Olivia Road,' she says. It sounds familiar but I have to consult the map book, and then I see it's one street down from where I used to live twenty years ago. Walking there, through the purple rain of the falling jacarandas, it starts coming back to me, and when I arrive at the house I realise I'd have known exactly where she meant if she'd said diagonally opposite where the old Black Sun cabaret venue used to be. (Now the African Sun – it's unclear what line of business they're in.) The house with the mosaic of broken mirrors on the wall.

I ring the buzzer on and off for what feels like five minutes (but is more likely two), and peer through the wrought-iron gate as though my gaze might conjure up somebody to open it. As I start pacing up and down, a man steps up from the street and pulls back the bolt of the gate for me. Turns out it's not locked. I assume he lives here, but no: 'I'm Robert. I'm a taxi driver, and I park here.' Is it safe to not lock the gate? 'Oh, they all know each other. And I park here,' he reminds me. In the northern suburbs it's high walls and alarms. Here, it seems, security is people.

After wandering around the property for a few minutes and asking at an open doorway, I'm finally directed to Fiona Fraser. She lives in one of the rooms in the main house, but with a separate entrance and kitchenette. The house is owned by her daughter Thandi, but for the past few years Thandi and her partner and daughter have lived out near the Hennops River. Thandi rents out the house to Isaiah, who lives in the house and in turn rents out rooms to others. Another Thandi and her husband, King, live in rooms behind the house; have done so for fifteen years. I'm becoming confused about who is who and where, but in the end it doesn't matter. What is clear is that there is a community here.

Fiona belongs to that group of people we see television documentaries about from time to time, wondering what will become of them: white, elderly, and living in Hillbrow – or in this case on the border, in Berea. There is a woman, according to one of these documentaries, who is so afraid to leave her flat that she's not been out in two years. This is not Fiona, whom I see regularly walking between Berea and Braamfontein. It's hard to miss her familiar figure: tiny, with a shock of white hair, and a fast, determined walk. 'Yes,' she agrees, 'I don't amble much.'

I had always assumed that she can't drive, but I find out that's incorrect. 'I gave up having my car in about the beginning of the Seventies,' she says, 'after Bill died,' referring to her late husband, the entertainer and music journalist, Bill Brewer. 'Before that I had a car for thirty years. It was a great blow not to be driving any more, as you can imagine. It was economic, partly, and then also living here in the city, what is the point really? It's very convenient. You can get almost anywhere you want now by taxis. I'm a great user of black taxis, I think they're wonderful. They're the lifeblood of Johannesburg. And since I haven't got a car I couldn't survive without them.' Fiona is seventy-six years old.

'People all gasp and say, "You go in black taxis? Aren't you terrified?" But I think it's actually much safer being in the taxi than being a pedestrian when the taxi's in a hurry,' she says, echoing my thoughts. 'And you know, most people have very good manners. When a girl with a baby gets on, a young guy sitting in the front will usually get up and move to the back. And they're very sweet to me, they'll say, "*Gogo*, sit here." And being small, if there's a full cab and the big Mamas are sitting there overlapping each other, they can shove me in and I fill up spaces.'

'It would be so much more expensive to run a car. I mean, sometimes I curse. Especially if I've been called for a voice-over and it's somewhere like Rivonia and it's at short notice. Then it's absolute hell. But you can go to most places quite conveniently.'

Fiona earns her living as a freelance actress and voice artist. Last year she opened her one-woman show *Growing Old Disgracefully* at the Grahamstown festival and, after a run in Johannesburg, toured the schools with it. 'But it's more difficult than it used to be in the old days,' she says, 'because the school set-up is different. And it's tiring, because you've got to do the business side of it too. At the end of the show I stand on my head and do the splits and things like that.' She does yoga regularly and frequents the gym.

'I must warn you, it's an enormous shock the first time you hear someone call you old,' she says. 'About fifteen years ago, it was New Year's day, seven o'clock in the morning, and I was on my way to the gym – at the Summit Club in Hillbrow. My hair was red then, and I was wearing a T-shirt and tights. I bought a paper, and a young coloured guy passing behind pinches me. I turned around and he was shocked, and very drunk. To excuse himself he says, "Sorry Merrem, but from the back you got a sexy bum for a ol' lady!"

'One of the regulars at the gym came up to me recently and said, "Can I ask you something?" I said, "Of course." He said: "We all wonder how old you are?" So I told him, and he said, "Why do you still practise?" I said, "Because I want to die healthy!"' Her biggest fear, she says, 'is no longer being able to earn my living'.

I comment that many of the elderly white people living in the area feel too vulnerable to venture out. 'Yes, that is very sad,' she says. 'You have to be careful sometimes. You just get a feeling, and you think, Oh, I'll go and get some milk, and then you suddenly think, No, I don't actually need it. I know it's just around the next corner, but… And then other times you'll not give it a second thought. I try not to do anything stupid.'

For a while Fiona lived at the Park Royal, a block of flats owned by the Johannesburg Association for the Aged, which was in the news when JAFTA was short of funds and at risk of having to sell the building. 'It had a lot of advantages,' she says. 'We only paid R309 a month. But I didn't feel nearly as at home there as I do here. They were very... Ag, you know elderly white people. They're very us and them. And... "You can't go out, *now*!" I mentioned it once to one of the girls at the fruit stall, and she said, "Oh, they don't realise we're not criminals, we're just people." I find black people much more tolerant on the whole.

'I think it's a shame... You know, people are lonely. They don't get paid much attention by their young relatives. Sometimes over a weekend there would be five or six of them just hovering around the phones, waiting for the call to come, which didn't come, and you do feel awful about it. And white people are very naughty, you know, the younger ones, they forget their relations, with great relief.

'I'm much happier here, because it's more of a home. Isaiah, who runs the house, said to me one day: "I must tell you we think it very lucky to have a grandmother in the house." And Khosi pops in first thing in the morning to see if I'm all right, if I need anything.'

Fifteen-year-old Khosi has lived in the house since she was five, and grew up with Fiona's granddaughter, Cody, also fifteen. 'Khosi is the daughter of Em and Mandla, and then Mandla moved out on her mother and left her and got another family together, leaving Em and Khosi to just manage as best they could, so Thandi got Em a job. And then we got Khosi a bursary to study ballet at the National School of the Arts. She's a very talented dancer. It was noticeable from early on.'

I wonder if Fiona's unusual ease about race is because she didn't grow up in South Africa. What seems to set her apart from other white South Africans is no trace of a sense of entitlement. 'Well, I think it must be,' she says. 'Someone once said to me, "You know, you have no idea how difficult it is, growing up in South Africa and trying so hard to be liberal." Whereas with me I had no troubles like that. I was very fortunate because one of the very first people I met here was Bill Brewer, and he worked with black musicians, and I met the black actors before I met the white ones, and I enjoyed getting to know them. I thought apartheid seemed somewhat strange, but... You know, you're from another country, and you don't want to comment too much.'

Her mother was Irish and her father Scots, and Fiona was born in London. But when the Second World War came she was 'evacuated to a stud farm, just outside of Stilton. You know, where they make the cheese. And I became pony crazy. And while I rode I'd think and imagine stories. If you needed to get to the village, then you got on a horse. And if there weren't four legs available then you just walked.'

In 1956, when she was twenty-eight years old, a friend invited her to visit South Africa, 'and I thought, why not, let me go and see. My father was dead. My mother came over later, but she died very soon after.' And Fiona has been living in and around the inner city of Johannesburg ever since.

'I especially liked walking with dogs,' she says. 'I was always much happier when I had a lot of dogs. But of course here I've only got the two of them left. That one there,' she says, pointing to 'Cassandra. And the cat, Boris. But Cassandra doesn't like Hillbrow. It's not her scene. And food shops aren't designed to have little dogs walking around in them.'

At this point Fiona's granddaughter Cody arrives. She's just finished an exam: 'Apartheid,' she says. (She's struggling to speak as she's 'just had my tongue re-pierced.) And it's *so boring*.' Apartheid, it seems, is the new Great Trek.

'I've never been particularly political,' Fiona picks up. 'I've always been too busy earning a living! When I've had spells out of work, I've organised courses on presentation for a management consultancy. I do that about once a month. And I've taught. And been a dialogue coach.' She got her Honours degree in English literature from Unisa 'two days before my seventy-third birthday. I loved studying,' she adds. 'I absolutely adored it. I still attend classes at the Actors Centre, at the Civic Theatre.'

One of her biggest challenges these days, she says, is hills. 'I used to think nothing of going to Mass at the cathedral and coming back up the hill, but these days I find it too tiring. I dislike hills very much. There is a beastly one going up to Dunkeld. It's on the way to several studios, and there's no taxi and no bus. I've finally given up now. I've found a taxi rank with metered taxis along there, and now I just give them a ring to come and fetch me because walking up that hill is a stinker. It's gradual and it's steep, and it's a killer. I arrive at the studio not being able to speak, let alone act.'

I turn to the inevitable question of experiences of crime and violence, and remarkably, she tells me, she's had very few. Her daughter Thandi was shot and injured during a burglary. But this was out in the country.

'Somebody tried to stab me once,' Fiona says. 'Two guys were coming towards me and I thought, uh-uh. One of them put his arm around my neck, and I bit it so badly it bled. He let go. That was about five or six years ago.

'I use the ATM in Hillbrow. I know it's silly and I shouldn't, but these days they have five or six security guys. But one day they didn't have all these security people, and a guy behind me does that old gag of dropping ten rand and saying "Oh, you've dropped a ten rand". I said, "Thank you so much" and I put my foot on it and went on with what I was doing. Then I bent down and got it and said thank you and walked off.'

I'm aware throughout our conversation of the urban hum of voices around us. 'The guys next door are quite noisy,' she says, 'but they're very sweet. Mostly Nigerian, I think. They said to me, "We'll protect you. We're not like that rubbish!"' she laughs, gesturing towards the street. 'The police come there from time to time. Probably taking bribes.

'The noise doesn't bother me. I'm so used to it. Actually, it was when I was stayed with Thandi out in Hennops, where everything is so quiet, that I struggled to get to sleep.

'I don't know how many people would be happy living here,' she concludes. 'I haven't got many friends who will come here.

'But where else would I go?'

Stepping into the Future

Gordon Bruce was born in 1922 in Bath, in the west of England, about twelve miles from Bristol. In those days, as he puts it, 'cars were never even thought of in my family'. His father was a schoolmaster, and he recalls the 'picture in my mind of him walking home with the headmaster, walking side by side – I've never forgotten this, I don't know why – and they were deep in serious conversation, and for the whole of their lives the idea of getting into a car, and doing this by car, would never have entered their minds.'

By the end of the Second World War, Gordon had joined an organisation called Federal Union 'which was trying to create a world federal government, during and after the war. All this was very interesting, but suddenly I realised that world government wasn't something you could just fish out of your hat, by working hard for it and all that sort of thing. There were certain obstacles in the way and one was of course racism, and one or two black people pointed out to me that I might see world government as a thing oriented on the Western, predominantly white, countries – America and the European countries.' And this is what brought him to South Africa.

'I thought the best opportunity to study racism, and to become familiar with it in practical terms, was to come to South Africa. My original intention was only to stay here a few years, but when

I returned from London in 1958 I met my wife and we married.'

His late wife Ursula and her family were refugees from Nazi Germany. The Bruces settled in the Yeoville area, where 85-year-old Gordon still lives, at the Larmenier Village at Nazareth House. Though run by the Catholic Church, the residence is nondenominational. 'I, for one, am, a rather inadequate term, but we'll call it an agnostic,' he explains. 'My wife was Jewish, and many people here don't have any religious observances, but they enjoy the benefits of the building and eat in the dining room and so on.' Alongside the retirement village, Nazareth House runs a home for HIV-positive orphaned and abandoned babies, a hospice, and an outpatient antiretroviral clinic. Many of their patients are 'non-citizens', whom government hospitals and clinics turn away. So, while to many eyes Yeoville appears to have changed beyond recognition over the past decade, in one respect it hasn't changed at all: it remains a haven for immigrants and refugees. Though now, for the most part, they are from the African continent.

Yeoville has always been an accessible area for him and his family to live in, says Gordon. 'I've always found it quite easy to get around on buses. My outdoor excursions normally take me particularly to Rosebank. I go to Hillbrow police station, and I get off the bus there, cross the road, and get on the other one. I have used minibus taxis. I find it very convenient to get a taxi to go into town, but coming back I find it much easier to get on a bus.'

And Yeoville has always been a pedestrian-friendly suburb. 'I think that walking gives you a different experience of your environment,' he reflects, 'because if you're car-borne the whole time you almost have a blind eye to certain social realities. If you walk you have decidedly closer contact with others, if only because you're moving at a much slower rate than you would do in a car, and you absorb the atmosphere around you.'

His observation about having a blind eye is unexpected, since his wife Ursula, with whom he enjoyed many walks, was blind. 'Going over rough ground was a problem, of course, so I tried to avoid that kind of walk with her. But she wasn't a person who cowered within her living quarters.' And he adds, almost in answer to my unspoken question: 'You don't have to be blind to do that, some people seem to do it psychologically.'

Strangely, though his son David is also a dedicated walker, they have not done much walking together. Gordon recalls one of his favourite walks, showing me on a map: 'If you walk right up Webb Street' – the street in which he lives – 'to the end… at the very top, as far as you can go, there is a green place on the top of Bezuidenhout Ridge. You walk two to three kilometres and eventually you get back onto the main road, through Rockey Street and up to Observatory. David and I did it once about six months after he came out of jail.' David, who had spent two years in jail for refusing to do military service during the worst days of apartheid, had commented at his trial on his decision to go to jail rather than leave the country. He said that he did not want to flee from racism in the way that his mother had been forced to.

I suggest to Gordon that some would argue that the streets of Yeoville are no longer safe, but he disagrees. 'Yes, well you see this is a creation of people's minds. Shall we say in 33 per cent. It's how you view yourself and how you feel about things around you. My conviction of walking through Yeoville is that 99 per cent of the people walking past, apart from the colour of their skins, they're just like me, just going about their daily business. And the odd number of people who are gangsters, or what I would like to call make-believe gangsters, don't bother about an old man with a walking stick! I'm always a bit mystified by people who talk about "Ooh, Yeoville, it's such a dangerous place."' He agrees, though, that it's inadvisable to walk at night.

His only negative walking experience was not in Yeoville but about twenty years ago in the upmarket shopping haven in Rosebank. And 'this wasn't a violent experience,' he says. 'Two or three men… I used a little narrow path with bushes on either side to get from the back end of the Mall down to a lower street, because I had to visit a doctor in the street below after I'd done some shopping. As I went down, I was about halfway down, two men approached me from behind, and they were amazingly courteous about it. I didn't have any violence in the strict sense at all. He just said: "I've got a knife here. Don't do anything, and you'll be all right. I want to go through your pockets." Luckily I didn't have much money on me. What I did lose was my watch, and that was all. There was nothing else they could take.'

For the most part, walking is what has kept him healthy. 'I was a very sick person as a child,' he says, 'and consequently I virtually never played games, sports, or anything of that kind. But I was fit enough to join the Air Force at the age of nineteen, and that was in a way what made my life for me because I'd been living a very protected life until then. It was quite a shaking experience for the first few weeks, as you can imagine, but I managed it, and I went through all the normal drill that you have to do for the first four weeks in any armed force, and the physical exercise.

'I survived all that and worked on a bomber station on the Eastern side of Lincolnshire. I joined up on the 31st of December 1941. I had volunteered for flying before, at least twice, but I was rejected. At the first medical they said my eyesight wasn't good enough. So I wasn't accepted for flying. I probably wouldn't be talking to you today if I had been because they had a fantastic death rate, about eighty or ninety thousand Air Force personnel who were involved in flying during the Second World War. But I did a lot of other work, checking on intelligence reports brought back by bomber pilots on their return from flying over Germany, collating this information. Then I was sent to Burma. We got to Rangoon about two or three weeks after the Japanese had walked out. They were evacuating Burma, and British Services came in behind them.'

There was a time when Gordon attempted to get a driver's licence. 'It's a rather doleful topic, really,' he says. 'I took driving lessons here, and during the period that I went overseas I continued them in London, and finally returning here I carried on again. I'd taken the test many times, and I was with the test official. Finally he said, "You know, until we came to that last robot I was just about to give you your licence, but then unfortunately you made a mistake, so I can't give it to you today, but I'm sure you'll get it next time." I became so disillusioned with this that I just gave up at that point. It was very stupid of me actually, I'm sure I would have got it the next time.' It makes me wonder how his life, and his attitudes, would have been different if he'd become a driver.

'It's been quite exciting living through transformation in South Africa,' he tells me. 'White people here had got into a way of thinking racism was a natural part of life, having a group of people who you more or less regarded as your inferiors, at least those who did all the work, and who occupied a place that was convenient for the working of the industrial nation.

'It's a triumph for all the people of South Africa. Perhaps not an unmitigated triumph, but it's still a triumph all the same. There is an element of disillusionment in it. It seemed before that we only had to have a black government and we would be on top, as it were. People are beginning to realise now, painfully I think in some cases, that having a black government is not the only thing. You need education. You need training and industrial skills, and those things cannot be done in five or ten years, they take a much longer period, perhaps twenty, thirty, forty, even half a century. You quantify the growth of freedom with being able to be a skilled worker, for one thing, and not just doing all the unskilled jobs. Being able to share in the education that you've seen white children having in the past.' Until his retirement, Gordon worked as a clerk for Afrox, African Oxygen Limited.

I wonder what he imagines for the future of South Africa. 'I often give this some thought,' he says. 'One of the things that will happen is that there'll be tremendous integration between the countries on the African continent; shall we say southern Africa, I think. And by integration I'm not thinking merely of black and white people living in the same suburb, but more in the sphere of what you do, in life, you know. I think these things will change dramatically.

'I mean we already have a black president, but he isn't really representative of what I'm thinking of. Because what has happened at the present moment is you have empowered a certain group of people, and they are predominantly middle-class black people. And those are the people who are really beginning to wield power here. But there's still another group, the unskilled worker for example, the person who is virtually a slum-dweller, if you ask those people to express what they really feel they would probably tell you something along the lines that we haven't really got what we were looking for. But that can only come with education. It's not an easy thing to do.'

In June 2007 the government reported that 43 per cent of South Africans live on less than R250 a month; and 14 million South Africans don't know where their next meal is coming from. As of 2007, South Africa is also 'the planet's fourth most efficient producer of dollar millionaires'.

When I ask Gordon what he thinks historians will make of the time we're living through, he returns to his earlier thoughts. 'It's a period of adjustment to what is virtually a kind of world citizenship. It's quite clear that not even the United States has the power to control the world, in totality, in the way that Hitler visualised controlling Europe. All that is passé as far as I'm concerned. We're living in a period now where we're all adjusting to being citizens of a single society really. It'll take a long time, but there's no going back.

'It's the end of the old system in Russia. We've come to the end of that historical period, and we're now embarking on a period of integration, some form or another. Spiritual integration perhaps is almost a more realistic way of looking at it, because technology and the material unification can only be achieved over a long period. But I think we're at the moment coming into an era of envisaging that in some way or other the world belongs to everybody, in a spiritual sense. We move all around all over the world. The only limit to moving around the world is your bank balance. It's possible to move right around the world in a few days. A week, ten days perhaps. So all this is something which we're beginning to come to terms with.'

And his personal future? 'I'm reasonably fit, and I hope to be so for some years ahead because, if I don't crumble, I hope to do some writing on the subject of people who emigrate to a satellite of another sun in our galaxy.

'I started being interested in science fiction many years ago, and then of course I realised that we have already embarked on the early stages of something that seemed almost fictional twenty, thirty, forty years ago. Now there's no reason why we shouldn't accomplish the rest. But it will be very hard, because the bulk of the colonists will never return home.'

I comment on the parallel with his own environment, in Yeoville, surrounded by exiles who for one reason or another might never be able to return home. 'Yes, indeed,' he says soberly, and recalls that he and his wife returned to Europe only three times throughout their lives. Though his younger son Eric now lives in Bristol.

Returning his attention to beyond the borders of our planet, he says: 'You see all these institutions, and space ships, are primarily now in the hands of the United States, but that won't last forever. So I rather think that before too much time has passed there will be a new kind of exploration. This would be with the purpose of finding suitable places for us to live in our galaxy.' And the consequences of man's desire to colonise other spaces is never far from his mind. 'What happens if we meet intelligent beings? What is going to happen to them, to us? Are we going to be able to forge any kind of good relationship, or is it going to involve further war? If there are other beings, are they already watching us, wondering what we're going to do with our newfound power, preparing to defend themselves, perhaps?'

Walking to a New Rhythm

In the mid-1990s, while many South Africans were returning home from exile, Adam Levin was developing itchy feet and turning the other way. Of his life in Johannesburg, he wrote: 'I am growing weary of life in this jungle. This savage hunting for money and things … it is time to walk again. To walk till my feet turn a tar road back to dirt.' This led him on his *Wonder Safaris*, through twenty African countries, in search of what it means to be an African. It restored his 'miracle eye' and changed his life.

As he moved through Zanzibar, Senegal and Morocco, it didn't enter his mind that less than a decade later he would be immobilised by Aids – that the journey would turn inwards and he would need to learn to walk all over again. He describes this in his *Aidsafari* as 'a terrified crawl from the door of death back into the great wide world of life'.

'It's a weird irony for me,' he says, 'in that when I published *Wonder Safaris* I'd finally achieved my dream, which was to be able to go wherever I wanted. That gave me the credibility to keep travelling and walk the journeys that I wanted to make my life about. And at that point I physically couldn't walk. So it did force me to think about different journeys. I stressed in *Aidsafari* how far one can walk without leaving.'

In 1790 a French soldier, Xavier de Maistre, after being sentenced to forty-two days under house arrest for taking part in a duel, wrote a travel book called *A Journey Around My Room*. It seemed to echo Pascal's theory that 'the sole cause of man's unhappiness is that he does not know how to stay quietly in his own room'. According to fellow travel writer Paul Theroux, this was one of Bruce Chatwin's favourite books. Chatwin, a student of nomadism and a cult figure among Western walkers, is best known for his account of the 'invisible pathways' traced by the Australian aborigines in *The Songlines*.

Adam has spoken out vociferously about the silence that perpetuates the stigma attached to Aids in South Africa, and I wonder what he thinks of the way Chatwin mythologised his illness and subsequent death from Aids in 1989 – exoticising it and claiming that he'd contracted a rare blood disease after being bitten by a fruit bat in China.

'It's a hard one,' says Adam, 'because Chatwin's really one of the people who set me walking. I remember reading *What Am I Doing Here?* and *Utz*, and him and Naipaul are really the people who made me want to be a travel writer. It was a different time, but I do think he was quite calculating.'

According to Chatwin's biographer, Nicholas Shakespeare, 'The official reasons were that it was to protect his [and his wife, Elizabeth's] parents ... But there were many, many reasons why he was probably afraid, he didn't want to kind of be pigeonholed, this disease would have pigeonholed him beyond doubt as a homosexual in people's eyes. He wanted all this to be ambivalent and elusive.

'One of the interesting things is that he actually didn't think he had Aids, and the doctors gave him reason to think that. They'd never seen before the fungus that was manifested in his bones and typical of Chatwin, it was the first time it'd ever been seen in a Westerner. This fungus is now a well-known pathogen of the HIV virus. But at the time, and rightly for 1986, it had only been seen in the bamboo rat in southern Asia and in some Arabian whale. So Chatwin was thrilled, it meant he was unique, an A-1 medical curiosity and that this was what he was suffering from. And the doctors kind of blundering about, not realising that this allowed him to think that, so I think that also he hoped that if this fungus could be got rid of then his illness would cure.'

'I don't necessarily damn marriages where it might be a marriage of some convenience,' Adam adds, 'because I think he did love her. But it helps... anyone who died of Aids and disclosed it – the earlier the better – would have saved lives.

'I can also say what's upset me is that I've got close friends who watched me near death, stayed at my side, and came to me now and told me that they've been positive all along. It would have helped at the time, when I felt like I was the only person in the world... But even intelligent, educated people are still highly burdened by stigma.

'I am now rehabilitated to a point where I can travel again. And in the last few months I've been to Thailand and I've been to India, and that's just so rewarding for me, and such a relief that I can do it. I can't do it the way I used to. But I did rattle around Rajasthan. Where I did just hop and skip around any foreign city before, now I had to be driven up to the Amber Fort in Jaipur. But still, what an amazing prize to be able to walk around something.'

One of the cruellest symptoms of Aids is neuropathy, a disease that causes the feet to be numb but, paradoxically, in constant pain. About 35 per cent of HIV-positive people are affected by neuropathy.

'The thing with neuropathy,' Adam explains, 'is that surfaces are so key. That's another thing you can't take for granted. For me to cover an area of a few metres on cobblestones is a complete nightmare. I still can't walk at all without shoes, because the muscles have died in my feet. They say they may regenerate, but there's no guarantee. And nerves grow back at half a millimetre a day.

'There were moments when I thought, if I chop them off, will the pain go away? But it won't, because I'll feel it wherever the nerve endings are. That's improved, the sensitivity on the surface of the feet is much better. But without the muscles I'm walking on bone, so it's not really any easier. It's just my taking control of it that's made it bearable. It can totally annihilate me, and I can just feel useless and immobile and crumple up in a heap, but if I'm on top of it I'm much better. It's hugely psychological.'

As for painkillers, he says: 'I went through a morphine addiction and came off it and am on a very mild restricted opiate now. I'm going to gym and cycling because I need to ensure circulation in my feet, because they get very cold without the blood vessels getting to them. That's a huge fear for me because you can land up with amputation if you don't have blood there. So I'm doing what I can to heal that. And I'm much more active in terms of getting around.

'I got to a point where I realised that the pain is there constantly, whether I walk or whether I lie in bed. So what the hell. Being immobile, psychologically the pain takes over. Basically, at this point exercise helps, because it stimulates the production of endorphins – the body's natural painkillers – but it also helps psychologically. That spirit of independence, you know. You walk on your own. Whether it's to the bathroom, or through the desert, I think it's part of defining your existential reality and affirming it in the process.

'So I've regained it in a makeshift way. I drive. I can't feel the pedals, so it's fairly dangerous. But I can get around, and then I can walk to places once I'm there. And that's been miraculous for me to be able to do that again.

'I've got an automatic car because I can't push on a clutch. You're supposed to drive an automatic with one foot, but I can't because I wouldn't know which pedal I'm on, so I drive it with two feet so I know which is brake and which is accelerator. But I can't feel which is which.

'I would never have dreamed that I would not be able to walk. I took it so for granted and it's an amazing luxury. I've been coming into contact with disabled people now, and just negotiating a flight of stairs is such a nightmare for me.'

Even when he could walk easily, though, Adam rarely walked around Joburg. 'I'd walk down the street, or to the shop or whatever, but no… It was more the adventure of arriving in a new place. It was always standard for me, because of my fascination with maps, I'd arrive at eleven at night, and I'd go out to get my bearings, walking to make sense of the geography of the place. That was always an adventure.'

Of course walking at eleven at night in Johannesburg is not an option. 'Joburg is also very class-bound,' Adam reflects. 'And I think danger is one of the factors that plays into that.' Yet during the day you are arguably as safe walking on the streets of Joburg as you are in a car. According to a newspaper report, South African roads have 'a daily casualty toll higher than the killings in Iraq … every day there are, on average, 38 roads deaths, three taxi-related accidents, 16 involving pedestrians, 21 disabling injuries and 125 serious injuries.' In *Aidsafari* Adam muses, 'After everything I've battled, will I die in a car crash?

'People miss out,' he adds, 'with all their comforts and fancy cars, I think they miss a lot by not walking.'

He has been mugged 'quite a few times. The most recent was when I ventured back to Diagonal Street, researching a craft tour to send people on.' Diagonal Street is famous for its Indian traders – including Kapitan's restaurant, where Nelson Mandela regularly ate lunch as a young lawyer before he was sent to prison – and the Mai Mai Market and muti shops. Anglo American's domineering 'diamond-shaped building of reflective glass' towers over them.

'I was crossing the street,' he says, 'that end of town's pretty rough – and these guys knocked me, and then I apologised for bumping into them, only to find that my phone was missing afterwards. Then I felt very violated, the fact that I'd apologised.'

Speaking of walking in the city, 'A great walking memory for me,' he recalls, 'is New York. I think that was my greatest experience of liberty, to be able to hop on a subway and then walk that city, which is walkers' paradise. It's just amazing. There you have these really wealthy people who'd never dream of owning a car. And then there's walking, which is usually associated with poor people, as a daily routine of the wealthy.'

But he admits he did feel vulnerable walking in Harlem. 'I was missing Africa, so I moved up there, and I've never felt so alienated: there's no bullshit with black Americans. There isn't the kind of politeness that we have here. And walking in Harlem was very dangerous. Just getting from my house to the subway was scary. All the more so in drag! But I did it.'

When it comes to walking, rhythm, he reckons, is key: 'In New York everyone has an iPod or a Discman, because you're alone, on the subway or whatever.' Everyone trying to create a little personal space in the crowded city. 'So there we all sit with our separate rhythms beating, and walking to our separate rhythms. I defined three kinds of rhythms – the one of all our memories, all our songs that have carried us so far; what we currently listen to; and then what will take us forward. I've always got to have an anthem of the moment, that I play to death.' Currently his anthem is 'Lord Raise Me Up' by the 'reggae rapping Rabbi', Matisyahu. 'At first I thought it sounded like a gimmick,' he says, 'but his songs are wonderful.

'I think rhythm affects us subconsciously quite profoundly. I love to dance, and it's crazy that I really struggle with walking, but sometimes if I numb myself with alcohol my feet are better and then I can really get down to dance music. If I hear a great song, like I did in Cape Town this weekend, I was phoning my friends and holding the phone close to the speaker.'

Despite his illness, Adam has been remarkably productive over the past few years, publishing three books (*The Art of African Shopping* in between *The Wonder Safaris* and *Aidsafari*) with another, on the history of dress in South Africa – 'a look at historical crossovers of style' – on the way. But he insists that he's 'prolific by default, because I'm a lazy ass! When I get an idea, though, I get very excited and I get things going.

'There I was,' he recalls, 'unable to get out of bed, and I suddenly found myself as "the country's top fashion writer", crawling to fashion shows. That was very important to me because I wanted to be not only about Aids.'

He is also organising an 'urban runway as part of fashion week, which again will be individuals promenading. And it's real people, it's not models, and we're doing castings based on individual style. That thing of the catwalk and the promenade, I think there's something very powerful in that. There's an irreverence to it, as well. I don't take it too seriously.

'The urban runway is the first fashion thing I'm producing, so actually organising an event is exciting for me. They're launching the Fashion Kapitol in Pritchard and President Streets. It's going to be a fashion district of twenty-six city blocks, so for the launch we're doing this parade of people walking. It'll either be in the square where they've got a public runway, if it's ready, which is going to be on sand-blasted glass with lights underneath, outside. Or we're going to close Pritchard and walk along the street. What's interesting there for me is the cycle from street as inspiration, to catwalk, back to the streets. So in this show I want to have celebrities, grannies, hobos, young punks, to really reflect Jozi's style. I think that's key for the Fashion District, but street fashion is always much more exciting to me than ready-to-wear collections. How people customise their clothes, and then communicate something to the universe as they walk. Urban identity is powerful, and street style is key. I think clothing is very intimate and very political, because what touches our skin is so close to us. And what we wear subconsciously says so much to the universe, as we parade about.'

In *The Wonder Safaris* he recalls the observation of a friend who lives near Ponte City, the 54-storey 'grim concrete phallus of a tower downtown' with the nervous tic of its giant neon Vodacom sign. Notorious in previous years as a magnet for suicides, now it provides shelter to Africans from all over the continent. From his window, the friend sees the stylish Francophones walking around the neighbourhood. 'Only they don't walk,' he chuckles. 'They promenade – long purposeful strides down the hill. I watch the locals watching them from the pavement, transfixed, then trying to copy the walk after they've left.'

I ask Adam about his spiritual beliefs. In *Aidsafari* he wrote that 'my father went to great lengths to instil a committed sense of atheism in his son – and for the most part, I thank him for it', but since he took a leap of faith when he was at death's door and prayed to a God to help him get well, he feels it would be disingenuous now to disown him again. 'You ask me if I believe in God,' he says, 'I believe in this: Every now and then I meet a master, where instinctively I know this person is a teacher for me.'

One of these was Emerson, the enigmatic hotelier in Zanzibar who invited Adam to come and work for him. What was required of him was never clear, but his first instruction from Emerson (for whom a single name seemed to suffice) was: 'I think you should go and walk today … Lose yourself. Find yourself. Walk off where you've come from.'

And so, he writes in *The Wonder Safaris*, 'I slipped quickly into the maze of streets … My lostness frightened me, and yet I knew how important it was for my initiation. It would be weeks before I could tell one crumpled palace from another, for just when I thought I recognised a route, it fizzled into an alleyway …'

German writer Walter Benjamin observed: 'Not to find one's way in a city may well be uninteresting and banal. It requires ignorance – nothing more. But to lose oneself in a city … that calls for quite a different schooling.'

'I walked alone as much as possible,' writes Adam, 'but it was difficult, for most times, moments into my stride, some bright-eyed local boy would slip in alongside my gait and begin asking questions…. The content mattered little, but the combination of walking and company was sacred here…. In this busybody of a town, one dared not breathe a sentence while standing still, for it would ricochet through the delta of plank-thin alleyways, like a paper aeroplane aimed perfectly into the ears of the streets. Here, each mildewed cornerstone was a telegraph pole. Each glassless window, a live microphone…. So you walked, and as you walked, you talked. Secrecy danced to the shared rhythm of stepping feet.'

Another person who has been a mentor to him is his Indian friend Tarun, who showed him a side of India beyond the poverty on the streets. 'He took me to a party full of maharajahs and princesses and Delhi dowagers, dripping in rubies and emeralds. And just seeing that world… A tourist would never get access to that.

'The Taj Mahal was very disappointing,' he adds. 'It could have been the Oriental Plaza in Johannesburg.'

Less glamorous but no less valuable teachers for him were the Hadzabe, East Africa's last surviving hunter-gatherers, who he spent time with in Tanzania in the late Nineties. I picture him taking leisurely strolls with traditional people who have all the time in the world. 'Not if you're a hunter,' he points out, 'and have to chase after your next meal! And not if you've never been in a car.' The Hadzabe are his fastest walking companions to date.

They 'own nothing and share everything', so it is with ambivalence that he notices 'Njegela eyes a pair of my sneakers.' He recalls in *The Wonder Safaris*: 'I have another pair of shoes with me and his are wearing through. Still, this pair was an indulgence from Diesel and I retain a shiver of nausea at the thought of their price tag.' Later, after joining in pursuit of a wild pig (if he'd understood the language he'd have been less reckless and stayed behind), 'We wake the clan, who are truly delighted and feast until it is almost daybreak. My Diesels, I notice, are stained with pig's blood.

'It was such a turning point for me when I went on that journey with the Hadzabe, with my friend James,' he tells me 'without even thinking, What the hell am I going to do living with this tribe?, only realising the car wasn't coming back for a week once I was there. I didn't think, I just spontaneously went with it. But I remember what James said to me, in his profound American tone: "You have to take that leap of faith across the canyon without knowing whether you're going to make it to the other side." I think without that leap lives are wasted,' Adam adds.

'A physical journey, creates for me a written journey, creates a read journey for someone else, that then inspires a physical journey, that then may inspire yet another written journey… And so there's this magically infinite quality to journeys that can only happen if you catalyse it by taking one step. Without taking that step nothing will move, it's static. But making that step, and committing to walking a certain distance, be it in words or physically, you set into motion something magically exponential that just continues and continues. And that's been one of my greatest lessons through all of this.'

For the Hadzabe, time, though a foreign concept, is running out. Along with wildlife conservation and the development of international game-viewing destinations comes fewer and fewer animals for them to hunt. They are one of 120 Tanzanian tribes, and by 2005 their numbers had dwindled to fewer than 1500.

As if mirroring the fate of the Hadzabe, Adam says: 'The thing that I live for is my fear of missing out. I know there are more surprises, and even right now there are more things hanging and possibilities, and that's why I get up in the morning. And that is truly what drives me, and probably why I made it, because I feel very hard done by if exciting things happen and I'm not there for it.'

Walking into Dance

1.

I remember bumping into John Cartwright in Braamfontein one evening, at dusk, on his way down into town to the Market Theatre. This was before the Nelson Mandela Bridge was built and nobody I knew who had the option of calling a taxi would willingly choose to walk into Johannesburg's city centre at night. Yet there he was. It seemed to symbolise his way of exploring unconventional routes. After two decades as an academic at the University of Cape Town, on the eve of his retirement he had decided to move in a different direction.

'I'd been dean of the arts faculty in the early Nineties, which was very interesting,' he says. 'I enjoyed most of it, because the dean at that stage had not yet been turned into an executive managerial role with budget responsibility and all that stuff, but rather had a very much more central role as an academic facilitator. But I could feel the bulldozer on the horizon of university corporatisation. Then I was made head of the English Department, and it was not pleasant. Nothing to do with my colleagues,' he assures me, 'they were only too pleased to have someone do the job, but all the increasing bureaucratic pressures... it was just like a blizzard of trivia, and after a year I couldn't go on. I decided it was time for me to leave. I was just repeating myself.

'I'm glad I made that decision because I was then persuaded by my friend Clifford Shearing to get involved with the Community Peace Programme, and that's been another adventure for eight years.' Shearing is the director of the Institute of Criminology at the University of Cape Town.

In late 1997, Shearing – with the help of the late Dullah Omar, the minister of justice at the time – initiated a pilot project in Zwelethemba ('Place of hope' in Xhosa), in Worcester, about ninety kilometres from Cape Town. 'Omar thought it was a good place to start,' says John, 'because it was a medium-sized community that had a history of activism in the Eighties. It was not without its problems, but not overwhelmingly so, and it was not gangster-ridden. The aim was to build a model that would be well grounded enough to be widely replicated.' Since then about twenty similar peace committees (as they have come to be called) have been established, mainly around the Western Cape. As with many independent initiatives, though, funding remains an ongoing challenge.

'Then it became very clear to me that I was coming to the end of that as well. We've done a lot together, building this thing, and we have new younger and darker people coming in, and I was simply not needed except for a bit of backup and follow-up.' So, while most white men his age are afraid of becoming redundant, he is only too pleased to be liberated from these responsibilities, 'particularly in order to do more work in acting, performing and writing'.

No longer needing to be near the university, he decided to sell his house in Kenilworth, at the centre of the southern suburbs of Cape Town, and move back to his roots at the coast, to Muizenberg. This, too, seemed counter to the perceived wisdom. Author Mike Nicol, returning to the area in 1998 after a year in Berlin, was horrified by the changes he found: 'Our street was littered with broken bottles, half bricks, discarded shoes, the wrecks of cars. Men loitered in groups on the corners, music blared from windows. Babies crawled in the gutters, children played cricket in the middle of the road using tins as stumps. Women in curlers stood at the gates smoking. I groaned. I wasn't ready for this.'

'When I bought the house in Muizenberg there was a lot of decay and grunge,' agrees John. 'And within the next couple of years the Americans gang bought a cottage around the corner, and that kind of thing, but it never struck me as being a downhill slope. It was perfectly obvious to me that things were getting better, and that the kind of houses we have, the kind of community there is, the physical location of Muizenberg, the railway line, the beach, all these wonderful things, could only mean that it would revive. And the kind of people who chose to come and live here were people who understood that, and kept an eye open for each other and had a sense of certain kinds of community values.'

Perhaps, as a friend put it when he advised Nicol to move: 'Something had come to an end, something new had to be started.' Nicol, whose writing is beautiful when exploring history and reflecting on the past, is on more shaky ground when it comes to the future.

So how did they take control and stop the slumlords and drug dealers from taking over the area? 'It was not through some kind of community committee particularly,' says John. 'I think the Community Police Forum in Muizenberg did a valuable job in putting pressure on the local police to come up to scratch, but also it was just people bugging City Council, for example, about houses falling into disrepair.'

An estate agent, who has also been a resident in the area for twenty-four years, tells me that many of the residents bought up buildings that were in danger of being exploited by slumlords. When I visit her, her dogs announce my arrival, but – with only a low wall around her house – I am able to walk up to the front door and ring the bell. She obviously has faith in the suburb.

'There's been increasing pressure on the kind of relatively minor slumlords that there have been in Muizenberg to clean it up or get out,' says John. 'Just recently, there's been a very much more explicit building on this sense of community, with people getting together and very peacefully going walking through the streets on a Saturday evening with the kids.' This calls to mind the Jewish community where I live, in northeastern Johannesburg, on Friday nights. In fact Muizenberg, too, has a history of Jewish migrants, from Lithuania early in the twentieth century. So much so that, when I was growing up, the area was sometimes derogatorily referred to as 'Jewsenberg'. Now, however, as with Yeoville in Johannesburg, the migrants are a different colour and hail from other parts of Africa.

Historically Cape Town has been very 'good' at keeping its own small black population on the margins. As a white South African visitor to the city once remarked: 'Cape Town is better because the coloureds keep the blacks in their place.' Because of South Africans' xenophobia, other Africans, unwelcome in the townships and haunted by ghosts from their own countries but not the memories of apartheid, are moving into the city centre and the formerly white suburbs. This has been disconcerting to many Capetonians.

'Most of the new inhabitants' of Muizenberg, wrote Nicol, 'were refugees, young men who'd fled the warring, hopeless regions of Africa.' And, while Nicol had previously 'felt as comfortable in its streets as I had in my living room', he felt less at home in someone else's. 'They took possession of the streets because there wasn't enough room in the houses.'

Nearly a decade later, John is very positive about the area. 'I don't have dogs now but when I had dogs and we'd go out, I'd very deliberately walk through the street where the Americans' cottage is.' I can almost see him doffing the panama hat he wears as protection from the sun. 'There was pretty obviously no physical danger to me unless I was really stupid, but they just needed to know, they don't own the place.'

But Nicol's discomfort was not about race or nationality, it was about class. When the bohemians in Muizenberg began to be replaced by *bywoners*, South Africa's equivalent of so-called 'trailer trash', he found that equally hard to live with. He knew one of his worst nightmares had arrived on the day they moved into his street, when 'they revved their cars, they swore, they shouted, they played loud music, and that afternoon they drank brandy and Coke on the pavement.'

Those who have chosen to stay in the area, however, are taking action to preserve the community. 'A small group responded to the request of a couple who own a house which they'd been letting to some young people who had not paid the rent for several months and had resisted all attempts to get them to pay or to leave,' John tells me. 'We have to do this very carefully,' he reflects, 'so that it doesn't become vigilantism. A group of about twenty or so, with their kids, went along at the time of the deadline for the eviction and just stood outside in the street, and started engaging in a conversation: "Oh, I believe you're moving today…" And they left in the end.'

Interestingly enough, it is John's work in township communities, with the Community Peace Programme, that continues to inform his thinking on community building in the suburbs. 'For the so-called African, so-called black, African-language-speaking communities, they have at least a memory of a tradition where there were no Western courts and police, where somehow conflict was resolved in the community. Sometimes it might have involved punishment or exile or whatever, but there were attempts to resolve it. Very likely in a very patriarchal kind of frame, but nevertheless there was that sense of there being other ways of doing it.'

The important thing, he says, is 'valuing local knowledge, local awareness, local capacity. The project is not about crime, it's about governance. Though expressed in this particular project through questions of security, it could equally be expressed through questions of environmental control. It's really about: "Do we want to go on living on this planet? And how?" As the late Sixties and Seventies saying has it, "Think global, act local". That's very much my view.

'And what we're doing in the Community Peace Programme has been to try and build, co-operatively, a model of how that local knowledge among people, who don't necessarily have very much formal education and are poor, how can the kind of knowledge that they have of their community be most effectively and sustainably expressed in practices. In other words, what is it that a citizen is?'

There is a fine line though between a community taking control of itself, and vigilantism, so nonviolence is central to the CPP's philosophy. 'If you think of the way that Pagad went,' John recalls, 'people could imagine in the beginning, We've got to take back the streets; but when it becomes associated with violence and vicious judgementalism, a holier-than-thou attitude, that's not building anything worthwhile.' Pagad, People Opposing Gangsterism and Drugs, an organisation formed in 1995 to fight crime on the Cape Flats, was responsible for more violence than it prevented, including a gang leader being burnt to death by a mob that marched to his home.

'I think the search for community is such a powerful one, whether it's conscious or unconscious,' he observes. 'The nuclear family, without a broader community, can't take the strain. The Religious Right, here recently and obviously in the US and other places, is completely obsessed with the nuclear family, and it's a dead end. It's not a matter of rejecting the so-called nuclear family, but it's not the be all and end all, it can be a horrible trap.'

Looking out his living room window towards the sound of squealing swimming children at the Pavilion, and the Promenade, often frequented by inebriated *flâneurs*, his thoughts turn to his love of walking. 'I think it's a question of temperament. I enjoy physical exercise, and it gives me great pleasure to do that – a feeling of one's body working. There are various aspects of it. Part of it is just the physical pleasure of walking. And you're also more conscious of what's going on around you.'

It was this consciousness, however, of the decay of his

neighbourhood that began to irritate and unnerve Nicol and stop him from enjoying his daily walks. 'I no longer wanted to walk through the streets of Muizenberg,' he wrote. 'Not because they were dangerous but because I couldn't stand the filth, the noise, the sights. The beach, too, became a no-go zone. Too much litter, too many uncouth drunken people, too many full-volume car radios playing funk…. Graffiti defaced the coastal path, even the rocks were sprayed with the nonsensical patterns that had been used to vandalise so many cities throughout the world…. I couldn't stand the sight of plastic bags in the rock pools, smashed bottles, chicken bones in the sand, and everywhere cigarette butts more numerous than shells.'

And so a car became the main item on Nicol's shopping list. It allowed him and his wife to drive away from Muizenberg, finally, onto the mountainside in Glencairn. Here, apart from a neighbour who was afraid that Nicol's building his house on the edge of the cliff would steal his view, it is the natural environment which became the biggest source of stress. 'The southeaster is a phenomenon we have been forced to take into our lives,' he wrote. 'Although we have lived with this wind for twenty years and know that it can topple buses and snatch off roofs, the narrow streets of Muizenberg were remarkably protected … But after another season of southeasters we have become acclimatised: not used to it, rather hardened against it. The wind still frays our nerves and after three days of a blow I can sense a tightening of the skin at my temples and a brittleness in our conversation. We are far out to sea on a roaring trade wind. We listen to the house, to its creaking and thumping the way sailors must have listened to the timber and rigging of their ships as they rounded the Cape.'

2.

John grew up in Glencairn, and it is there that he developed his love of walking and climbing. Having witnessed him scampering barefoot over rocks, I'm amazed at how confident he seems on rocky ground. 'Well, I was always out of doors, because it was a very small place there, and there was the beach, and there was the little vlei, and then there was the mountainside. And we were on the mountainside, so I was always going up and down and exploring around and about. Up the mountain is somewhat more strenuous exercise, and I love the fynbos.'

I wonder if he is ever deterred from walking by Cape Town's wet winters. 'It depends on the circumstances,' he says. 'If it's a matter of walking to the station, or whatever, I just try and see to it that I don't get soaked by the time I get there. But you must remember also that I spent eleven years in Toronto, not living in a comfortable suburb but living out on Toronto Island, where you caught a ferry into town. And to get from my cottage to the ferry was like a different country from where you got off the ferry on the other side and hopped onto a bus, in that you might have to wade through snow, or mud, or gales or blizzards.'

This calls to mind William Wordsworth and his sister Dorothy on their treks across the countryside to visit Coleridge, which upset a number of people, particularly because Dorothy was often drenched. On the 16th of April 1802 she reported to a friend in a letter: 'A heavy rain came on ... When we reached the Inn we were very wet. The Landlady looked sour enough upon us ... but there was a young woman, I suppose a visitor, very smart in a Bonnet with an artificial flower, who was kindness itself. She did more for me than Mrs Coleridge would do for her own sister under the circumstances.'

'Of course,' John reminds me, 'what we see among the Romantics is this growing consciousness of it being a deliberate choice', since at that time only the poor walked, and pedestrians were viewed with suspicion in case they might be 'footpads' – the equivalent of contemporary muggers, known to beat up their victims, as they didn't have the means to flee the scene of the crime in the way that highwaymen did.

John has had his own experience of footpads, but he is pragmatic about them. 'I've been mugged a few times,' he says. 'One of them was not while I was walking, but just as I got out of my car near the place where I worked in Observatory, having picked up thousands of rands in cash to pay community members. As I got out of the car, this chap with a gun was right there. They'd obviously had someone in the bank and they'd followed me all the way, and he just said, "Give me the bag or I'll kill you." I looked rather astonished and he said, "I'll kill you, I'll kill you", and I handed it over and they went off.

'Another time was when I was walking in Newlands Forest, and I just was not paying sufficient attention. I should have known better. But when he came from behind a bush, my friend, she and I created such a noise that he just took one thing which he could see, my cellphone in my pocket, and pushed off.'

I raise the issue of muggers often coming in threes, and he says: 'That happened to me in Durban, on the beachfront, about two years ago. Out of the dark. They took my brand new running shoes and my bag. I was so pissed off, I sprinted after them, yelling. I was so bloody cross, the chap who took my bag dropped it. But the other two had gone off in different directions, each with one of my shoes,' he laughs in hindsight. 'Well that was silly of me too, because I should have been on the other side of the road where there was much more light.'

Though he isn't glib about it, he is unwilling to become paranoid. 'Under certain circumstances I'm very conscious of who's approaching me,' he says 'and who's behind me and who's across the street. It just becomes a kind of alertness. But that's the kind of price to be paid for all the privileges we have, I guess.

'I am fatalistic only in the sense that what happens happens, but you have a responsibility to yourself. So I do have a walking stick in my car. Even to be carrying it may be enough. If you are walking quite firmly and looking confident *and* carrying a stick then they may just decide, "Oh well, I'll try something else." I don't carry it all the time, by any means, but it is there in the car if I want to go and take a walk somewhere where I'm a little dubious. And it might just help me up the stairs or something,' he laughs. 'There have been quite a lot of muggings on the mountain, and when I'm going on a path where I know they have been, I might just pick up a stone and carry it.

'People talk about the kind of vibes that you give off, and it's hard to know, but when I have visitors here I do not discourage them from catching trains and walking and so on, but I warn them: "Just be confident, and don't wave cameras around."'

He recounts the Sufi parable about an Arab travelling in the desert. 'He's very worried about his camel, which is his main possession. What does he do about it, does he tie it up overnight, or does he just trust in God? So he goes to his spiritual adviser who says: "Tie up your camel, and *then* trust in God."'

Returning to the Romantics and present-day South Africa, he reflects, 'The funny thing about walking and class, when you're uncertain about your class position and you're very conscious of other people's opinion of you and how they place you in terms of class, you will be very careful not to do things that could be interpreted by them as bringing you down, like going walking. And we have gone now very much, over the last fifteen years, into a huge new nouveau-riche, nouveau-bourgeois dominant culture in which you don't walk because it's a sign that you're poor and you haven't made it.

'I was very amused reading the paper just the other day,' he says, 'about a parking crisis at the Waterfront, quoting a young woman sitting in her car in the heat for forty-five minutes, waiting for a place close to where the shops are, and saying it's really terrible because it's much too far to walk to where the parking is. Imagine how far you could walk very slowly and coolly in forty-five minutes,' he laughs. 'It's such an ideological blindspot.

'A discussion document from the City Council has just come out which puts forward integrated public transport as the most important issue in developing the city,' he observes, 'but it's been a dreadfully low priority for the government since the political changes. I think what happened is that there are so many obvious priorities, people simply hadn't recognised the really fundamental role that effective public transport plays in developing a country. It was just regarded as a trimming, which is what it had been increasingly seen as by the National Party, because fewer and fewer Nats would ever have been seen dead on a train.' This is ironic, since the railways, along with the post office, was one of the main areas of job reservation for working-class whites – predominantly Afrikaners – during the apartheid years.

Returning to his new career as a performer, as he approaches seventy, John says: 'I've had small parts in couple of films. In *To Be First*, about the first heart transplant with Chris Barnard and Co., I played the father of the young woman, Denise Darvall, who was killed in a car crash and whose heart was used. And I've done my first commercial, which was profitable, which I need because I don't have a pension.

'But on this whole question of movement and walking,' he says, 'walking's only one aspect. I really value dance. I always enjoyed throwing myself around on the dance floor from when I was very young. And around 1990, when I was deeply engaged in academic stuff, I suddenly found myself at Jazzart Dance Studio. I still can't figure out quite how I got there. I started in the first class and then took part, to my astonishment, in the studio concerts. And it was wonderful – such a different dimension of oneself.

'I remember saying this to Alfred Hinkel,' the artistic director, 'when they said after the first couple of months, "We're going to have the studio concert, and of course you're going to be in it," and I thought, I haven't a clue. It ended up with myself and another much younger guy just working wonderfully. And that was a real revelation to me, because walking is great physically and it gives you time to reflect on things a lot of the time, and you observe the passing show, but dance has an even more personally expressive dimension, which I think at that time I was clearly lacking because of all that other stuff I was doing. It was a wonderful thing for me, about exploring one's humanness in different ways.'

Moving into dance is also allowing John to explore different aspects of his masculinity, echoed in the part he played in Brett Bailey's production of *Orfeus*. 'I was one of the creatures in the Underworld, simply called the Forgotten Man. I said nothing, it was all expressed through movement. It's such a powerful theme for me and, when I look around, for many people, particularly males who have a lot of power and position but at the cost of what it was in themselves that might have been different. The dominance of men is at an enormous cost. Moving into the stereotype of the breadwinner, the provider, the boss etcetera, actually means stepping into a cage.'

Recently John has been exploring a box of letters exchanged between his father and mother during the Second World War which he'd like to develop into a stage production. 'He went as a volunteer in the South African Army, the Cape Town Highlanders, up north to North Africa, and he and my mother exchanged letters for years, several times a week, and they are extraordinary.

'He had to leave school without even getting Standard Eight, and he became a clerk with what was then the Colonial Orphan Chamber. And then he went off to the war, leaving behind his wife and two small children, and it's so interesting to read how he responded to the challenges as a very junior officer, and the kind of alertness to where he was and his descriptions of the people and the environment. His amazement at his capacity to command respect and affection from his men, and his capacity to go through the desert for miles by compass reading and come to exactly the right point at the right time. And then he was with the British Army War Graves Agency, based in Tunis, going looking for the graves, the temporary on-the-spot graves of airmen, soldiers. All over the place, in the mountains, by the sea. Learning French, talking to a huge range of people to get access and starting to think, as the war was obviously coming to its end, well now I can do something different.

'He was about thirty-six or so, the age my son is now, and thinking, I want to join external affairs, Foreign Service. There's going to be a new international agency, United Nations, Smuts is involved, South Africa's going to play a role, and I want to be part of this. And then realising he doesn't even have matric, let alone a degree. Then he starts making plans, getting my mother to send him documents, and starts studying French for matric. So he was excited at his own capacity. And then increasingly through the letters finding the obstacles and starting to say, "Well maybe I'll have to go back to that job, just while we sort things out." And then of course he comes back and the letters stop. So when I knew him he was doing a job looking after other people's money, which he did for the rest of his life with great integrity. But he withdrew a lot. His presence was always there, very courteous, interested, but… I don't want my son Thomas to have any regrets about me or my life,' John says finally. 'I want to do it now.'

As an English professor, one of his favourite courses was Speculative Fiction, particularly Ursula Le Guin, for her 'sense of possibility'. In *The Dispossessed* she wrote: 'Unless the past and the future are made part of the present by memory and intention, there is, in human terms, no road, nowhere to go.'

Grace Notes

'It was a Sunday afternoon. I'd been down to the municipal dump once already that day and, as municipal dumps go, there are always loads of scavengers around, basically trying to earn a living. They asked me for money, which is pretty normal, and I said, "Don't worry, I'm coming back." So I left and went back for another load of stuff, branches that I'd cut down. And when I came back with my stepson, it wasn't more than twenty minutes later, the place was dead quiet. It was about five o'clock so I thought, okay, obviously they've knocked off and gone home.'

The way he says knocked off suggests Dex recognises scavenging as an occupation, just as many South Africans believe, too, that crime is a job.

'So basically, I was at the back of my trailer,' he continues, 'busy loosening the tailgate, and I heard a very soft-spoken voice saying, "Look at me, *baas*, I'm going to shoot you." At the time the images that went through my head were of a kid who'd found a toy gun in the rubbish, and I wasn't particularly fazed. And eventually – I'm not sure of the time frame, it could have been seconds – I thought I'd better look. When I looked up there was a guy standing on the right-hand side of the trailer pointing a .38 Special at me.' He is obviously a man who knows guns. 'So I looked at it, just trying to see if it was real and it was loaded. It was a rusty old gun. I thought, the chances are it's actually been lying in the water and

121

may well misfire anyway. And I just managed to ascertain all that, when another guy came and grabbed me from behind.'

Seeming to feel that full disclosure is necessary at this point, he adds: 'Okay, the reason they attacked me is because I was carrying a firearm myself. The first time I was there I unhitched my trailer and emptied it into the pit, and I had my firearm in my belt, so my T-shirt probably lifted up and they saw it, so by the time I came back they were actually waiting for me.' His use of the word firearm sounds academic, and has a distancing effect. It seems less lethal than a gun.

'The municipal dump in Walkerville is about a kilometre and a half off the main road, so it's really out in the bush. And I thought, the only thing for me to do here is to struggle. Even though I was carrying a firearm the last thing that crossed my mind was actually to use it. They were young kids, about seventeen, maybe even a little bit younger. I thought, you know, I'll give you guys a bloody good hiding and send you home. And as I managed to free myself from the guy who was holding me the other one shot me. From their perspective I can understand,' he says, 'I'm a big guy and I've got a firearm. I'm pretty sure he shot me out of fear, because the guy who was holding the gun, he wasn't cocky; he was pretty shook up himself. And basically as I hit the ground, another two guys appeared, and they went straight for my firearm.'

This was the 17th of December 2000, when Dex's life changed completely. He was shot just below his shoulder blade and the bullet went through a lung and into his spine. He is now paralysed from the waist down.

'My oldest stepson, Nick, was with me at the time. At that point he was fourteen. The attackers had just pulled the firearm off me when Nick got out of the car. As he opened the door they pulled him out of the car, and one of the guys got in from the passenger side looking around for whatever he could find. He tried to get the ignition keys out but he couldn't do it – with the Corolla you've got to push the key in and turn it to get it out. So they ran off saying they're coming back for the car. Then I sent my son up to the main road to go and get help.

'He was probably about two hundred metres away when two little kids came along, maybe nine, ten years old. My first thought was, Now they're coming to rob me as well, but they said they wanted to help. So I got one of them to go and have a look to see if the ignition key was still in the car. It was. Then I got them to try and help me to the car, but they were small kids, they couldn't lift me. So I eventually managed to drag myself to the car, and up onto the back seat. Two kids in the car, and then coached the one little kid to drive... Ag, and he was great,' he recalls. 'Stalled the car about four or five times, and then off we went... He'd never driven before. By the time we got up to the main road Nick had flagged someone down. So now the other driver sees the car coming up the road, two young black guys driving, so he's now standing with a 9mm on top of his roof, ready to start shooting. I managed to get the window open, waving and shouting, "Don't shoot!" Then twenty minutes later, ambulance and police, the boys and my wife, they came down.'

He never had the opportunity to thank the children who helped him. 'The cops then took their details, and a week later came to me asking me if I knew who they were; they'd lost their information. Apparently these kids knew the guys who shot me.'

At this point he was not yet in pain. 'Adrenalin is the most amazing thing,' he marvels. But about an hour later the pain began in earnest, and it wasn't made any easier by the poor quality of healthcare available to a self-employed South African without medical insurance. 'You're with the paramedics,' he recounts, 'and now you've got to decide where you're going to go. Not having any medical aid you can't choose which hospital you want to go to, so you've basically got the public facilities: Baragwanath, Sebokeng, or the Joburg Gen. I was closest to Bara and Sebokeng. Sebokeng was a little bit further, but the paramedics said they deal with a lot more violent injuries, so I went to Sebokeng.

'It was awful. Really rough. Very unsanitary conditions, blood all over the place. People with really severe injuries. There was a guy with an axe in his head. I lay there for about six and a half hours before anyone looked at me.

'Obviously they did the right things, but it was in a very harsh manner. They don't really have any facilities there, so I was lying on a steel table, no cushions, nothing. And eventually two nurses came and they asked me to sit up – I've just been shot and paralysed, but they ask me to sit up – because they need to take my clothes off me so they can take my X-rays. I said if you want to get my clothes off me then cut them off! So that's what they did. Sent me for X-rays, came back from X-rays, went into this operating room, about four metres square. In there were two beds, with two overhead lights, doors on either side so you've got people walking in and out.

'This Cuban doctor walks up to me while talking to someone else, didn't say anything to me, walked over to me with a scalpel, shoved the scalpel into my side and made a hole, put in a piece of fairly hard plastic pipe and forced that into my lung to drain the fluid. Basically that was the treatment, and he said, "Okay, now you can go off to the ward." The bed they'd allocated for me was caked in old crusty blood. My sister arrived at that point and said, "No way you can stay here." So she made some phone calls trying to get me into another hospital. Milpark wanted either cash or a bank guaranteed cheque for R100 000 before they'd admit me, and eventually Mulbarton said they need R13 000. When I arrived we had to give them R3000 in cash, and the rest by ten o'clock the next morning. So we managed to scrape the money together. But just getting onto the Netcare stretcher was like being in heaven,' he recalls. 'All soft and padded. Then the paramedics had to fight with the hospital at Sebokeng to give me a pain shot for while they transported me. At that stage, still no painkillers, nothing. Also, because I was leaving, they wouldn't let me take the X-rays with me. So the next morning at Mulbarton I had to go for another set of X-rays.

'Ja,' Dex reflects, 'that was the start of another journey.

'Up until that point I'd been carrying a firearm for eight years, living in a really dark headspace, in a bad marriage, under financial stress, working long hours, and all of a sudden that changed. I'd been carrying the firearm for that sort of eventuality, and it all unfolded. Before that nothing would have made me give it up. The area we were living in was quite rough, and then a friend of ours was attacked and raped by three guys, and the day after that I went out and I bought a firearm for my wife and one for myself.

'But when I was shot I realised that you can't run and you can't hide. If there's something in your path, it's in your path, and you're not going to change that. And that in itself was such a release, just learning to accept things. When I moved to Orange Grove,' a Johannesburg suburb close to the city centre, 'I lived there for four and a half years – I never locked my doors. If someone wants to break in they're going to break in anyway.' This reminds me of a friend's wry observation about car thieves who smash the windows even when the car is unlocked.

It is a popularly held belief that it's in South Africa's cities, particularly Johannesburg, that one is most likely to become a crime statistic, yet those who live in the countryside and on the smallholdings on the outskirts of the city are really more vulnerable. Some analysts go so far as to suggest that, as operations against organised crime in urban areas intensify, criminals begin moving out to the rural areas.

Walkerville is described on its website as a 'rural retreat south of Johannesburg', and is seen as idyllic for its wide open space, 'but it's actually very closed,' says Dex. 'I think in Walkerville, and places like that… people actually live in prisons.' There may be fewer walls than in the suburbs, but 'they live behind burglar bars and security gates and electric fences – this whole experience of angst all the time'. In Walkerville the disparity between landowners and the poverty of the nearby Orange Farm township – begun as an informal settlement of laid off farm workers in 1988, now grown to over 350 000 residents – is also brought into stark relief. And yet, like Zimbabwean farmers, many Walkerville residents refuse to cut their losses and move, and continue to live as though under siege.

'In the time from me getting shot, my son running up to the road to try and get help, and the kids arriving,' says Dex, 'I don't know how long it was, it could have been five minutes, but it also seemed like a lifetime of thoughts. I had blood gushing out of my mouth, and I thought, okay, I'm going to die now. About two months before, my life insurance had lapsed because I didn't pay it, and I thought, what's going to happen to my family now? What are they going to do? And then actually realising that what you've done, you've done. You can't change anything. Everything is exactly as it is now, and you can't do any more. And then also facing one's own mortality and realising that actually I can do this. I can let go. It was a great sense of release in a way.

'That's the point where you're really pushing your beliefs, because you sort of think, well, I believe all of these things and maybe in that situation I'll start praying, and it was nothing like that at all. Everything was peaceful, and the things I believed in were more true for me then than any other time of my life because they were real. Being able to come to terms with myself... that's probably one of the greatest gifts one could ever get. At that point is where you start realising what is important.'

Remarkably, Dex seems to be without any anger towards his attackers. I wonder if his compassion is because he has three sons himself. Did part of him see them simply as someone else's children? 'Ag, what's there to be angry about?' he asks. 'It wasn't personal. They wanted my firearm, and ultimately we did a dance together. We exchanged energy, and we moved along in our respective journeys in our own directions. From there my life took a positive turn, and I can only think that their lives went down a negative road. The guy who shot me, I'm pretty sure he'd never shot anyone before, so that was a step in a new direction for him too.'

Dex's experience is consistent with Gun Free South Africa's research, which found that 'victims in possession of a firearm were nearly four times more likely to have their firearms stolen than to use them in self-defence,' and 'firearms were robbed from victims in 78 per cent of the cases in which victims were known to have a gun'. Even if you do manage to use your weapon in self-defence, they say, this increases 'the likelihood that the perpetrator would fire his firearm between three- and fourfold'. And surprisingly, 'given the increased likelihood that a man will have a firearm and will attempt to defend himself, hijackers appear to target male victims', which seems to suggest that carrying a gun may 'have the perverse effect of increasing the incentive to commit a robbery.'

Though he seems exceptionally fatalistic, Dex reminds me that he has choices. 'You have to decide how you're going to deal with a situation. There's negative in every situation and there's positive in every situation,' he says, rolling another cigarette.

He's beginning to sound like a Taoist, but assures me he has no allegiance to any particular faith. He recognises our interdependence as human beings and sees order in things, but as for its orchestration, 'I have no idea. I know there's amazing energy, power, but where it comes from, what it is, I don't know. I don't speculate, because ultimately I'm not going to get any answers anyway... Things actually work in an incredible way. The more you try and control things, the more you basically fuck them up, or just delay them by resisting.' I recall the words of Caroline Myss: 'Becoming conscious is the capacity to enter and live within mystery full time and feel that it's the answered prayer and not the unanswered prayer.'

A cynic might argue that Dex is simply in denial, that his fatalism is unrealistic, that some part of him must be enraged, and yet it is the directness of his gaze that strikes me and makes me believe he is telling the truth. Sometimes it is so intense it unnerves me, and I have to break eye contact and look away.

'Strangely enough,' he says, 'about three or four months before I got shot I started becoming aware of people in wheelchairs. Seeing people in shopping centres and that sort of thing, and realising in a number of ways it seemed like they were invisible. And three months later I ended up being disabled myself.'

While being slowed down dramatically by being unable to walk, it is cars that can give the wheelchair-bound their independence. Dex says he was never much of a walker. 'I'd walk around a bit, but I always felt more comfortable on a motorcycle. I've been driving since I was thirteen, riding motorbikes since I was eleven. The need for speed and adrenalin, and pushing things – I still do it. My most favourite thing, apart from playing music is, two, three o'clock in the morning, taking Ou Kaapse Weg in my car and knowing that I'm the only one on the road and being able to fly over there. It's the most awesome experience ever.'

I wonder if he's someone who has ever defined himself by the kind of car that he drives, but no, he says, his needs are purely practical. 'It has to be automatic, and it has to have power steering, and that is it… The speed… I'm very much in touch with my vehicle, I know what it can do and what it can't do, how hard I can push it. I've done two hundred thousand kilometres in it, and we're very close. We've been through many situations.' I'm shocked when he tells me, 'I used to do Orange Grove to Fish Hoek, a 1400-kilometre journey, in nine hours. I'm very alert. If you're taking on 1400 kilometres after having been up for sixteen hours,' he reasons, 'if you drive slowly, chances are you're going to fall asleep and have an accident. While when you're driving at speed you're alert and aware all the time. You're involved.'

In 2001 Dex's ex-wife moved to Cape Town with the boys, so until he moved here a few months ago, he has been 'driving down every month. Thursday night after work, drive down, spend Friday, Saturday, Sunday, then Monday afternoon after lunch drive back to Joburg.'

At first he hated being in Cape Town. 'I was staying either at my sister's place in Muizenberg or at their flat in Fish Hoek, which has vertical stairs. My sister's place is up stairs as well, and also the bathroom facilities… So it's always really just been a very uncomfortable place for me.' But now that he has his own house, 'there couldn't be any other place for me to be. The world's opened up since I've been here. I've met really awesome people.'

One of the biggest things that has changed in his life is learning to ask for help. 'And getting to know the nature of people as well, because the majority of people actually want to help. Even getting in and out of a car, people are frequently coming and asking, "Can I help you?" Getting someone to help has never been a problem.'

No longer slave to a high-budget lifestyle and the IT industry, he's spending most of his time doing what he really loves – playing the saxophone and compiling the *WhatsOnSA* website. 'At least four nights a week I'm at music venues, and the majority of them are upstairs. I'll get the closest person who's there to assist me.'

So how does he advise his children to live their lives and keep safe? 'Well, all three of my boys have been mugged,' he says, 'in Fish Hoek. Never at gunpoint, but at knife point, usually by gangs. Last time my youngest son, who's now fourteen, about seven o'clock in the evening, he'd gone down to the shop and three guys pulled him into an alley and took his cellphone and his wallet, some of his clothing.'

Fish Hoek, known for being populated mainly by elderly people and dogs, and thought by some to be the one place in South Africa that hasn't changed since the Fifties, is famous for never having allowed alcohol to be sold in the suburb. But this hasn't prevented another problem from developing in the area – teenagers addicted to hard drugs, particularly 'tik', crystal methamphetamine.

'I tell my son obviously to be sensible,' says Dex. 'I sincerely hope and wish that nothing bad will ever happen to him, but it's his journey, and I can only be there to support him and help where I can. As long as he knows that I love him, no matter what. More than that… I try not to put any of my experiences in his way.'

As I walk along the beach before catching the train from Fish

Hoek back to the southern suburbs, I recall something he said: 'Obviously there's stuff I miss a lot, like feeling the water and the cold sand on my feet… Going for walks to remote places with beautiful scenery like dams and waterfalls, places that I just don't go to any more.' I imagine suddenly finding myself unable to walk, and that it would feel like my life was over. But no, he assured me: 'The first thing I did when I got back from the hospital was go and blow my saxophone. I was shot in the lung, and I was terrified I wouldn't be able to play any more – then my life would have been over.'

Inside Out

In 1964 a small boy watched through the window of a third-floor flat in inner-city Durban. 'My best time was Friday and Saturday nights, watching this amazing spectacle. Right opposite was a hotel, the Himalaya Hotel, and there was a club in the hotel called Mountains, and I'd watch people going in. It was always fascinating to me how they would disappear and then reappear on another floor. There were these ballroom dancers. All these really glamorous couples. Very well dressed and well heeled. And then at midnight the fights would start. Invariably these big events would break up into monstrous affairs.

'We lived on the corner of Grey and Beatrice Streets,' explains choreographer Jay (Jayendran) Pather, 'in a seedier part of Durban. It was a very small room, and six of us lived in it – my mother and five children: three brothers and my sister and myself. My parents were separated. My father lived in the suburbs, in Clairwood. And my mum walked. We walked everywhere.

'We moved from there when I was about nine or ten and lived in houses and in the suburbs and so on, but when I look back on my childhood that was my happiest and most buoyant time: when I had the freedom of the city.

'Those formative years made me aware of a kind of time that is possible in the middle of the city. I felt that I could do just about anything. With having to rely on your own feet, or your own body, you feel like you can interact or not. Whereas if you're driving you can't. You can hoot,' he says. 'But when you get off, you arrive, and then there's another process that starts.' We reflect wryly that the first point of entry, after arriving at one's destination, is often a complex and fraught negotiation with a car guard.

Jay's choice not to drive 'started, I think, with the fact that I was the youngest in the family. I had three brothers who drove when they were about twelve and, faced with that, I just paled into insignificance and was quite happy to be driven. But when I could have driven I moved to New York and lived there for three years, in the early Eighties.' He had won a Fulbright scholarship to do an MA in multimedia theatre at New York University. 'And then straight after that I moved to the University of Zululand at Ngoye, where I was posted for four years, teaching choreography and drama, so then I didn't need to drive. But after all that time I think walking was quite important to me; also being a passenger, and being able to watch and dream. The desire to watch the world, and dream onto it, superseded driving into it and getting somewhere.

'But then I have a partner who really loves driving,' he adds. 'For him, driving is a way of relaxing, so when we go away the fact that he doesn't have someone to share the driving with is not an issue. Even if I could drive, I think he would do the driving.'

Until recently Jay was based in Durban, where he was artistic director of the Siwela Sonke Dance Theatre ('We cross over together' in Zulu). With admittedly ambivalent feelings about Cape Town – he has been quoted as describing the Mother City, where he spent seven years in the past, as 'too beautiful and sometimes bland' – it seems surprising that he has chosen to return here to live. He explains: 'I think Cape Town was the ideal apartheid city, and that Durban is much more prone to on-the-street intercultural and interracial encounters than Cape Town, because this was the foundation of the apartheid city, and the formation of slave quarters. It worked at pushing away the bad stuff and black people from the centre of the city, and did it really well, because it takes half an hour to get to any of the townships.

'Whereas in Durban, for some reason, the townships just encroached further and further into the inner city, and in combination with an active migrant labour system – more Indian than in Cape Town – because of the sugarcane, or whatever, you have a situation right now where people from the townships and the suburbs and the city intermingle. Whether they actually touch is another typically South African psychosis, but Cape Town is an eloquent treatise of apartheid, because it makes touching very difficult. It's really very hard for people living in the townships to get to where it's all supposed to be happening. During New Year and the festive season people take possession of the city, but it's only really in town. And the transport system is also so bad.'

Personally, I find the transport system in Cape Town quite good, because of the train – certainly compared to Johannesburg – but of course this is travelling on the main suburban line. Getting to and from the townships is another story.

'While I was running Siwela Sonke,' Jay continues, 'I used to do quite a lot of work for the University of Cape Town – as external examiner for the Masters drama programme. I had taught here before, and the school offered me a post, and because Siwela Sonke had developed a solid leadership base – funding is notoriously unstable for dance companies – I decided to accept the offer.'

In recent years, he has become best known for his site-specific explorations of public space, in the form of performances and installations. Together with a range of collaborators – collaboration being the essence of his work – he created *CityScapes*, *Home* and *The Beautiful Ones Must Be Born* – inspired by Ghanaian author Ayi Kwei Armah's novel – among others. Usually these consist of a series of five or six pieces, performed at various locations, from beachfronts to shopping malls and restaurants; from Constitution Hill to Mandela Square, and the steps of the Cathedral of St John the Divine in New York. Working with video artists, who document the events *in situ*, the performances culminate in an installation and re-creation of the dance in a gallery.

'Then it becomes not just about where you're seeing, but how you're seeing. The video artist on the *Hotel* piece in *CityScapes* had a single security camera, and filmed six different versions, and then installed six television sets, with the bed, and showed black and white footage of what had happened from different angles.' Performances of this piece, at the hotel, accommodated an audience of about twelve. 'You got a sense of the claustrophobia. And the levels of how these discrete realities occur.

'When I think about how much walking has inspired… My site-specific project work would not really have transpired if I didn't walk as much as I do. In fact the performance of my first work was at 320 West Street, which was a place that I had walked when I was a teenager, and I remember looking at those escalators and thinking, How nice to do a dance here!' The performance at 320 West Street featured *pantsula* dancers in pinstripe suits on cellphones and concluded with a bunch of red balloons being freed to float up past the office windows.

'I remember looking at buildings and thinking, at that time already, how incredible that these spaces people walk through are like living sets. And I forgot about it. And then it was much later in my life when I went back to the idea. Invariably contemporary dance attracts quite a middle-class audience, but to do it in a public space, in a way that people have access to it, is a completely different thing. People are taken by the spectacle, but there's some element in it that they're familiar with. It's very satisfying to stage these pieces in public spaces for pedestrians who don't ever put a foot inside a theatre. And it really has made me understand that there is so much discourse on the street that is available to walkers, that is not available to drivers.

'There was a piece done by a foreign choreographer on a residency in South Africa, set in the Warwick Avenue Triangle,' he recalls. The Warwick Triangle is described in a travel guide as an 'Africanized *Bladerunner* setting west of Grey Street', where

Jay lived as a boy. A commuter hub, and the largest informal street market in Durban, as the 'western gateway' to Durban's central business district, it's estimated that pedestrian traffic reaches 300 000 on weekdays. Typically, it has also been identified by investors who are renovating old buildings and cashing in on the student accommodation market. 'Anyway, this choreographer depicted a world so chaotic, people bumping into each other, and running… And it's so funny because I never see any of that. There are tons of people, but it is so ordered. There is so little pushing and shoving. This notion that in a pedestrian space there is chaos is just so untrue. It's very interesting to me how people, who you can see are daily professional walkers, use the space economically. They understand the space between themselves and somebody else, and move without touching.

'If you look at the sweet sellers, they'll have a red crate, with a blue strip, and pink sweets and yellow sweets, in intricate patterns. There's a coherence that is unavailable to people who are driving past, the desire to make the space around you beautiful, but if you walk through it you can get in touch with that logic.' Contrary to Michel de Certeau, author of *The Practice of Everyday Life*, who writes of pedestrians 'whose bodies follow the thicks and thins of the urban "text" they write without being able to read it', Jay says: 'My argument very often, to intellectuals in their ivory towers, is that unless you make contact and are in synch you can't see that logic.'

This highlights the ongoing argument between pedestrians and drivers about notions of time. 'If you're driving it goes by in a flash,' says Jay. 'Both time scales are fighting with each other, and so it's a constant battle. Drivers constantly trying to get pedestrians out of the way, "Why won't they move faster?" And it's almost a negation of the human flow, anatomy and physiology.' Walking he describes as 'lingering. It helps me to take in things, to process, and readjust them. It sharpens a subconscious awareness.

'I think invariably the prejudice is on the side of the drivers, and the notion is not one of different modes of transport, it's that one is superior to the other. Pedestrians have to "get with the programme".

'I've seen so many kids on their way to school who have almost been run over. People blame the taxi drivers, but very often it's not the taxi drivers, it's BMWs and Mercedes Benzes that are being driven by suburbanites. I sometimes feel I need to carry a stick,' he adds, mirroring my own frustration. This would be to keep drivers, rather than muggers, at bay. For while some might consider crime to be the biggest threat to South African pedestrians, nearly six thousand pedestrian deaths due to fatal crashes in 2006 challenge that argument.

There is no doubt, though, that being an associate professor has shifted Jay's relationship to time. 'I used to travel by minibus a lot when I was in Durban. And when I lived in Cape Town many years ago I used to travel on the train a great deal, but my schedule used to be such that I could cope with any kind of transport delays. Now I can't possibly. I'm privy to all kinds of other people's schedules, so I have to manage my time, and have a lot of information. But in a curious way, walking also makes you quite appreciative of things. You figure out a more lean way of living. Invariably I position myself in relationship to my work, so I take ten minutes through the Gardens from home to work, while most people are struggling in traffic. In my professional life now there are many more places that I have to get to quite quickly, and be on time. But if I need to get somewhere I'll invest in a metered taxi.

'It would have been a problem if I really wanted to live in a suburb. I would have struggled. But the kind of person I am, I look forward to walking in the middle of the city. When I was in New York I lived between the West and East Villages, and when I was in Durban right opposite the City Hall, and now in Cape Town I'm living right next to the Slave Museum, next to Parliament. It's fantastic to be in the centre of the city. It's very inspiring. I'm aware of all kinds of people, and it feels like people are much more open-minded and easier, and actually I feel the safest in the middle of the city. I often look for crowds – that's not a safety issue, I just look for the energy. I walk through the station a lot, to get to the theatre at Artscape.'

Walking in the countryside holds less appeal for him. 'When I lived in Zululand it was quite rural, and I walked quite long distances and it didn't really matter. But I think as I grow older there's a level of anxiety that I associate with lack of access. I can walk five kilometres without stopping, but I must see someone.'

On the obligatory question of crime, he says, 'I'm not paranoid. I think it's as safe as you make it.' He has had no violent experiences. 'Well, there was one time,' he recalls, 'in the Seventies, when I was harassed by young white thugs, but that was a racial issue.

'What interests me is where it's a good space to walk and where it's a bad space. For no apparent reason. The Roeland Street area, for example, in a very curious way it just doesn't feel right,' he says, highlighting an industrial area of Cape Town's city centre, where what was once a prison now accommodates the National Archives. 'And it's not more unsafe than anywhere else.

'There's also an area in the Durban city centre, near the Workshop shopping centre. The Workshop is heavily populated with people, the City Hall is close by, and the KwaMuhle Museum, but there's an area in between that nobody uses. There's a hall nearby where we tried to do a performance, and no one came. It's a vast open space that's just dead. And it's literally two minutes away from the thoroughfare.'

Patterns are a recurring theme as Jay talks, and it calls to mind a little story I came across years ago: 'An architect built a cluster of office buildings around a central green. When construction was completed, the landscape crew asked him where he wanted the sidewalks. "Just plant the grass solidly between the buildings" was his reply. By late summer the new lawn was laced with paths of trodden grass between the buildings. These paths turned in easy curves and were sized according to traffic flow. In the fall, the architect simply paved the paths. Not only did the paths have a design beauty, they responded directly to user needs.'

'I've found that I'm more likely to follow patterns, existing pathways,' Jay agrees. 'I have a friend, when we're walking she often says, "Let's go the other way," and I like drawing patterns in a new space, but I often find if I keep to certain patterns I find new things. Sometimes it is because I want to be efficient, and I know this takes that amount of time, but it's often about seeing what has shifted and changed.'

I wonder if it was his time in New York, with its friendly public spaces, that prompted him to move his work outside. 'In a curious way,' he says, 'at that time I didn't think to make work on the street. I was on another path then. All of this was happening during the two states of emergency in the early Eighties, and because my work was around multimedia political theatre my thing was about agitprop; so the engagement with public spaces during that hectic apartheid period, your sense of creativity and art was never about being outside. It was about being out, or open, but how to make these works in smaller spaces, in community halls and that kind of thing. Because as soon as you went outside you were likely to be arrested.'

In post-apartheid South Africa, concerns have moved from purely political to economic issues. One of the pieces in *CityScapes* featured a black *kugel* in a ball gown rapp-jumping down the side of the Musgrave Mall in Durban. Basically abseiling, but with the ropes attached to her back instead of her front, she went down facing the ground. 'She was very brave!' he recalls with admiration. 'At once powerful and vulnerable. It was about the taking over of this white middle-class space by the black Middle Class. She had shopping bags, and she walked all the way down, and then at the bottom there was a performance with traditional singers. They were like praise singers, and they praised Calvin Klein.'

To recontextualise something Jay has said in the past: as a result of 'the thirst for lavish spectacle that reinforces notions of power and sophistication' and the consequent 'symmetrical favouring of the high arts' which has made opera and ballet fashionable once more, nowadays 'the hot-shot black entrepreneur' is likely to be found 'swanning around at the opening of Swan Lake'. So in the Musgrave Mall piece 'I wanted to capture the combination of dread and admiration that comes with a rise in class. The shifts of consciousness from rural to urban, from cash to credit cards, can be very giddy. The video artist who worked with me on that piece did a beautiful video. All she did was film the rope and the dress, and created images with that.'

His next works, in collaboration with Jazzart Dance Theatre, Dance for All and Vandini Dance, called *CityScapes Cape Town*, will be performed at Thibault Square, Sea Point Promenade, and Cape Town Central Station. Then 'there's a piece that I'm wanting to do called *Body of Evidence*, which looks at the placement of pain inside bones. The notion of memory and pain being interred in bones. Because you can never really express your pain, and no one really understands one's pain, so I'm looking at how it becomes part of one's bone structure, and gets passed on. We'll be drawing connections with Truth and Reconciliation testimonies and burial sites, and probably performing it at the burial sites.'

The street discourse he speaks of extends also to passers-by offering advice during rehearsals. 'At the Workshop – quite a working-class area – people would stop, and then they would come to me and tell me how I should direct it. Because we can't play music during rehearsals and so on we'd just be marking the space, and they'd go: "You should get better dancers, they can't really dance!" There was one guy, he looked like an office worker, who came repeatedly to give me suggestions as to what I should do.

'When we're performing at a shopping centre or whatever, I have to negotiate very carefully with management and security and so on, because the bottom line is that I do not want to be safe. There's no point. We need to be in a highly dangerous space, in the sense that anything can happen. It has its own anarchic kind of logic.'

Though he has moved a long way from the little flat in Grey Street, his fascination with hotels has never faded. The piece in *CityScapes* was performed first at the Albany in Durban, and then at the Devonshire in Braamfontein in Johannesburg, on the border of Hillbrow. 'It spoke about the way that the inner city is a fortress, as well as a space of refuge. At night you're too terrified to step out, so you remain in this fortress, and then it becomes a space of all kinds of secrets, all kinds of liaisons and night encounters.'

The late Phaswane Mpe once wrote: 'On first visiting Hillbrow in 1989, at night, I felt that it was a surreal place, what with the activities going on; with so many people seeming to enjoy themselves in the streets ... [but] one of the people I was with pointed out that, in fact, there were far more people in the buildings around us, hidden from our view. I wondered what I would encounter if those people decided, simultaneously, to come out into the streets ...'

'The Dev,' says Jay, represents 'for me, a peripheral, transient space, looking as it does onto traffic moving in and out of this city, people mostly leaving and, if arriving, then only for brief sojourns ... a site for unquestioned states of being unfolding beyond the cropped verges of the suburbs.'

Sadly, it was on the steps of another Braamfontein hotel that Darryl Kempster, a crew member of the visiting production *Lord of the Dance*, was shot and killed in 2004. Having been advised, and offered security to accompany him on the few blocks from the theatre to his hotel in the early hours of a Sunday morning, he decided to walk alone. As he reached the hotel he was shot for his laptop. A newspaper reported that the cast and crew were then 'moved out of central Johannesburg to a smart hotel in the prosperous Sandton financial district'.

The core paradox at the centre of hotel and city: 'the desire for both security and freedom, for recognition and anonymity,' says Jay, offers a space 'which continues to make the chest tighten with a combination of anxieties – from fear to infinite possibility'.

Mom's Taxi

'Approaching in bright orange shoes,' I SMS her as I get out of the taxi, and she comes down to meet me in the Main Road in Woodstock. We have not met before. I have been referred to Miriam, as remarkably she has raised two children as a single mother using only public transport. Not so remarkable amongst the working class, who have no option, but few do it out of choice.

'I started using the minibus taxis in about 1984, when I was a student,' she tells me, 'but they weren't all over Cape Town yet, they were only in certain areas. I was using them from Wynberg to Grassy Park because there was no train there, so that was the only way to get there. I lived in the southern suburbs and I'd visit friends there quite regularly.'

Though there were buses to the Cape Flats, these would have been for 'non-Europeans' only, effectively preventing whites without cars from travelling to the townships. 'The great thing about the taxis was that they were taking me right to where I wanted to be,' she says, 'so I got familiar with the whole culture of using them. This was still when very few white people used them, I would imagine, because I caused a bit of a sensation. But then you know how people are, they get used to you and then that's just the person who gets on every Friday or whatever.

'So by the time my children were born I was quite accustomed to them. I was familiar with how it all works. And as it evolved and spread out, I just carried on using them.

'It's been challenging over the years. My perception now is that it was easier getting around in those years, when the children were small. I nostalgically remember times when I happily hopped onto third-class coaches on the train. There were less people, and I breastfed, and people stood up and gave me their seats, and I felt very comfortable.'

During the apartheid era, while first- and second-class coaches with their padded seats were identical – people were divided exclusively by racial classification – the cheaper third-class coaches were used by people who were both non-European and poor. As apartheid was dismantled, a few whites began to enjoy the cheaper price and more convivial atmosphere of third-class coaches.

Travelling now at peak hour from the city along the southern suburbs line, I find the class system on the train has begun to reflect one being entrenched generally across South African society. First-class coaches have come to resemble London's Tube, with commuters sitting silently side by side reading.

While second class no longer exists, divisions happen in the third-class coaches themselves, with what appear to be office workers – predominantly so-called coloureds and a few whites, nearly all women – sitting silently at one end of the coach, and black labourers, mainly men, standing at the other talking animatedly in Xhosa.

Resources are spread thin, and even standing room is at a premium in third class now. It looks unlikely that anyone will give up their hard plastic seat even if you are elderly or breastfeeding. It looks like the more convivial atmosphere has migrated to the taxis.

'I've had very happy experiences with the *gaartjies*,' Miriam says, referring to the 'little guards', a nickname historically given to Cape Town's bus conductors and now to the 'helpers' in the taxis. In Joburg taxis things seem to happen organically, with passengers sitting where they choose, and the customary tap on the shoulder and the cupped hand of the passenger in front of you reaching backwards to receive the money being passed forward till it finally arrives at the driver. Cape Town taxis are more orchestrated. And yet curiously they feel more chaotic.

The *gaartjie* also acts as the *Caayype Tyyyowwn!* crier, who calls out the destination to potential customers along the way. In Joburg this function is filled by the taxi driver leaning on his hooter.

I'm intrigued by this difference in taxi culture between the two cities. 'Well, you know Cape Town,' a friend reckons, 'you always have to have a *handlanger*', described by the dictionary, depending on which way you look at it, as a helper or an accomplice.

'There's quite a space between my two children,' Miriam continues, 'so I had a 5-year-old and a baby, and the 5-year-old would sit next to me and I'd be carrying the baby, and then I'd have a pushcart, and then the *gaartjie* would grab the pushcart, fold it up quickly, shove it under the seat, and do the same thing for us on the way out, so I always felt like I was getting more taken care of than I was on the train. There are inconveniences; and occasionally the door falls off,' she laughs. 'But in recent years I've felt safer in taxis than on the train. I try to avoid stations.'

This goes for Cape Town's central taxi rank as well. 'I'm not liking the taxi deck at the moment, which is the place at the station where you leave from if you need to go from town to anywhere else in Cape Town; and where, if you go from here to town, they drop you. And it's crappy right now. It's not that safe, and it stinks.' This echoes the threats that women at taxi ranks around the country have to deal with, constantly open to sexual harassment, in what have often been reduced to public urinals. At some taxi ranks the possibility also exists that you might get caught in the crossfire of rival taxi association wars.

'The inconvenient thing,' says Miriam, 'is when it's really bad weather; when you've got a tiny baby, and you're getting drenched.' I recall someone once telling me that what consoled her at these times was the thought of 'all the other mothers, thousands of women all over the city doing the same thing'. 'But you just dress for the weather,' Miriam says, 'and if it's pouring with rain then you get to school and you change.

'When my older daughter Wendy was a baby I tried to learn how to put her on my back, African style, because I reckoned a million African women can't be wrong, carrying babies in blankets. And it didn't work: small breasts, fell off. So when my younger daughter José was born I thought I'm going to get someone to show me properly, and I did it.

'Partly why I was doing it… it was a long time ago and the technology's improved a lot, but the backpacks that you got to carry them on your back were uncomfortable in those years. They really dug into your shoulders, and as the baby gets older and heavier it's more uncomfortable and you can't walk for any distance. So I learned how to carry her on my back for the pure and simple reason that I walked. And I got funny reactions to that. Most middle-class mothers have babies in car seats, and then you take the car seat with the sleeping baby and strap it into your car, drive to wherever you're going, and put them into a pushcart.'

As a preschool teacher, when her children were little she would take them to school with her, 'so we had to leave really early, earlier than we would have had to if we were in a car. But then I also have to say I've noticed that people who use public transport usually arrive first, because they plan better and they're more punctual, because you know you're not so in control of those issues.'

From 1995 to 1998 Miriam lived in Jwaneng, a small mining town in Botswana, and 'then it was a different kind of deal because we lived very close to school, and we basically all just walked there and walked home – you know how it is in small towns. So in cities, ja, it's been challenging over the years.

'My older daughter went to a school where most of the children were middle- to upper-class, at Pinelands High. And there are no taxis to Pinelands.' A formerly white middle–class suburb, Pinelands, with its trademark thatched roofs, is oddly located on the increasingly rough Cape Flats train line and is difficult to get to safely by public transport. Commuters from the townships to the suburbs travelling on this line often speak of changing at junctions, and switching modes of transport at different stages of their journeys in order to avoid more dicey parts; leaving hours early and taking long routes around in order to arrive safely. 'There was one bloody bus!' says Miriam. 'That was very tricky. I almost moved her quite a few times and then I was just like, okay, stick it out.

'Once I got a Thornton taxi that goes near there, and I ended up sitting on somebody's lap. The taxi squeezed me in, and I was just sitting on this guy's lap going, "I'm so sorry but there was no bus!" I was hitch-hiking and nobody was picking me up. I hadn't hitch-hiked since the early Nineties. You just don't. Not unless you're absolutely desperate. All these business people were driving past me looking at me like I was a serial killer, and I was thinking, I'm just stuck!'

I wonder about peer pressure on the children in an environment where it's expected that every family has their own car. 'When the children were small, little children asked me, "Where's your car?" You know when children perceive you to be different they ask you a very straightforward question. As the kids got older and became teenagers it was, well, that's just what I do. I think children are much more accepting of difference. Adults find it weird. If you're not poor they think you must be on drugs or something,' she laughs.

'My younger daughter goes to Queen's Park, a very mixed school in this community where there are lots of children whose parents don't drive, and they walk to school. It's a five-minute walk, and if I need to go to a parent meeting I walk there. A lot of the children also commute long distances in taxis and buses and trains to get here from the townships.

'It's something I would perhaps change if my children were younger now – they're nineteen and fourteen – but when the eldest was about thirteen they were getting the taxi together. I don't know if I'd let them do it now. You see thousands of children doing it, but my sense is that I'm having to be a lot more cautious than I was.

'But that's not because they're using public transport, it's about them being in public. For example, my 14-year-old, who now walks around this community, by the time her sister was that age she was very independent, getting into taxis, going to Claremont, shopping, coming back. Her sister doesn't want to do it. It's just, like, you walk to your friend's house, your friend meets you half way, you let me know that you got there safely, when you want to come home I walk half way and meet you. And it definitely wasn't like that four or five years ago.

'She also has a brown belt in karate, which helps in terms of her own confidence. But generally, whereas her sister was going off alone – "See you later, oh are you coming home at five o'clock?" – there isn't that freedom any more. So with public transport, like everything else, you have to be more cautious, better planned. Especially with daughters.'

Miriam grew up in affluent Camps Bay which, before the days of the minibus taxis, I found particularly inaccessible without a car. And yet, she reminds me: 'How did domestic workers used to get to Camps Bay? They had to get to work. They used buses. And the bus service has now basically fallen away; the taxis have definitely taken a lot of the buses' business away.

'But it's still a mission,' she observes, recognising the struggle for the working poor, without the luxury of choice, who have to trek every day to their places of employment, often a long distance from the townships where they live.

'With the taxis it varies according to the time of day, the time of year. In December, when there are loads of people coming to the beach, you're more likely to get a taxi at midday filling up fast. Or four o'clock when people are leaving the beach and there are tourists. But during the year I can sit on the main road from eleven to twelve waiting for the taxi to fill up, because they won't go until it's full, it's uneconomical for them to do it. But I know that, so I know that if I stay over at my parents' and I'm in a hurry, I must leave at eight in the morning. I don't know what those guys do for the rest of the day. They sit and they will not drive unless there are eight people, and then there's seven people and you're sitting... Who knows, maybe they like to sit and watch the sea!'

She laughs, recalling a taxi driver's interaction with a passer-by at the taxi rank in Camps Bay. 'The guy's calling: "Come, we're filling up, we're about to go, get on, *Caayyype Tyyyowwwn!*" and this woman was doing her, like, power walking, and she said: "Over my dead body!"'

Of her time in Botswana, she recalls: 'What was very interesting for me was that, although we could walk to school and the immediate logistics of daily life were fine because it was a small town, getting to the next town, which was three-quarters of an hour's drive away, and to Gaborone which was two hours away, was very tricky. We really were in the middle of nowhere, and my lifestyle was... I experienced it very differently to if I'd had a car.' She echoes the theory that it is cars that have given city people the freedom to move to small towns.

'Someone would say to me, "I'm driving to Joburg this weekend, would you like to go?" And I'd say, "Fantastic, we can share petrol," and off we'd go. That type of trip became more spontaneous. And then I had a few driving lessons when I was there, and I just decided this is not for me. And I realised if I'm not going to drive in a mining town I'm sure not going to drive in the city.

'My feeling is, if you're sitting in rush hour traffic for an hour, whether you're driving or in a taxi, you're going to get stuck in it, so I could sit behind the wheel and have to deal with everybody else getting frustrated about being in a traffic jam, or I can be doing my SMSing or reading or whatever in the taxi, and be pretty relaxed. I've always said I don't buy newspapers because I get to hear the news in the taxi. If there's some big news people will be discussing it.' The taxis have a bad reputation but, since they carry fifteen passengers, as someone pointed out: 'Just imagine if everyone using taxis was driving their own car.'

Inevitably using public transport involves a fair amount of walking. 'Whenever somebody tries to persuade me to join a gym,' Miriam says, 'I always mention that I don't need to go to gym because my travelling is also my exercise. When I have to do it to get from point A to point B, I get into a rhythm, and start walking in a more, like, exercisey kind of way. I love walking up hills, when you can feel your legs are straining and you're getting some good exercise.

'I love walking in the centre of town. My older daughter lives in town now, so we walk around there. Even if I had a car I wouldn't drive to town. That would be bizarre, getting there by public transport takes five minutes. Finding parking would take longer. We live in a beautiful city, and Cape Town's got some wonderful historic things in the centre of the city, so I pop into museums just spontaneously because I'm meeting someone and I've got half an hour to kill.

'I get a bus or a Rikki to town, because I don't want to be on the taxi deck.' The little shared, circuitous but door-to-door Rikki taxis – at about four times the price of minibuses, but half the price of the one-person metered variety – are a convenient compromise, often used by tourists.

'I've always wanted to go to New York,' she says. 'I love the idea of walking everywhere, in between hopping in and out of those yellow taxis.'

Walking to town, though, while a relatively short distance, is no longer an option, she says, reflecting on those 'nowhere' spaces in between – as author Marlene van Niekerk refers to them – as we dart 'from safety to safety'. Van Niekerk was examining South Africa's gym culture, where people walk on treadmills designed for prison inmates rather than on the streets they've come to fear.

A mugging at 9 a.m. a couple of years ago has made Miriam

more cautious. 'I'm sorry about that, because otherwise I probably would walk to town, for the exercise, and also for the fun and the interest and the great shops and the cool people that you meet along the way, but unfortunately the dodginess hasn't been outweighed.' Just a few seedy blocks and a couple of thugs can often determine our choices. 'But I have to say, as well,' she adds, 'that I've become a lot more intuitive now, so wherever I am, if I'm putting out my rubbish at eleven o'clock at night, if I get a strong feeling I shouldn't do it, then I listen to it.

'I want to be able to walk more, obviously because then it doesn't cost me anything and I get more exercise. Six months ago I was asked to start a playgroup by people in the community, because my daughter and I also babysit at night – she babysits for her pocket money. And then I started thinking, I really like this idea of being able to walk to work, and I haven't done it in years, and I'm doing it because, although I like taxis, I'd still rather walk there. And there's enough business in this community because there are hundreds of children. There's enough to generate not having to go and be anywhere else. And that is a huge plus for me.' With sharply rising fuel and transport costs, ongoing power cuts, and more toll roads proposed, working within walking distance of home may become increasingly popular.

'The hardest part for me about being a mother who doesn't drive is going out at night, and that means me involving other people. I've never had to do it, but if there was an emergency, I've always said to my kids, "You call a private taxi from a reputable taxi service" – there's a crowd on the corner here, they run it from their home, so we know a lot of the drivers personally – "You get one of the guys who we know and we trust, and I'll pay him when you get here."

'I must also say that I do have access, and I always have, to an extended family, so if there's an emergency in the middle of the night I won't have to wait for an ambulance. I have that resource, which I know a lot of other people don't have, so my children haven't been at risk, being at the mercy of...' she trails off, and reminds me of a recent report that South Africans have a one in eight chance of an ambulance arriving when Emergency Medical Services have been called.

Apart from their time in Botswana, Miriam has lived in and around Woodstock since her younger daughter was born, and witnessed it changing. Over the past decade, as Cape Town's coastline is bought up by 'foreigners' – the wealthy kind, rather than 'illegals' – and Capetonians are priced out of their neighbourhoods, so too has gentrification hit many formerly working-class suburbs, and many long-time residents have been squeezed out.

As a friend remarked wryly, what were considered *skommie* areas when we were growing up are now considered fashionable, particularly among middle-class arty types. These are the only areas that middle-class Capetonians can afford that are not in the unfashionable northern suburbs, where you may get 'value for money' but you also get a lot of ugly architecture, long commutes to the CBD and the more insular aspects of suburban life.

'Upper Woodstock has become very developed,' she says, referring to the upper and lower labels given to the areas above (closer to the Mountain) or below the Main Road. 'Older houses got sold, and renovated, and prices shot up. Rents have doubled.' Consequently crime has increased, and 'there's less of a street culture. There are fewer kids playing in the street than there used to be, and that in itself makes the area feel more like other suburbs, where I choose not to live because I don't like suburbia, so I find that a bit of a pity. So wherever I can I promote children playing in the streets, and also parents being in the street with their children, and parks being used and all that kind of thing.

'I like the fact that my daughter can walk to school and she's got a bunch of kids that she walks with. She's also now become very aware of which times of the day she can walk. Like now, late afternoon, she walked up the road to her friend, and I walked up to buy the vegetables, and there's a recycling place on the corner. And then you go along and there's the corner café, and you've known those people for fourteen years. I've always said that if that goes then I will just move to a small town, because it's so important to me. It's what nurtures me.'

There is a saying in Cape Town, 'I'll walk you half way'. It doesn't mean literally half way, but rather I'll see you on your way. She walks me back down to the Main Road, where the *gaartjie* is calling to me – *ClaremontKenilworthWynbeerrrrg!*

Shabbat in Glenhazel

It's 5.30 on a Thursday evening, and there are few white people in the streets as I walk over to Anat and Greg's house. But at the same time tomorrow the picture will be very different as people in the religious Jewish community collectively put down their car keys for twenty-four hours and take their weekly sabbatical from any form of work.

'From the minute Shabbos starts to come in,' says Greg, 'you park your car and you know that you're not going to get back into it until at least Saturday night, or Sunday. It's great.'

'We take over the road,' says Anat.

'There are people walking, and people on the street. Especially in these areas,' he says, referring to northeastern Johannesburg. 'Wherever you go there are Jewish people walking.'

'And waving to each other, and greeting each other. It's nice. Sometimes you see people walking, and then suddenly there's a car, and you completely forgot there are still cars around'.

Even in cities where walking is considered everyday, unlike Johannesburg, busy people don't generally have time to take leisurely strolls.

'The thing about Shabbos is that it's not about time,' Greg explains. 'There's no rush to get anywhere, so you put your kids in the pram and you walk. You have a destination that you're going to, whether you're on your way to *shul* or to have a meal with people, you're walking, and it's a beautiful thing. There's no other way to get there than to walk, you have no other alternative.'

'On Shabbos you don't really look at a watch because you don't need to,' says Anat. 'You put your cellphones aside, you put your laptops away, close everything, so there's never this rush.'

'You feel like you're a part of the world again when you walk,' says Greg. 'You see what's really going on in your neighbourhood, because when you're in a car you're pretty separated and you don't see it. Like there are two houses that have been demolished. You really see what people are doing and what's going on. And it's the most amazing thing.'

'A lot of the domestic workers get very excited when I come with the double pram,' adds Anat. 'They chat with the kids.'

'On a Friday night, someone's had a child,' says Greg, 'and you walk to celebrate the birth of their child. And you might walk four, five kilometres, and you walk home at two, three in the morning, because there's no other way to do it. And it's quite an empowering thing, especially in this country.'

Neither of them grew up in a religious home. Anat was brought up on a kibbutz and, though Saturday was the weekend, that didn't necessarily mean a day off for her. 'If the cows needed to be milked, they needed to be milked.'

I met her in a yoga class when she first came to South Africa. Her parents are South Africans who emigrated to Israel during the apartheid years and, after South Africa's first democratic election, at the age of eighteen, she decided to explore their home country. At that time she was eclectic about her spirituality and engaged in alternative spiritual practices.

'The thing about the esoteric world,' she says, 'is that there was nothing that held it together. I just saw it getting to people's egos too much, in all the different workshops I'd done. Like, "The universe provides, but look what I can do." It was a bit too airy-fairy, too unstructured, so what do you go home with, a meditation?' Now, with three children, her life has changed. 'It was just not enough.

There wasn't anything to hold a family in place.'

Though Greg grew up in Glenhazel, he says it wasn't always a religious community. 'It's only been, I would say, the last twenty years or so that there's been this turn towards religion. Since about 1986, and the state of emergency. Before that it was more traditional than observant.'

I don't understand the difference. Anat elaborates: 'Well, it was more symbolic, so you'd light your Friday night candles, have a meal, and then go off to a movie.'

'But I think, because of the uncertainty in the country at that time,' Greg picks up, 'it created a feeling of togetherness, of being in a community, especially for young people.'

For Lauren, Anat's cousin, the experience is different. Her approach to spirituality is to draw from different paths she's explored, and walking on Shabbat is a big part of that. 'I love it, that's why I keep it up. My Shabbat… a perfect day for me is we walk to *shul*, hang out at *shul*, walk home, not have lunch – Shabbat lunch to me is like the absolute bane of my life – have a light lunch, and an hour-and-a-half nap, and then go around the corner to visit friends. And that to me is a perfect Shabbat. It sounds like the most mundane day, but… My body knows that by Saturday afternoon, by one-ish, my whole system has stopped and I have to sleep, it's mandatory, non-negotiable. If I don't get that sleep I become vicious and my whole week is ruined.'

She walks with Piki, her 6-year-old son, 'and we love it. I drag him out on Shabbat morning and he moans. Normally it begins with this one trying to follow us,' she says, pointing to their little dog Ziggy. 'We have to throw him back in the house about five times and eventually he learns he can't come. And then we start walking. And we stop at the same places, because this is where we watch the ivy change colour, and then there are lizards at a certain spot. And in summertime there's a guy who waters his lawn as we pass, so even though we're not supposed to on Shabbat, we walk through the sprinklers because it's cool. There's a whole bunch of things we do. And he always moans, and I have to explain to him that we do it for a reason. I don't think he's quite bought into it yet, but he enjoys it once he gets going.

'The thing about walking when you walk as a single girl,' she says, recalling the time before she was married, 'is that it's actually quite lonely. You see all these couples and families walking past and, even though you're part of the club, you're still not in the club.' I recall that Lauren's husband, Rajend, once described himself as a Hindu atheist. 'Well, he's a scientist,' she says.

When she was still single, 'sometimes I'd walk and think, what the heck am I doing, why am I walking? What for? And then eventually I decided I really enjoy the walking, so I turned Shabbat from just going to *shul* to a walking day, and I'd walk to the shops, and to Rosebank to have coffee. I used to love it. And I miss that. It was a nice 40-minute walk for me. The one thing about Rajend is that he just doesn't like to walk like that.'

Beverley is in the process of converting to Judaism and says, for her, 'What is nice about it is that it's very good family quality time. It actually brings the family together. You walk together and you chat. When you're under a roof together you're not necessarily all together and talking, you're in front of the television. But this forces you to actually talk, and most of Joshua,' her partner, 'and my discussions happen walking to *shul*. And of course Daniel,' her 8-year-old son, 'participates as well. We make it a lot of fun because on a Friday we'll fetch a friend of his, and he'll sleep over and spend the day.'

Though she was raised a Baptist, and went to church and Sunday school, she stopped when she was about thirteen. 'I just felt no connection.' The turning point to Judaism came for her when her mother died.

'My parents had been going to the same church for twenty-five years and I don't recall one person knocking on the door with a meal for them. Myself and my sister used to cook and drive out to Florida. When I used to go there, every month, at the end of the month, my mother would be cooking these meals for the old-aged home for the church. And she would walk, because she couldn't drive – my mother walked everywhere – and she would take these down to the old-aged home and deliver them. And when my mother was housebound and couldn't walk for six weeks, I didn't see anyone come and bring food. When she died my father was there on his own, and I don't recall once, ever, anybody from the church, including the minister, inviting him for supper. And that was a turning point for me. I just realised, it's so different in Judaism. I find the warmth of the people and the caring, nurturing... They have a genuine care and compassion for one another.'

Something I have found refreshing living in a predominantly Jewish community has been the lack of proselytising. 'The first thing that you hear, when you want to convert,' says Beverley, 'is, "Why on earth do you want to be Jewish? We've been persecuted for so many years, we're still being persecuted, why do you want to be Jewish?"' Rather, energy is invested in calling 'lapsed Jews' back into the fold.

'When we registered at Daniel's school, the first thing they asked was, "When are you converting?" Because about 60 per cent of the high school kids end up marrying each other.'

Dana is one of those who would prefer not to walk, and doesn't see the point of it. 'I used to do it a lot. Sometimes I do it with the kids,' her daughters are eight and nine years old, 'to my mom or my brother or whatever. But other times I find it a bother. It would just take two minutes to get in my car and I'm there. Why do I have to walk there?'

For her it's also an aesthetically alienating terrain that she finds off-putting. 'I like walking where it's pretty, where there's something to see. But I find it the opposite of relaxing walking around with cars hooting, and exhaust fumes, and impatience. I think it also disturbs me to an extent... the problem is you can't walk and look at pretty houses or whatever. When you walk you just look at everyone's walls.

'Whereas when I used to take my students into town, to Newtown, I enjoyed it very much. It was close to the college where I taught, and we were doing photography, so we'd just walk. I enjoyed walking over the Nelson Mandela Bridge, it was culturally interesting. I enjoyed walking in the streets of the city. Most people say: "Don't do that, it's dangerous!" But I found it interesting, because you come across other aspects of life in Johannesburg that aren't just white experience. And I found that my students were like my teachers there. They knew more about what was going on, and what people were selling, what people were doing. That kind of walking I enjoy, if it's relaxing in the countryside or culturally stimulating.'

But, for many, walking on the Sabbath is a time to reflect inwardly rather than focus on the outside world. 'It gives me time to reflect on my week,' says Anat. 'There are days I go to bed and I haven't even thought about my day.'

'Our lives are just so hectic during the week,' says Greg, 'that come Friday night, and Saturday, it's just incredible that a completely different energy is present. It gives you a sense of peace, knowing that you're just this tiny little thing in a much greater world.'

There is something of a dance that happens between pedestrians and drivers on Shabbat. 'You see Jewish people, who are driving, looking at you,' says Greg. 'Maybe it was me feeling uncomfortable about doing it in the beginning, but also you do notice people looking at you in a different way, people who may recognise you. And then some people don't like to look at you while you're walking because it makes them think about the fact that they're driving. So then you don't look at the people in the cars because you don't want to embarrass anybody. I think it gets taken as an arrogant thing, but it's done to not make the person feel embarrassed that they're not observing Shabbos.'

Lauren confirms this when she talks about her experience of driving on Shabbat. 'I can't drive to *shul*, that's just too hectic, but I can drive to the shops and watch TV. When I have driven on Shabbat, and I've driven through Glenhazel, it's quite a joke. I sometimes want to drive with my head down, because I think, Oy…

'But it's also about us and them. It's very much this thing about, I'm walking and they're not, and I'm definitely special. I'm more unique because I'm walking, and it's quite obvious to everybody that I'm walking. But it's also kind of deceptive, because people see you walking and they assume you're religious.

'If you're walking on Shabbat in a skirt everyone knows you're going off to *shul* or coming back from lunch or something, and you see everybody else doing the same thing, and everybody assumes that everybody is observant, and actually at the end of the day when you bump into them on Sunday in their bikinis and their shorts they say, "Oh, I thought you were *frum*," and you say, "I thought you were *frum* too!"

'It's amazing. That's why I'm saying to you, it means very little. You walk on Shabbat… It's a form of projection, people sort of assume everything is different and they throw all kinds of assumptions at the person walking which in fact are all rubbish. Because he's just walking from his girlfriend who he's been sleeping with, they've had a good afternoon *shtup*, but he's still walking. That evening Shabbat will end and they'll go out and smoke dope and go to a club or something and dance until three in the morning.

'You don't know a thing about anybody. My feeling about religion is that the only difference between secular people and religious people, all religions, is probably their dress code, besides that you don't know a thing about what goes on behind closed doors.

'You see people at *shul* and you assume that they're moral, that they don't have affairs, they're financially sound, they treat their servants well, but actually when you see somebody walking on Shabbos, all they are doing is walking on Shabbos.

'The thing is, do you have to be religious to be Jewish? I think the whole Jewish intelligentsia is being lost because of this belief that you have to be religious in order to be Jewish. They're losing a lot of good minds.'

Linzi tells an amusing story about her experience of walking during her religious years, as a teenager. 'I became orthodox at the age of sixteen. I loved being with my grandmother and grandfather, so I would spend most of Shabbat at their home, and the nearest *shul* was a good hour and a half's walk away. I think there is a law for Shabbat which states that if you walk too far you are in fact breaking the Sabbath, so I might have been guilty of that.' The rationale behind this, explains author Douglas Rushkoff, 'would be that if it takes too long to walk to *shul*, then you're not living close enough to a community of Jews'.

'My grandmother was determined to accompany me,' says Linzi. 'She loved being with me, but she also did not want me to come to any harm, so she drove alongside me, with us singing, talking and sharing stories with each other. Sometimes people slowed down behind her and hooted and shouted obscenities. Once someone stopped and asked me if I was okay – was I being followed? By my grandmother!

'As we got near to the *shul* we would make jokes about the rabbi seeing her driving, and I'd encourage her to head off before that could happen. Sometimes she came back to meet me four hours later to accompany me on the second half of my journey, another hour's walk to my home.'

Anat's rabbi has a sense of humour about the driving. 'He says every Saturday he used to go out and say goodbye to people after *shul*, and this one guy drove past him every Shabbos and the rabbi waved at him, and he said, "You know what, after a year he's not driving any more." He says you can't not look at somebody, you wave, you greet, hopefully they'll join you one day.'

Strictly speaking, because the Torah forbids moving an object from one domain to another on Shabbat, carrying anything outside the home, including one's children, is also forbidden. But orthodox neighbourhoods usually have an *eruv* (from the Hebrew, meaning 'mixture'), an imaginary boundary marked by overhead wires that symbolically extends private space out into the public, in which necessities may be carried: house keys, water, holy books, reading glasses; and prams and wheelchairs may be pushed. 'It creates a walled city,' Joshua explains, an imitation of the walled Old City of Jerusalem, the original *eruv*.

Imaginary walls added to Joburg's notorious real ones. These 'walls', though, are to keep the observant in, inside one's own home, rather than to keep outsiders out. The *eruv* metaphorically extends the family out into the community. Carrying is then happening within one large home.

Security is always a consideration on Joburg's streets, and it becomes further complicated when you're forbidden to carry anything. 'I know my ex-husband asked, what do I do to protect myself on a Friday night?' says Dana. 'Because at one stage there were a lot of people being attacked on a Friday night, and the rabbi said he wasn't allowed to carry a weapon. So he strapped a gun to his ankle.' I try and imagine, in the event of an attack, if this gun would be of any use to him. Would he even be able to reach it fast enough?

Lauren has experienced a few anxious moments. 'Sometimes I feel threatened,' she says, 'but when I walk with Piki I don't feel too bad. The scariest thing was one Yom Kippur, Rajend dropped me at *shul* and I wanted to walk home. It seemed nobody was walking to the Cheltondale park, so I went to Torah Academy, and everybody had already gone home. And I had to cross the park. It's funny how… you're standing all by yourself in the street, and yet why is it that I can't bring myself to go into the park? And funnily enough the security guard walked me to the edge of the park and also wouldn't go in!

'Anyway, thank God a group of about six men came past and said, "What are you doing?" And I said, "Please just take me across the park," and they all walked with me and dropped me on the other side. And as we crossed the park and went up one of the side streets, there was this bliksem drunk guy weaving his way down the street. And all these guys... you could see they were just about as chicken as I was! But I think if I had encountered him by myself... I remember being absolutely petrified.'

A response to fears about safety has been the establishment of GAP, the controversial Glenhazel Active Patrol, 24-hour, armed security guards with a visible presence on the street. 'It's not only in Glenhazel,' Greg corrects me. 'Now they've done it in Waverley, Savoy, Cheltondale, Sydenham, and it's helping. It's brought crime down by about 80 per cent.'

'I think the thing is that people feel safe now,' says Anat. 'You don't look over your shoulder any more.'

Though she is in the minority, Dana doesn't feel safer. 'My family think I'm mad, they think it's wonderful, but my initial reaction was, "Gosh, what kind of community am I living in?" It was such a show of force, you know, the guys standing there with those Uzis or whatever they are. Just the whole image of it. It's quite a shock, I think, to see someone in a black army uniform holding a gun.' Though post-apartheid South Africa aims to transform its police force into a police service, these new private security companies look more like a defence force. Many of the recruits are from Angola and Mozambique, with Portuguese as their lingua franca. It seems ironic, in the light of the xenophobic attacks in South Africa in 2008, that foreigners are being recruited to keep South Africans safe.

'It's very militaristic,' Dana continues. 'I just found the whole concept very frightening. On two levels: the one is that it's necessary, and the second thing is, what does it say about us? It made me think of South America, you know. You hear of these communities living like this, and children are taken to school in armoured vehicles and helicopters. It doesn't make me feel more secure. It means that we live in a very violent society. And even though I knew it, maybe what's happened is that it's made it more conscious. Now you're faced with it all the time. You see the cars driving around; you see the guys standing with their guns. You are always unconsciously aware, but now it's continuous.'

Perhaps, I suggest, a visible presence is a good thing, and acts as a deterrent to criminals. 'I don't know,' says Dana, 'you expect to see it outside the bank, but you don't expect to see it outside three shops and a school.' There is also the threat of being caught in the crossfire between criminals and security guards, as happened recently in Johannesburg when a child was killed. 'I guess in extreme situations people do extreme things,' Dana reflects.

'I know that preceding this a lot of people got involved, many of the rabbis got people involved as police reservists and they had patrols on foot on the streets, and if they saw anything they'd call a reaction unit. And then I know they put a whole lot of money together because the Sandringham police station only had one vehicle, which was in very bad condition, and they bought a new vehicle for the police station. And in fact to get the community to go ahead and do this, Rabbi Tanzer became a police reservist himself. People still do it, but it wasn't very effective.

'The thing with GAP is that it's all done with CCTV. There's a station somewhere near Yeshiva College that monitors the whole area, and they have an aerial view. So obviously that's more effective than people being on foot.'

'You are now in a GAP zone,' the posters warn: 'GAP is watching', 'Zero tolerance to crime', '<u>Hoot</u> if you are being followed' and 'Have you signed your debit order?'

GAP was initiated by the Chief Rabbi and sponsored for the first year of its existence by a few businessmen, but now that the burden of payment is beginning to fall to the community, on top of their regular rates and taxes, some people have mixed feelings about it. 'I do have certain issues about it,' says Greg, 'we're also still paying for our regular security company, who we've never even seen, on top of what is needed to run GAP.'

Researcher Achal Prabhala sheds some light on this: 'The walking classes,' he writes, 'have their own ways of making night life safe. When, for instance, people need to get back home – after working the kitchens and tables in Midrand, Melville and Norwood, or just enjoying a good night out – they take South Africa's safest form of late-night transport: the Armed Response Taxi. Security company employees, driven to boredom on their late-night patrols and eager for a quick buck, will pick you up and take you home for the same price as a taxi.'

'On the whole I'm very much for GAP,' says Greg, 'it's making the streets safer.'

'And on Shabbos sometimes they follow people at night,' says Anat. 'They drive slowly, without you asking them, sometimes a single person walking. You feel safe.'

'They have certain points where they wait,' says Greg, 'and they're a presence on the street. Their system works on the principle that if you see two or more males in a car that look suspicious, walking or hanging around, they just want you to call in and alert them to the fact, and they go and they check it out. And the more they check it out, the less people want to hang around in the area. If they see a suspicious-looking car they'll follow it until it leaves the area. So they're pushing the criminals out. And that's why Sydenham has had to come in, Waverley and Cheltondale, because the criminals are leaving this area, and they're going to those areas. And now they're pushing them out of those areas.'

Writer and scholar Jonny Steinberg hesitantly predicted that 'the current escalation of violent predatory crime will not last … South Africans will not tolerate it'. But in the process, he asks, are we becoming less of a nation and more a collection of inwardly-turned villages – and at what cost?

Anat considers returning to Israel. 'The soldiers are a big issue,' she says. 'To bring your boys up knowing they'll have to go to the army. But Israel's much safer. The life here is just not… there's no sense of freedom, to walk around, or let your kids go out in the streets and ride bicycles, and give them money and say, "Go and buy milk." I don't feel it's normal here, the way we live. It's all very nice that we walk on Shabbos, and people try and create the space, but kids growing up... It isn't what I want for them.'

'There you don't have to own a car,' says Greg, 'you can get on the bus and go into the city.'

'To me that's normal, that's a normal life.'

'And the kids can go to the beach, or meet their friends, at ten and eleven years old.'

'There's more of a sense when you live there that this is your country and these are your people and at least when terrible things happen you belong somewhere and somebody cares about you. To go to a country where everyone's pretty much equal.'

The Palestinians wouldn't agree, I suggest. 'Well, the occupied territories are a problem,' she says. 'They always have been, and they always will be. Nobody's right in that situation.'

'The Israeli issue is a very complicated one,' says Greg. 'I don't think anybody has the answers, and I don't think there's going to be peace there. Israel will always be seen as the aggressor.'

Lauren doesn't want to go anywhere else. 'I'm happy to stay here. I like the country. Though I battle with this poor child,' she adds, pointing to Piki playing among the building rubble, 'the fear that he has to deal with. And the corruption gets to me.

'I don't want to be an old lady here – that I do know,' she says, after some thought. 'That worries me. I think sixty, sixty-five is a time to seriously start thinking about where to go. We went to India in December, I could see us living there in the south somewhere.

'I was thinking about it as I was driving to get stuff for the building.' They are renovating their house. 'To me this country is an exercise in sort of Buddhist concepts, that you have to learn to focus on what you can do and not get caught up in what you can't, because I've realised I can't control any of this stuff.'

Though Linzi isn't religious any more, she has fond memories of her teenage years spent with her grandmother. 'She had the most wonderful circle of friends, from Lithuanian intellectuals, free thinkers and armchair Zionists, to writers and singers. I loved this world of Eastern European Jews. While the rest of my school friends were out meeting, dating and probably having an exciting time, I was hanging out in Yeoville in the homes of rabbis and their many children, learning about Jewish mysticism, Chassidism and the Torah. I didn't want to be anywhere else for a long time.'

It is said that about 80 per cent of South African Jews can trace their ancestry to small Lithuanian towns and villages within a radius of about a hundred kilometres of each other. Lithuania was 'the seedbed of South African Jewry'.

'In this area where we live,' says Greg, 'within a three or four kilometre radius you'll probably find over thirty *shuls*. So wherever you live here you could find a *shul* within walking distance of your home.'

'I round the corner,' wrote Chandrea Gerber nostalgically. 'Almost there, I say to my freezing feet … People are arriving from all directions … with few of the worries that burden us during the week … A blur of singing wafts into the street … It feels as if the Jews of Glenhazel step back in time, reliving the world of their ancestors, and of all that has gone before them and will go on from them.'

(in brackets)

'By the sheer pounding of my feet, and the rhythm of moving, and the dropping of awareness from the mind to the body – without thinking, now I've got to hold my thoughts and regulate my breath and count to five and try not to think of anything – all the things you want to achieve in meditation just happen. You're so much more in the unselfconscious moment. And you drop down from the overly cognitive sphere, and god it's a relief! Just to get out of that space. And to allow things to emerge according to a different rhythm.'

Spending his days as Head of the Wits School of Literature and Language Studies, by dusk poet Leon de Kock is ready to head out onto the streets.

'When you run you enter into the somatic body. Many people work till five, six, seven at night, they've got stressful jobs; then they go home and straight into another sort of sedentary situation and never enter into strong engagement with the somatic body, strong breathing.'

Or when they do, it's very often in the artificially lit, thumping environment of the gym.

'What happens when you walk or run,' says Leon, 'is that you've got this concentration of stress from your working situation, which nowadays is quite hectic, and it's almost like the act of getting into your somatic body explodes it centripetally – Paaahhhhhhh, kind of blows it up. Stuff sometimes just cakes up so badly that I have to get out there and run.'

Marlene van Niekerk described this kind of aggregation of 'stuff' in her novel *Triomf* (which Leon spent a year translating from Afrikaans into English) with the term *saamgekoek*. Leon says, 'When things cake together, the notion of that coagulation, like mud and hair and blood and crap, they all coagulate and get hard, and I need the pressure of running to break that shit up.

'So in a sense running acts as a kind of switch, one that alternates your mode from a highly over-concentrated cerebral to a somatic body. It's a way of getting rid of these bad stress enzymes. We have these toxic encounters at work, or we have these toxically suppressed atmospheres of tension that you can cut through with a knife.

'And I need to go and pound the bloody streets. It's almost like a sense of expulsion. And the stuff somehow is expelled in the act of running. And then there's a rhythm. After about half an hour of running, you sense yourself regathering into yourself, minus that crap. And it's such a necessary act of recomposing yourself that, now that I realise how it works, I can't imagine not doing it.

'I do have lapses when I go through periods when I slip into more toxic cycles, like instead of running I'll drink a glass of wine, and that might lead to a cigarette. But then you take your stress into other places; into your liver, your spleen.

'Another thing – these thoughts emerged while I was running – is that it acts as a form of bracketing for me. At any given moment in our lives, let's say we're in a relationship, it's like that period of time becomes the expanding now, the now that has no closure. And it feels wonderful, like it has great unfolding potential. Then something happens, and it crashes, the bracket closes. And suddenly it's no longer an infinite progression, it's a bracket. It's a period of life in parenthesis. And you go into the next opening.

'So sometimes you have these brackets in your life, for example marriage and divorce, and you can be very cut up about the closing of the opening, when the bracket closes on you. It can feel like your life has ended. And then it can be very comforting when you get back into the running bracket and you realise, this is the biggest bracket of them all, this is who I was before, no matter what happens; the closing of an intervening bracket can feel like total bloody devastation, because some of what happens can really threaten your sense of who you are. This is the solace of the meditative bracket which is you alone in the world, the biggest one of them all, which cannot be trodden upon by anyone else.'

And yet there are others out on the streets, and this is part of the pleasure for Leon. 'The space is populated by people, and the people are part of it, and there is an engagement with the people. There's something about an equalling of relations between you and them. If you're in a car and they're walking, it's clear that there's a difference between you in terms of class, and standing, and wealth. Whereas if you're on the street, you kind of level that. Not completely, but there's a sense of comradeship of being on the streets, which I know from walking the streets of central Johannesburg, which is something I like doing. I love walking in the Diagonal Street area.' This, he writes in *Bloodsong*, is 'a quick step pleasure, on my way through, / going somewhere else'.

'I grew up walking the streets of Mayfair,' the formerly white, lower-middle-class, now predominantly Indian suburb of Johannesburg, 'and when we were kids we walked nonstop, to the extent that nowadays,' having recently returned to Joburg after living in Pretoria for twelve years, 'when I ride my motorbike around there, it strikes me that I have walked every one of those streets. There is not a single street in the entire broad circumference of Mayfair and Brixton that I do not remember walking. So I have a somatic memory of those streets.' He's on a roll: 'those pavements, those houses, those corners, the shape of the topography, the lie of the land, the slants upwards and downwards, the S-bends, the Ash Veld, there's a church, there's a steep alley going down there, that's where we used to go down on our skateboards. I think that's really important. And you have a memory of those streets being populated by people as well, and by a way of being on those streets.'

'We streamed / from pug-faced brown houses' and 'week-weary parents' listening to Springbok Radio; 'the evening doors leaked children / from 6 o'clock baths / mobs at play,' he recalls in *Bloodsong*. But the streets are no longer a reliable babysitter: '30 years on ... There's no fun left / in these frightened avenues. Now the kids / are washed in blue TV noise ... they're inside. Outside / are dogs and killers.'

'I really like engagement on the streets,' he reflects, 'even though, sure it's dangerous, and the issues about danger are different now than they were when we were growing up.'

There is a sense of loss when he writes in 'Nights I Remember': 'It seems it's only me, and my son, awed by night's cold silence as he rides / Dad's fear and Dad's sober back, / who think these streets are worth remembering.'

Protecting a child has become a wide-eyed responsibility, as he observes: 'I am left with the unspeakable burden / of making your joy ... of helping you envision / in this blighted arc, / indifferent to its dead, a life of making, / when all views disclose, in dumb show, the advance of shadows.'

But as a solo runner, 'I don't feel vulnerable,' he says. 'I can look intimidating, even though I don't really have the heart of a street-fighter.' As a six-foot-three, ninety-kilogram man, his experience is different from mine at five foot two and fifty kilograms. 'It's certainly more difficult for women,' he agrees.

Somatics scholar and 'recovering philosopher' Don Hanlon Johnson describes these literally different 'points of view' in his *Body, Spirit and Democracy*: 'As I came to feel, not just acknowledge philosophically, the uniqueness of how and where I stand on my uniquely shaped feet, I came to realize that my more abstract ideas about such exalted matters as morality and death bore the idiosyncratic marks of my high-arched feet and hummingbird-like hormonal rhythms ... I believe there is an elaborate web of intimate connections among seemingly ethereal notions about reality, narrow-minded attitudes towards other people and very fleshy postures and emotional reactions.'

'You know, the interesting thing,' says Leon, 'is a lot of New Age-type people have this theory that I sometimes find quite reprehensible, that they say, "Oh well, people who are scared attract crime."' This teeters on the edge of blaming the victim. 'And yet,' he's come to the conclusion, 'there is something to it. I was running one night in Pretoria, across the Austin Roberts Bird Sanctuary, and I witnessed a mugging, these guys mugging a man who was walking his dog. He ended up with blood spurting from his wrist, and I helped him find someone to take him to the nearest hospital. And those three guys were just sauntering off in the distance; they looked so unconcerned, it was such an easy thing they did.

'And a couple of nights later I ran across what I'm almost certain were the same three guys, and I thought, how am I going to handle this? First of all, I'm running with nothing on me. But as I approached them I thought, let's try something, and looked at them, smiled and said, "Howzit". And they responded, "Howzit, sharp-sharp". And that to me in a way proves the point. Even people who are out to get you, you can somehow undercut their approach and their engagement with you by transforming it – making eye contact with them, greeting them – because you're pulling them into the domain of the street on a level with them. You're with them out there on the street, you're not a rich tourist about to get mugged. And I think a lot of rich people about to get mugged behave like rich people about to get mugged.' A similar view recently prompted someone to form the *Stop Crime Say Hello* campaign.

'Humberto Maturana, an idiosyncratic Chilean biologist,' Leon explains, 'says love is not a sentimental thing or an attitude that is soppy or sweet, he says it's an entire bodily inclination towards others. And basically love is a bodily predisposition, or a "bodyhood", an entire predisposition of your whole orientation towards people that either brings them into being, or negates them. And he says that if you negate people your world shrinks; if you bring people into being by acknowledging them, allowing them to "arise", as he puts it, in equal coexistence with yourself, your world expands.'

In Zulu this is implicit in a Hello, *Sawubona*: 'I see you.'

In other words, if you are regarded with suspicion and treated like a mugger, perhaps you're more likely to behave like a mugger. Equals might return the respect they are given. And the pragmatist in me thinks: Just don't carry any valuables, in case.

'Some people argue,' Leon continues, '"What about all those people at the robots? I can't let them all arise into being because there are too many of them!" And that is a difficult one. How do you deal with this whole industry of begging out there, which many people believe is passive and indulges in a form of coercive, subtle exploitation of people.'

Filmmaker Sipho Singiswa once observed: 'We have this growing phenomenon of these small islands in the middle of busy traffic intersections, of the woman with a baby on the back and one or two toddlers, begging. So there's this culture developing. These kids growing up getting accustomed to the fact that their mothers, every day, when other people are going to work, go to these places, particularly targeting predominantly white areas. These kids are not getting any other stimulation other than to look at these cars, with mostly white people giving them money. So the impression that's being inculcated in these kids is that this is okay, that it's normal. And my fear is it's leading to a generation of beggars. And in addition to that, it's reinforcing a race issue.'

Recently I've noticed another trend on the rise at intersections around the city. A blind beggar being led up and down between lanes of traffic by a sighted person.

'When you're in a car,' says Leon, 'you're trapped, they target you. There is something very exploitative about their approach to you. It's not a genuine human interaction. Stereotypes are leveraged by people out of desperation, but everything is not what it seems in that transaction. I've got to the point now where I decline engagement with those people. I don't like the nature of that engagement, because of that disparity, and it draws me into an uncomfortable and an unpleasant sense of human engagement on a manipulative level. It certainly doesn't allow for people arising in each other's regard in a mutually healthy sense.

'But when you walk or you run in the streets, and you pass someone and you say, "Howzit Bru" and he says, "Ay, howzit", that moment is actually ennobling. It's a moment of human amplification instead of a moment of human narrowing.'

On the outside of the glass it is the machinery that intimidates Leon. 'When it's getting dark, I find the approaching cars extremely menacing, the way they bear down on you, the way they assume occupation of space; it's very aggressive. One feels quite threatened, and lesser. One feels almost predated upon, as though: "What are you doing out here? You shouldn't be out here." The system doesn't have space for you. If you think of the human ecology of this, what we have is a system in which locomotion, which metaphorically is the movement of life, is done in cars, which are aggressive, which are noisy, which are eating the planet up, but which are especially highly competitive and full of anger; compared to this sub-ecology of walking, which is another sphere of human travelling going on at the same time.

'The relations are unequal between them. The big guys have got the high ground, the advantage of speed. But time is running out for that system. Firstly we're running into gridlock, secondly it's too expensive, and thirdly we're killing the planet. At what point do we all realise we're just going to have to get out of our cars and do things differently, like walk, like move in closer to where we work, like create different communities based on different assumptions?'

Perhaps only when we no longer have a choice. Hopefully not in the way Zimbaweans have been forced to. On holiday in Bulawayo in December 2002, he wrote that half the city's cars had been 'abandoned to the hungry but immobile petrol queues. All over the city you see them,' he wrote, 'spread around long suburban and city blocks ... Cars that have become utterly useless.'

But the upside of this was that 'on the street, the petrol queues are so long, and the supply of fuel so erratic, that there's little point in waiting there along with your car. So you get out and take a walk. Go home and drink a Pilsener in one of the city's lush tropical gardens. In the unlikely event that fuel should arrive at one of the garages, you'll get a call on your cellphone. The city is buzzing with intelligence about the movement of fuel. But unless you're connected to the black market for petrol – which involves hefty bribes and premiums – don't hold your breath.

'Surprisingly, the result is exhilarating ... Everywhere, people are getting out of their cars to talk. Life is slowing down. There's not much choice in the matter. People are walking the streets again. Cycling is in fashion, and exercise has become a functional necessity ... And the streets are stupendously quiet. You can actually hear the insects buzzing.'

Of course the article was tongue in cheek. The Zimbabwean situation is a particular one brought about as an extension of systematic and brutal violence, which certainly affects the poor more than it does well-connected government officials. And yet, for different reasons, the steady creeping towards the possibility of this becoming a global reality has become more ominous, and less of a dystopian (or utopian, depending on which way you look at it) fantasy than it was in the past.

When he runs, says Leon, he creates a circumference around wherever he is living. Now in Parktown, on the border of the inner city, 'I run across Jan Smuts Avenue, up past The Ridge school, down about a hundred steps, then return by a long series of uphills, which I like – I like the challenge of uphills. The masochist in me likes the eating up of pain. Because you've got to do pain in your life. I think hardship is necessary in order to live in a balanced way. I don't think it's healthy to live without hardship. I think hardship gives you a sense of the balances and the rhythms and the tensions of things. If everything is too soft and easy ... Knowing that rough edge of things, it gives you all those good old virtues like appreciation.

'But one good way of experiencing a bit of hardship is by running, reminding your body of the economies of labour and reward. If you want a reward you've got to put the labour in. You've got to take the pain.'

Alan Sillitoe's classic long-distance runner says it 'makes me think that every run like this is life – a little life, I know – but a life as full of misery and happiness and things happening as you can ever get really around yourself'. For this juvenile offender – who 'had no peace in all my bandit life' – it was a place to learn to think, but for Leon it is a place to learn to not think; or perhaps, to think in a different way.

'When you stop thinking, it's not as though your machinery of considering things and being in the world and weighing up things stops, it's just that it drops down to a less active and over concentrated level. And I often find quite serious *eureka* moments happening when I'm running. But I don't summon them, I don't look for them. They just emerge out of that lower morass, that lower way of regulating and dealing with things. Almost like sleep. And one wonders, what is that lower process of thinking? Or maybe it's not lower, maybe it's higher. But it's certainly less cognitive.

'Alternatively, no thoughts happen at all. It's just the relief of going through a passage of time without being aware of that time. There are only two places in modern life where you really get that absorption: in work and sex.'

In his novel *Saturday*, Ian McEwan writes of his neurosurgeon: 'Operating never wearies him – once busy within the enclosed world of ... the theatre and its ordered procedures, and absorbed by the vivid foreshortening of the operating microscope as he follows a corridor to a desired site, he experiences a superhuman capacity, more like a craving, for work.' And, though diaries need to be coordinated to snatch time for sex, then 'he is freed from thought, from memory, from the passing seconds and the state of the world. Sex is a different medium, refracting time and sense, a biological hyperspace as remote from conscious existence as dreams.'

'That remission from the shackles of self-aware movement through time,' agrees Leon, 'is quite a gift in a way. I find sometimes that moving through time is painful; the awareness of every moment in time, and every moment's necessary conjunction with past moments and the causality and your part in it and your fault in it and your responsibility for it...'

This is complicated still further by author Siri Hustvedt pointing out that when we retrieve something from the tangled web of memory 'what we're really digging up is the memory of the last time we retrieved it'.

'The chronology of time is a very false adhesive for holding life together,' Leon nods. 'It's a false matrix because it doesn't take account of disruptive forces and achronological folds in one's being in the moment. And they play havoc with time. Things that happened a long time ago can be very close to one now, you can flatten the folds and have now and then very close to each other.

'So your memory's also a moving target. Memory is by no means a store that you can count on for being stable, like an archive. The same document's not always going to be in the same place in that memory. Which is partly why fiction does what it does because fiction plays with those perspectives that get presented in different forms at different times in memory. So life then becomes a series of shots from different angles, depending on your location in the moment.'

Or alternatively, from the same location at different points in time, as Auggie Wren – whose life's work is to photograph the same spot for more than 'four thousand straight days in all kinds of weather' – discovers in Paul Auster's *Smoke*: 'Sometimes the same people, sometimes different ones. And sometimes the different ones become the same, and the same ones disappear. The earth revolves around the sun, and every day the light from the sun hits the earth at a different angle.'

When he is writing poetry, Leon says, 'I try out the feel and the taste of words, because often poetry is about finding the first line. It's not about making a poem, it's about finding a sense of where that poem begins, and what that moment is; the first moment of the poem. The rest of it follows from there. And often that will come to me, or I'll have a feeling or a strong sense of something that might be a poem, while I'm running. And then I'll just be receptive to it. Poetry is not something you rap out, it's something that you get an inkling of, and you wait to see if it persists...'

'I have gone to the edges,' he wrote, 'the many edges ... from which / we have no choice / but to recover / and rediscover / breath.'

Grounded

At the age of eleven Alka had her first seizure and was diagnosed with epilepsy. 'When I was young I never really thought about not having it,' she says. 'I wasn't very conscious about it. Because it's something quite hidden – it's not an apparent disability, like being visually impaired – you're not confronted with it all the time; other people aren't, so they don't mirror it in the way they interact with you.'

But reflecting on it now, 'walking is where I've felt free from other people. I've always felt this huge constraint of having to be safe only when I'm contained by other people, like my mother not wanting me to be alone – which are natural maternal concerns; that I might have a fit, and what will happen – so it's a huge liberation. I'm on my own, I'm doing something for myself. I'm literally powering myself.'

In her early twenties she took herself to India, where she says 'I grew up', and spent time on an ashram in Pune, and in Mumbai. I imagine the anxiety of being in a strange, chaotic city alone with the threat of a seizure ever present, and yet she says, 'I felt so safe there.

'I made a friend and we took the train and walked quite far, hiked up the mountain to look at some old Buddhist caves: beautiful, exquisite. And he took a photo of me walking up these stairs that had been carved into the mountain, so I have this picture of me, embarking on my adult life.

'I stayed on the river in Mumbai, which was nice even though it was polluted. It was near the burning ghat,' where the Hindus cremate their dead. 'I somehow felt fine with that, I liked it. The way death is part of life. But the poverty is very hard. You see people shitting on their own doorstep, and it's very hectic. It's become more apparent in our everyday lives here now. Then it was more tucked away in South Africa.'

Though the divisions between rich and poor in India are also huge, they seemed less confrontational. And confrontations seemed less threatening.

'I had someone approach me in the street when I was living in Pune. It was one o'clock in the morning and I was walking along the road, walking back from visiting a friend, and this local guy drove past on a scooter, and he stopped and he said, "Sex please." So I said, "Oh fuck off!" And he drove off at a rate of knots. I think he was so terrified by my violent response.

'When I came back here I just felt the atmosphere almost thicken, you know. It's a much more overtly violent society, and there is always this tension.'

And then she began to confront the things that would be denied to her because of her epilepsy, like getting a driver's licence. 'For a while I lived out in Discovery, on the West Rand, and I felt very isolated there. It has a very good bus service but at first I hadn't worked out that there was a bus five minutes away, so I would walk half an hour every morning, wind or rain, with my laptop covered in plastic, to get to the bus. It was okay, but it wasn't really pleasant. And of course there would be all these people around me walking much further,' she adds. 'You just do what you have to do.

'At the Noord Street taxi rank in town, which is not a very nice place, I've seen tiny kids, under eight years old, holding onto each other with their little school backpacks, in their school uniforms, and I just think, I'm sure the parents or grandparents or whoever's looking after them must cringe at the thought of these kids, every day, happily sussed about what to do and where to go, nobody interfering, maybe here and there somebody lifting them up into the taxi, managing.'

Yet as a white person in South Africa, where race and class remain so intertwined, she is conspicuous at the taxi ranks. 'When I worked in town I used to walk to the Bree Street taxi rank, and I remember once, it was a bit late, and there was a middle-aged woman walking with her shopping and she said to me, "You can't walk alone here," so I helped her carry her shopping and we walked together. But she was walking alone. I suppose she thought, I was white, I stood out. But there are always people looking out for you,' she says, commenting on the solidarity of women who are, in truth, equally at risk from brutish behaviour. Not long ago a young woman was stripped and assaulted at the Noord Street rank by drivers who objected to her wearing a miniskirt. This was followed a few days later by a crowd of women in miniskirts marching onto the rank in protest. 'Some of the guys running the rank can be really hectic,' says Alka. 'And sometimes they'll only speak to you in an African language; they won't negotiate the interaction at all.'

Non-negotiation is something that was brought home to her abruptly, having moved to Craighall Park in the northern suburbs. 'I went for a walk along the Braamfontein Spruit, at the bottom of Delta Park.' Braamfontein Spruit is thought by some to have the potential to be turned into Joburg's version of Central Park. 'Every day I was walking,' says Alka, 'just for pleasure and exercise and getting to know my new neighbourhood, and it was very therapeutic, I was enjoying it; the cosmos was out. And the one day, it was just after five, still light, winter hadn't really started, and I was walking, and I came to a fence, a diagonal fence. And I could walk up the hill along the fence, but there was very high grass next to the path.

'I saw two guys walking towards me, and I thought, I wonder if it's safe. And then I thought to myself, you know what, let me not think just because they're young and black I should be afraid. So I

179

walked along, and the first guy, I greeted him and he was friendly. And the second guy said to me, "Hello Nice, give me a cigarette." And all my warning signals went up. And I said, "I don't have any," and I just walked by. And I sort of laughed nervously.

'And the next minute he was on me, and he had a screwdriver, and he held me down and he said, "I'm going to fuck you." And I screamed, I didn't know that I had that sound inside me. I think it freaked him out. It was like a house alarm, it was hectic, and he ran away. And then I was so mad that I chased him, and somebody came to my rescue. I didn't catch him, he ran up into Delta Park. But I just… even though I went against my instinct doing that, because my first instinct was, this is not a safe thing to do – the reality is that we live in a very high-crime society.

'One of the most shocking things about the encounter for me was that I always thought I would be able to at least try and negotiate in that kind of situation. You think you can engage reason, but there was no negotiation. And I thought, my god, this is going to happen. And that was hugely shocking for me. I've never actually allowed that into my reality before. I've never even understood it.

'I suppose it's their own sense of person or being that is so damaged – and I can understand that and feel compassion for it, but at the same time I felt so angry. If I had caught him I would have killed him. I felt violently angry, I would have stomped his head in. And I just thought, I hate you for making me feel like this.

'The other guy was just watching, standing a bit further down to see if anyone was coming. And I actually got more angry with him in a way. I thought, how can you just watch somebody… And then I felt really angry that I couldn't walk there any more.

'Anyway, I reported it to the police and the residents' association and the community policing forum. And since then they've mowed the grass, which is a bit sad because the veld was beautiful. Now I walk there again. Now I walk with my dogs, I don't walk alone. And I just don't go there if there are no other people around. I'll turn around and walk back. But it was very important for me to go and walk there again, because otherwise they take away that space. They make it their territory.'

Curiously, as you get older, if it's properly managed, it's generally very common for epilepsy to dissipate. And because Alka has been seizure-free for the past four years, she is now able to apply for a driver's licence. 'So I have a learner's licence.' But she's not finding it as easy at thirty-seven as she may have at eighteen. Apart from how difficult it is to get an appointment, 'I've failed my driver's licence four times. And it's just… I have a huge amount of anxiety. But I'm determined to get it!'

In the meantime she has a scooter, and 'it's changed my life so much. What I like about it is that you still have the sense of being in contact with the environment – maybe a little too much!' She has had her first traffic accident.

'I was going through a green robot, and the robot was broken on his side, and this guy didn't see me and just drove into me. It wiped out my bike. I was in shock, but I wasn't hurt or permanently damaged. I didn't break anything, luckily.

'It's certainly more dangerous than walking, but it's made me more mobile, it means that I can carry more. Not a lot more, but I can go and do some shopping. If I have to take the dogs to the vet then we walk, so there are still certain things… I can't go to the nursery and buy plants.

Because of her epilepsy, she thinks, 'I haven't always felt very closely tied to my body. I haven't felt that I could trust it. I feel deeply betrayed by my body as well, so there was a lot of resentment and regret. The accident forced me to realise how physically vulnerable I am on the bike. I just didn't feel it before. It's almost like, when I have a seizure, I jump out of my body. You never know when it might happen. Like in a shopping centre,' she imagines being trampled on, and cartoon-like 'the cleaners would just peel you off the floor in the morning and throw you in the bin.

'One of the ways that I stopped having seizures was, if I started feeling really stressed or tense I would drink something very cold and just try to watch it physically going down. I can't think of Coke as anything but medicine. And that would physically ground me in my body.'

Since the accident she has bought another scooter, which she describes as 'some sort of Hong Kong clone. I'd be happy with a really crappy little car,' she says. 'I don't mind, as long as it goes and it's safe. Just for if I do have to take the dogs somewhere or whatever – for practical reasons.

'But now I want a really big bike!'

Baby Steps

'The scariest thing for me, with both my daughters was, as soon as they've got their balance they want to run because – *Independeeeeence!* And at the same you're chasing after them because at any point they miss a step and, oh my gracious!' Sheila is the mother of 12-year-old Chelsea and 2-year-old Rebecca.

'The thing when you're learning how to walk is you're made out of rubber. And I think it's also a bone thing, once you're up on your feet and you want to go forward, you throw your head forward and your feet kind of follow, so it does become a running thing, because of your weight. *And... and... and... then...* you kind of regauge it, and then occasionally they land on the bum.'

It's the kind of confidence we sometimes lose as adults. I recall a time, crossing a log over a river, that I was hesitating, and a friend pointed out that 'you just don't trust your centre of gravity'.

'Yes, because you're actually thinking about falling and not about walking,' says Ruth, 3-year-old Raphael's mom. 'If you think about falling you're not going to be able to keep your balance.'

'Their ability to fall,' says Sheila, 'they can fall on their faces, on their bums, because they don't think about it, and they're limber when they do it. They're not tensed up about it.'

'Meanwhile you're thinking of them falling, so you're going "Ah ah ah!"' laughs Ruth.

'On no, we run!' says Sheila. 'Oh god, parents can run. And

we try so hard to catch them before there's a graze on the nose. But when your nose has bit the tarmac, *you* don't want to do it again, because it hurts, so when she's running out of control and I'm saying, "Rebecca slow down baby, slow dooooowwwn…" And the next time she's running down the road, and I go "Rebecca…" she's like, Okay, last time my mom shouted at me I got a really sore nose, so maybe I should balance a bit more backwards, maintain the balance, and I can still run forward, but…'

'And they ruuunnn… boom!' Ruth tickles Raphael, who seems to see this as his cue to get up and go. 'Where are you going? Come back. You can't go home, there's no one there. Come.' But he's determined, and we lose her from the conversation as she runs after him.

'He's learned to break his fall though,' says Ros of 11-month-old Griffin, 'because he used to fall straight to a lying position. He falls backwards, and he'll be holding onto something and he loses his grip. He was falling headfirst, doosh, headfirst, doosh… But now he's learned to break his fall by bending his knee, so he falls on his bum, as opposed to falling straight back onto his head.'

'With Chelsea,' Sheila recalls, 'her first walking was against the wall. So she'd get up against the wall, and then all I'd hear coming was ggghhh, gghhh, down the corridor, gghhh gghhh. I'd hear the nappy scraping on the side wall. And she'd realised, Oh okay… She was holding the wall with two hands and walking, moving herself down the passage. There was nothing else to hold onto, because with the baby there's minimalistic anything around.

'Chelsea was walking at nine months, but I think that was from needing to get things, because I was making movies and she and her nanny were on the set with me, so if she wanted anything it was like, get up and go, kid.

'A lot of the books say that your first-born walks faster than your second. I think there's a need to walk, to get there, but if there's an older sibling it's more like "Eh eh eh,"' she whines, 'and the older sibling can help you.'

'And they can also see what their brother or sister is doing,' adds Ros, 'it's on their level. Whereas if they're seeing an adult, they have to get up to see what's going on.'

'It can also work the other way.' Ruth is back. 'Like if they've got a sibling who is talking, they talk sooner than the first-born.' I think of my godmother's daughter and me, born three days apart. She is a big girl and was up and walking long before she talked, while I was apparently still down on the ground, chattering.

'I used to look after a 3-year-old with cerebral palsy,' says Ros, 'and he couldn't walk, he was on crutches, and his mental development was mind-blowing.'

'Mothers shouldn't panic either way,' Sheila stresses. 'The thing with moms is they read too many books and magazines. Children develop at their own pace. The crucial thing is, you have to crawl. It doesn't matter when, but you have to crawl. That's one of the reasons why overseas those walking rings are banned.' Canada outlawed them first, and then Australia followed. Though there is debate about whether or not they cause developmental problems, they have been responsible for many serious injuries, most often babies falling down stairs.

'When they're born the left side of the brain controls the left side and the right side of the brain controls the right side. The crossover happens when they're crawling. The most important part of having coordination, and the ability to read and write, is crawling.'

'It's crossing the midline,' Ruth explains. 'The two sides of the brain learning to work together.'

'I heard from a woman that I met,' says Ros, 'who said that her daughter, at five years old they realised that she wasn't able to do certain things and they took her to a therapist, and one of the things they did was give her a puzzle, and they saw that she was picking up the puzzle pieces with her left hand, and giving them to her right hand.'

'There are also other things that crawling is important for,' says Ruth. 'When you crawl you strengthen your wrist muscles and your hand muscles. You need a lot of strength in your arms to crawl.'

'With babies, their legs are stronger so they can balance, and you can walk along… but then you want to get there,' Sheila points across the patio, 'so you actually need to go onto your hands and knees to get there.'

'Eventually they get so frustrated they just do it,' says Ros.

'That's one of the reasons they say, put your baby on its tummy,' says Ruth, 'because seeing the world around them makes them want to move forward.'

But apparently many babies don't like being on their tummies. 'Rebecca screamed blue murder,' says Sheila. 'Rolled onto her back and said, Take your putting me on the tummy and stick it.'

'The nurse told me to just put him on his tummy for five minutes a day if he hates it,' says Ruth.

'That's all the screaming I could take!' says Sheila.

'To strengthen the neck muscles,' says Ros. 'And then one day I walked into the room and from lying Griffin was sitting.'

'From lying on the tummy they push themselves up, and they realise, Hey!' Ruth smiles, looking at the world around her, 'I can actually do something.'

'And then they tuck in their feet, they realise there's another part of their body they can use,' says Ros. 'And literally, within five minutes, he started crawling. And I was sitting there, watching this going, Omygod!'

'Raphael just pulled himself along on his tummy, for about two months.'

'Like a little leopard crawl,' says Sheila.

'And then two days before his first birthday he started walking.'

'And then, my baby's not my baby any more,' Sheila wails, 'and, oh god, she can walk!'

'I can't wait for him to be able to walk properly,' says Ros, 'so I don't have to hold his hand all the time.'

'Also, before walking comes getting off things, and getting onto things,' says Sheila. 'You have to teach them about the edge of the bed. You can't go head first, because if you go head first,' she claps her hands together, 'you fall on your face. You have to turn them around. And then going down stairs is either backwards or forwards. It depends on their personality.'

'I showed Griffin how to get off the couch, on his tummy,' says Ros, 'but his instinct is he just wants to do it, and he's learned, because I've let him throw himself off, and now he climbs…'

'I taught both my daughters…'

'*I'm* talking now!' says Ros, raising her eyebrows at Sheila in a mock reprimand.

'He climbs up the stairs on his knees, and now I'm showing him how to get down the stairs the same way, tummy down. I've tried to show him how to slide on his bum, but he hasn't got that yet.'

'Both of my daughters, I tried to show them how to go downstairs backwards, but they can't see where they're going, so both of them turned around and said, No, Mom, this is how we do it, we go down on our bum.

'The thing with moms,' Sheila reiterates, 'is they read too many books, and then they panic because "James Jones did this at…"'

'The only book that I absolutely love,' says Ros, 'is *Baby Sense*. It's a fantastic book because it explains how, because they can't communicate with words and everything is new, it's all about their sensory world and what happens when they get sensory overload. After Griffin has his supper and his bath, then it's quiet time, and we play on the bed, and I always give him a massage.'

'We roll our eyes in horror,' laughs Ruth.

'Ja, I wish, I wish,' says Sheila. 'I get home at seven o'clock at night, and Rebecca's almost asleep and she sees me, and it's Mommy! She's eaten and dressed for bed, and when Mommy comes home it's like another two hours of running around in the street.' Of course when she says street she means the driveway between parking garages in the gated complex in which we live.

No children play in the actual street.

Actor Paul Lückhoff, now six foot five and an intrepid walker who strides across Johannesburg for about two hours every day learning his lines, tells me the story of how he began to walk. 'Apparently I refused. I did not even crawl. My mother later went to the doctor with me, and he said there's nothing wrong with me. I started walking only at about eighteen months. And she said, one winter evening she sat there, there was a big fire, my father was out and I was lying there, and as she looked at me she thought – obviously a bit exaggerated, but you know that old saying: "Don't kill a good story with facts", *nè?* – she thought, what is going on with this child? And a minute after that I started to get up. And we had a long corridor going out of the sitting room, you know those old houses, *die ou klipgeboue, sandsteen*, and she said the next minute I was on my feet, and *a bietjie gestagger-stagger*, and sssssshhhhhhwwww – there I go down the corridor.'

I imagine him lying in his cot for months, playing with his toes, plotting how to walk. 'And they say since that day I just walked around.' Living in the small town of Kestell in the Free State, 'I walked the whole town flat.' When he was about three or four, 'the pharmacy would phone and say, "*Dominee*,"' his father was a minister, '"*Paul is hier*." And my father would say, "Yes it's fine, he walks around."'

One day, fed up with his family, 'I said I'm not living with them any more, and there were fabulous farmers about ten kilometres out of town, and I said, "I'm going to Tant Hettie now," and I packed a little suitcase, and my mother said, "Yes, goodbye, go." And I was apparently just out of town and then my father got worried, and he drove up and stopped next to me and said, "Ag, we'll go to Tant Hettie over the weekend. Come back home now." *En toe't ek huistoe gegaan.* But since then I've just loved walking.'

Listening to him I almost become nostalgic for small town life in the Fifties, before I was born.

'Children have got to learn boundaries,' Ros reflects, 'so

Griffin's fallen umpteen times and he's learned from that. But you keep them out of overt and serious danger.'

'When they're running,' says Sheila, 'and you can see the rise in the hill and you know when they're going to hit their face, you run after them, and they hit their face on the dip down, and you pick them up and you console them. The next time you go to the park and they run up the rise and down the hill, they're slightly more tentative because they know what's coming.'

'The thing is, in our day,' Ros considers at twenty-nine, 'we played on jungle gyms and swings; that's what we did all day, we played, we weren't cooped up. But now in Joburg, as a mom on my own, I would feel quite apprehensive going to a park by myself with my child. I just wouldn't do it.'

Metal and Flesh

'I'll tell you exactly where it was – Central Avenue in Illovo, in Atholl. It's a steep road going down from Illovo to Atholl. I was at the very bottom of Central Avenue, walking from the school bus stop a few roads up. I was at King David, Victory Park, and I was with my brother, my twin brother. We lived just further on in a cul-de-sac. And this van was obviously out of control, and he had to turn or he would have gone straight into a house. So he turned onto the pavement to avoid whatever was in front of him, and we were on the pavement.' Paul and his brother Michael were seven years old.

It was a hit-and-run – the car sped off, and the little boys were both left in a coma. Michael came around after two weeks with no long-term physical injuries, but Paul remained in a coma for four months, his family not knowing if he would survive. When he finally came to his vision was impaired and he had lost his left leg from just below the knee.

'It was like being reborn,' he says. 'I woke up in the hospital, and I can remember my life before that but it was like being a different person. I remember incidents, and I have some memories, but I can't remember being somebody. It's like remembering another person.'

The little boys' nursery school teacher has memories of him. 'He was delightful, full of beans. Both of them. They were very close, they loved each other. They were adorable, got up to pranks and everybody followed them. They were leaders. When we heard about the accident it was shocking. It just devastated everybody.' I try to imagine the twins' mother sitting by their bedsides.

'But this is me,' says Paul. 'I can't think of me having two legs. I know I did, but I can't remember being that person. This is how I've grown up, so I've grown since then.'

With mainly peripheral vision, and unable to read easily, the decision was taken to send him to the school for the blind in Worcester in the Cape so that he could learn Braille. One of the hardest things about this was being separated from his brother.

Having spent most of his adult life in London and never really having lived in the same city as Michael, and with his mother getting older, Paul decided to move back to Johannesburg a few years ago, to Oaklands in the northern suburbs. But he says that he finds the city's streets very unfriendly to pedestrians.

'I mean, in Johannesburg people don't walk unless they have to, mainly for safety reasons,' he is referring to crime, 'but I'm always walking around here because I'm used to not getting into a car for everything. But this little distance, from my apartment to the garage, one block, is like an obstacle course. You can't walk on the pavements because they're so unlevel. It's either unlevel or full of litter, cans and things. Pavements in this country aren't designed for walking. There are all these potholes and things, so it's easier to walk on the road.' The playing field between pedestrians and drivers in South Africa is certainly not level.

Coincidentally, a few days after our conversation I meet up on the same block with some friends, visiting from out of town, with their toddlers in prams. A pile of bricks means we all have to step off into the street. I'm struck by how people are always emigrating from Johannesburg, and yet there's always building going on in the suburbs; others are clearly staying, or moving in.

Perhaps because of the condition of the pavements, many home owners elect to take responsibility for the area directly in front of their property themselves. But in the process they colonise it to the exclusion of passing pedestrians, who have to step off these elaborate, pretty but unwalkable landscapes. This makes it difficult for the average pedestrian to get across, and treacherous for the visually impaired or anyone pushing a baby. As Paul puts it, 'You're walking, and they've built up their little area, and suddenly you get to the end of that and there's like a two-foot drop down.'

It was just a block from his corner that I had a bad fall. The combination of a sloping pavement, building sand, heavy rain and slippery posters advertising a dance performance, that had been discarded alongside a concrete rubbish bin rather than in it, meant I jeté'd unexpectedly and ungracefully up into the air. A few seconds extended into a lifetime as I anticipated broken bones and teeth, but thankfully reflexes had my hands shooting out in front of me, and I got away with just a gash on one hand and bruised fingers on the other. Miraculously even my umbrella remained intact. I can only imagine what this terrain is like for those who can't quite see.

Those sections of pavement that aren't cultivated, many drivers seem to mistake for extra parking space, with service contractors as well as private citizens routinely parking on them; and informal metered-taxi ranks springing up there.

I'm also struck by the way we compensate, like limping on a blister, when things don't work as they should. A while back there was a water leak in my street. Despite numerous phone calls, eighteen months later there was still a constant stream pouring down the street. Consequently, waist-high weeds grew up through the pavement and pedestrians simply navigated around them. Impossible for people with prams. Difficult for those with canes. My neighbours walking on Shabbat told me they resorted to crossing the street to avoid getting their shoes wet.

'When I was younger,' says Paul, 'I didn't want to walk around with a stick. And my older brother criticised my self-consciousness. But it wasn't because I was self-conscious, it was just that I never really needed it. But lately I've been using the stick because it's easier here, for balance and the pavements being uneven.' The cane can also have what blind poet Stephen Kuusisto refers to as a 'civilising influence' on traffic.

'That was my brother's argument,' says Paul. 'Drivers can't always see. So they see I've got a bit of a limp, but they don't know I've got an artificial leg. The same with my sight, no one can see by looking at me that I've got a sight problem.

'My brother used to say, "You know, in situations, people are going to make a gesture to you, and if you don't see it they think, what's wrong with this guy? Is he just totally ignorant? Or is he drunk or something?"' And in the South African context, where pedestrianism is linked to class, there is the insidious assumption that pedestrians must be poor and relatively illiterate. In a discussion forum on the Arrive Alive website, one user wrote: 'Pedestrians are a problem. Think about it, they are uneducated, have little access to TV and in many instances even to radio.' Historically this was born out of racial prejudice, but in the class-bound new South Africa, no matter what your colour, if you're on foot and not attached to something – dog, running shoes, pram, cane – you're likely to be considered a second-class citizen.

Paul says he found walking in London very different. 'The streets there are designed for pedestrians, for walking. The pavements are wide and flat and concreted. I could walk outside and stop a taxi, or walk to the Tube. I used the Underground a lot. I also used the buses, but I preferred the Underground because I knew it so well. I didn't have to look at maps. I get on this line, and I get off there. I felt very at home in London.'

In Joburg he has found it necessary to employ a driver. 'People have said to me, it must be a lot easier living here, you've got a driver. But it's not easier, it's just that without a driver it would be impossible. Getting a taxi here is a nightmare. Eighty per cent of the time it's this beaten-up car with a guy who often doesn't know where he's going. It's not like getting into a registered, comfortable taxi, and you give them the address and they know exactly where they're going. And there's a set price that you pay. Here you have to bargain.' I sense his loss of independence in Joburg.

Getting used to his artificial leg wasn't easy. 'It's very difficult to adapt to, especially when I was growing up, because my leg was changing all the time and they couldn't get it right. Now it's better. It's settled down in terms of growth, and things have stopped changing physically. If I get a good fit it lasts for a year or so. For the last year or two it's seemed pretty good. There was a stage that I went through in London when they just couldn't get it right. It was breaking down all the time, and I was on and off crutches.' While he was able to walk a lot more in London, it did place a strain on his leg.

More than a century ago in London, in 1896, housewife Bridget Driscoll was the first person to be hit and killed by a car. It was travelling at what witnesses described as 'a reckless pace, in fact, like a fire engine'. In truth the vehicle was unable to travel at more than four and a half miles per hour. At Mrs Driscoll's inquest, Coroner William Percy Morrison was the first to use the term 'accident' in relation to violence caused with a motor vehicle, and he said he hoped 'such a thing would never happen again'.

The driver of the runaway van that hit the twins thirty-four years ago was finally caught and found to be drunk. By 2006 there were nearly six thousand pedestrian deaths in South Africa due to fatal crashes, and many more people were injured. The World Health Organisation has predicted that traffic accidents will become the third-leading cause of death globally by 2020.

In the 2007 report on the National Injury Mortality Surveillance System, South Africa's Medical Research Council reports that, of the 33 513 fatal injuries registered at thirty-nine mortuaries in seven provinces, violence accounted for 36 per cent and transport-related deaths for 32 per cent. While violence-related deaths appear to have decreased, there has been a steady increase of traffic fatalities. Pedestrian deaths accounted for the largest number of transport-related fatalities, and was the greatest cause of death of children aged five to fourteen.

Surprisingly, the highest number of homicides was not in Johannesburg, but in Cape Town, which was found to be the most unsafe among the four largest cities in South Africa. Johannesburg is the least safe city as far as transport-related deaths are concerned.

According to the *Economist*'s *Pocket World in Figures* 2009 edition, South Africa is number one in road deaths, but only thirty-seventh in road traffic injuries. As journalist David Carte points out, when we are hit, we are hit hard.

Unlike in the United States, where driving is a skill learned at high school, the majority of South Africans can't afford and so don't have access to formal driving lessons. Together with the complicated K53 driving test and how difficult it has become to get an appointment to take the test, this results in bribery and many people 'buying' their licences. Numerous drivers are not qualified to be behind the wheel at all.

Perhaps it is something that comes with having been so close to death, but amazingly Paul has no resentment towards the driver who hit him. 'People often say to me, "You must be bitter, how can you be so happy?" But this is how I've grown up, this is who I am.'

One of his greatest pleasures is swimming, which he has done almost every day for the past twenty years. 'I'm not really disabled when I'm swimming.' So he is considering training for the 2012 Paralympics. 'When I was in London I couldn't do it because I was on a South African passport. But now that I'm here, why not?'

Footing with the Ancestors

Patricia Glyn is not as tall as I imagined. She is six foot, but somehow doesn't tower over me. There is a gentleness about her that makes her accessible. Her little Africanis dogs seem to be contemplating a suburban escape as she opens the gate for me, but she calls them back sternly – they will have to wait for their walk.

Historian Roger Webster has called her 'the only woman explorer in South Africa', and yet 'it can be argued that there are no explorers left,' she says, 'because the whole globe is now known. Now the thing about getting out there is that you stare at your own soul.'

When she was a little girl she had heard about her great-great-grand uncle, Sir Richard Glyn, who had travelled from Durban to the Victoria Falls on a hunting expedition with his brother and a friend in 1863, eight years after David Livingtone had 'discovered' them, but he remained little more than a myth to her. This was until she was presented in 2004 with a copy of his diary of the expedition. She resolved then to recreate the journey he had made, sticking to the timetable he had followed. She set out from Durban on the 16th of March 2005, exactly a hundred and forty-two years after Richard, and arrived at the Falls in Zimbabwe more than two thousand kilometres later on the 23rd of July.

There was one big difference: 'Sir Richard was riding a horse, I was the idiot who decided to walk!' 'Why walk?' her sister asked.

To test her mental and physical strength, she says. She would have to cover about twenty-five kilometres a day.

'I think it's something that happens to people in their forties. You suddenly realise you're running out of time.' For thirteen years she presented the radio programme *Patricia's People*, 'and I was in the studio talking to people who were doing things that I wanted to do. You realise that your strength is finite, so if you want to do things best you go and do them.

'And it's doing it slowly. When you're on foot you have time to greet people, to talk to them and to walk with them. Walking through the Drakensberg, that took a whole day, and in a car it would be about half an hour. It's the wonder of seeing things unfold really slowly. After Howick I was on dirt roads. And in Botswana and Zimbabwe sometimes there were no roads at all, I was crashing through the bush. So it was a privilege to be in rural Africa for about four and a half months. And to see the trees – Zimbabwe is still very pristine in the northwest corner that I was travelling through. Beautiful scenery, beautiful people, lots of wild animals. I was in Big Five territory for about a month, which I have to say was terrifying, when you don't have a weapon – you've just got pepper spray and a boat flare,' she laughs. 'I was walking with my dog. And I picked up another dog along the way. So to walk in Big Five with dogs is not funny.'

In *Footing with Sir Richard's Ghost*, her account of her journey, it is the interactions with children along the way that touched me. Sandile Madlala, who 'bounced' along beside her in Estcourt and informed her that he was off to buy an electricity card, the ten rand he was holding would provide his family with heat and light for a week; after that it would be back to candles. And the two little boys who told her the story of their dogs, Rex and Tiger. 'I say told me their story, but in truth I could only understand a tenth of it.' One of her resolutions on the journey was to learn an African language. And then there was Elizabeth, the 12-year-old Tswana girl and her two school friends who joined Patricia near Lichtenburg. 'Several kilometres later it emerged that they were staying with me in order to protect me against harm. "There are many bad men around here,"' the 'tiny slip of a girl' told her.

In fact the only 'bad man' she encountered was someone who ran up and attempted to kiss her, and 'it was clear within seconds that he was deranged and that he had no intention of raping and molesting me ... I pushed him away and screamed, "No! No! No!" repeatedly until he slunk away, giggling.' After guarded life in the city, this absence of any violence made a big impression on her. 'I was never once so much as threatened, let alone robbed. Never once asked for a bribe. So you tell me about crime on our continent, that a woman can walk on her own for four and a half months and be greeted by nothing but hospitality.'

Her walking companion, Tapiwa, was a 'gift' (in Shona) that she found in Zimbabwe three years earlier on the Blue Cross Challenge, a five-hundred-kilometre walk to raise funds for abused animals. As these things happen, she spotted 'an emaciated brown puppy grubbing for scraps among the stones on the edge of the tarred road' near the Beit Bridge border post as she was driving home. By the time her really big walk came along he was fit and able to accompany her. On this trip she found another gift – Mpho (Setswana), near the Botswana border. Both dogs are Africanis, an umbrella term from the words African and *canis*, for the many types of rural aboriginal dogs found in southern Africa. For about three weeks Tapiwa growled at the new puppy, and then they became good friends.

Though she and Tapiwa were walking alone during the day, she did of course have an entourage. Not quite as elaborate as Richard, with his three wagons, sixty-nine oxen, ten horses, twelve dogs and eleven servants, to take just three men hunting, Patricia was accompanied by two Isuzu 4x4s, a camera person and two organisers who transported supplies and went ahead each day to do research and arrange logistics and camp sites for the night.

In her book *Black Woman Walking*, sociologist Maureen Stone, who was born and grew up in Barbados, remarks on the world of difference between middle-class adventurers who choose to walk and rural women who walk because they have no other way of getting where they need to go. 'At about the same time that Ffyona Campbell is doing her great walk across Africa, in Zimbabwe in Southern Africa, two black women are walking along a road in Hwange National Park, heading for the tourist lodge forty-three kilometres from the main road, where the bus dropped them at 9.30 in the morning. It is 2.30, and they have been walking ever since. They are returning from a visit to their village, to join their husbands who work at the lodge. They are each carrying two suitcases, and an assortment of other bags and packages, as well as the inevitable baby on each back. Unless they get a lift from a car or lorry it will be 5.30 or 6 p.m. before they reach their destination. They are not "great walkers" in the style of Ms Campbell; they are just two African women going about their normal business, in the course of which they may walk forty-three kilometres or more. They think nothing of it. It's all in a day's work.'

According to Stone, the poor African women think Western women 'silly' for walking when they don't have to, and yet in Patricia's experience she felt it acted as a point of understanding. 'After the initial shock of African people I came across, their shock of finding me alone on foot, it was quickly superseded by a clear knowledge of what walking's about. And they seemed to understand the quest. As soon as I said I was following my ancestors there were no further questions.'

But she was sobered by the sexism that still exists. On the question of seeing people carrying heavy loads, she says: 'It was always women, and the guys walking alongside them with nothing. I'm afraid the sexism out there is just staggering.' A group of 'wizened old men who gave me permission to walk through their land and showered me with blessings for my journey' had only one question for Patricia: 'Does your husband allow you to do this?'

'One thing is clear,' Stone observed, 'For the two African

women walking … relief might come in the form of a passing motorist … What with having to carry the baby on her back, and having to tend the fire and get the water and cook the meals and feed and service the men,' walking for leisure was almost certainly the last thing on her mind.

Patricia recalls an elderly woman in the Marico area who 'walked up and down a sorghum field all day, beating a drum to keep the crows off her crop. She probably walked further than I did every day, and she was almost double my age.'

Born and raised in Zambia to South African parents of British descent, Patricia's family have lived on the African continent for five generations. She thinks of herself unequivocally as African. 'Every time I go to England, I am left with absolutely no doubt that I am not English, and that is not my place. I am an African. A white African. Telling me I'm British is about as absurd as telling an African-American that they're Liberian or Ghanaian. What I'm continually being asked is how I feel about my ancestors' conduct. And I'm not responsible for them. I'm not prepared to pay for the sins of my fathers. The sins of my fathers are theirs. I'm trying as best as I can to live as a modern, white African woman.

'But we are all in some way held hostage by our histories. Our forbears' decisions and actions are going to be playing out in our lives whether we like it or not. I think they're the issues that play out in many white Africans' experience on this continent, that what our forefathers did is being visited upon us constantly, and it's a heavy burden to carry because, while we are not in any way blameless and we have our own crimes to pay for, every year of my life I have to be held accountable for what my forbears did. And that I in many ways must make reparation for what they did, and not for what I have done in my life. There's this wrestling with being a totally committed African, but maybe not being viewed as an African by my fellow black Africans, because of the conduct of my ancestors. It's extremely painful to me that many, possibly even most, of my compatriots do not regard me as African.

'Karen Blixen put it so well when she said, "If I have a song of Africa, does Africa have a song of me?" And it's one of the pains of my life that I'm not sure Africa does have a song of me, however much I commit here, whatever my contribution is, however passionate I feel. I think Africa's impervious to that in many ways.

'But these guys were a wonderful launch pad for a great adventure for me. Who could have believed that two Victorian gentlemen, whose worldview I've got no time for, could be a contributing factor to this enormous change in me.'

Describing herself as tending towards a scientific worldview, she concedes there were some 'spooky' things that happened along the way. On more than one occasion they found themselves coincidentally camping in the exact spot where her uncle's party had set up camp, and tensions in the team occurred in precisely the same place where Richard had experienced a 'mutiny' in his.

'When I was really battling with research on this chap, a friend of mine said, "I know you don't believe this stuff but take his photo to a medium." So I phoned this woman to book an appointment, and I told her it was because I wanted to know more about these ancestors – I hadn't even gone to her yet – and she said, "You want to know about the little one? A very bad-tempered chap that. Rides very big horses, hey." And when I went to England and met his granddaughter, those were the three things that she told me. The only things she remembered about her grandfather were: small man, very bad-tempered, and he liked big horses. Now what do you say to that?

'I don't think I would have changed as much as I did if I hadn't had this 142-year-old diary in my hands to see the environmental destruction,' she says. And it strikes me – apart from witnessing the environmental changes along the way, through a landscape that didn't match up to her ancestor's century-and-a-half-old description of it – that having grisly descriptions of their hunting for bedtime reading must have contributed to her other decision, to become a vegetarian.

In one entry Richard wrote of a 'clerical gentleman of my after acquaintance' who had joined them along the way: 'he fired twice at an old bull' – a giraffe, which in those days was called a camel, short for camelopard – 'and brought him to a standstill; loading again, he found he had but one bullet left, and in his excitement got the ramrod stuck on the top of that; nothing could get it out, so he fired ramrod and all into the brute's shoulder, still he did not fall and parson was at his wits end, he tried a button but it did not go through the skin, a pebble no better, still the camel stood looking at him, thinking he must die; parson lit his pipe, and sat under a tree for a long time, but the camel showed no signs of death; at last he could stand it no longer, so cramming his gun with gravel he fired several times at the brute's eyes in hopes of blinding him, but could not do even that, so he rode off to an African station and got another gun and bullets, but when he returned the camel was not there and though he spoored him some way he never was seen again.'

This cruel sport was by no means confined to the past. Her meeting with a hunting party along the way was even more disturbing. 'Tim greeted me with bloodied hands ... I let the dogs out of the Isuzu and they rushed towards a pile of unidentifiable debris next to the kitchen ... Next they disappeared around a corner ... There, tossed and toppled on a concrete slab like barstools after a drunken brawl, were four grey, bloodied feet. Their treads were worn and their toenails scuffed and they'd clearly served one of Africa's great elephants for fifty or sixty years. Nearby were his dentures, smooth and creamy, but topped by the mushy remains of his skull flesh.' Just a few days earlier she had watched from a distance as three bull elephants, quite likely including this one, drank at a nearby water hole.

For some reason killing an elephant seemed to be the measure of success as a hunter, and even as Richard stood looking at the Victoria Falls, which 'we had come so many thousand miles to see', his mind was still on the elephant he had not yet shot. And as if to taunt him, 'As we stood to admire, lo! 6 bull elephants appeared on the opposite cliffs. Quietly they tore up a great tree and fed on the leaves. As if they knew they had chosen the only place in South Africa where they would not be made to feel the weight of our bullets for, for 40 miles or more down, nothing without wings can scale the cliffs and cross the stream of the boiling Zambezi.'

After going back to check on their staff where they had left them at Pandamatenga, and making sure that they were not going hungry, Richard and his manager returned on foot for one last try. On the 16th of August 1883 they 'crept up to the last bush and fired at a bull's shoulder. The herd was off at once, but after following them for about 400 yards, I came on the bull on his knees and head, quite dead … Directly I saw four elephants coming towards me, the last with trunk in air, trumpeting wildly. I fired at her; she turned at once and chased me. I ran for my life, but she kept sight of me, and got most unpleasantly close, till I felt like a mouse before a cat. There was no real cover, only mopane trees the size of hazels scattered about on stony ground. At last I gave her the slip by dodging round some bushes and, much to my joy, she left me.'

When Patricia reached the Falls – 'The Smoke that Thunders', as Chief Sebitwane had described it to David Livingstone – 'elation and triumph were mixed with emptiness and loneliness … What does it matter that I've just walked 2152 kilometres to get here? … I thought about what I should do with the second half of my life on the continent that I love.'

Back in Joburg, she did 'what I usually do when I'm sad – I walked.' But the Braamfontein Spruit just didn't compare. 'Do you ever settle down again in a postage stamp when you've seen a full page?' she wonders. 'I see it most in my little dog. I sometimes wonder if I did him a disservice by showing him how big the world is, because he's never been satisfied with this little square that we live in. But we still explore a lot, and a lot on foot because it is ultimately the only way of knowing ourselves and knowing the world that we live in.'

I get the impression that she doesn't like Joburg much, but I'm wrong. 'I love it,' she says without hesitation. 'Look at this weather for a start. Look at the way things grow here. And it pumps. It's not some sort of mushy treacle at heart.' She is comparing it to Cape Town, where she spent ten years after first moving to South Africa at the age of fifteen. 'Cape Town's got this mushiness at its centre, because they're all so bloody laid back and life doesn't appear to be too much of a struggle. Here, there is a grating, grinding, pumping heart at our core.

'It's about its African-ness. I was brought up in Africa, and this is an African city. And if you like going to the bushveld this is the city to live in.'

But like a typical Joburger she rarely ever walks in the streets. 'I only walk where my dogs can walk. They are integral to my experience of walking and to my enjoyment of it, and walking them on the leash is just a ball-ache. I think it's cruel to the dog. They want to run and smell. They need three times the exercise we need, so I walk every day, but it's always in places where my dogs can walk.' Never in her boom-protected neighbourhood. 'And I drive there, and I drive back, which is silly,' she recognises, highlighting how most people who walk for leisure drive to where they're going to walk. 'I know, it's ridiculous,' she says.

Her love for Johannesburg seems contradictory, though, because apart from their daily walks, weekly grocery-shopping trips and occasional visits to friends, she rarely sets foot outside her suburban wall in Craighall. Joburg, it seems, is a state of mind. 'I don't know, maybe I live inside my own head rather than in a physical space,' she reflects. 'Where I lay my head I can make my home.' Perhaps her extreme walking is a response to this, an intense need to bond with the earth.

'I feel connected to places like the Zambezi Valley. As soon as I'm north of the Zambezi River then I feel real connectedness. But everywhere else… Joburg is a great place that I just happen to be in it at the moment.

'We're all deracinated in Africa, actually,' she reckons. 'White Africans are usually deracinated, because we've been ripped away. Our lives were ripped apart by the politics there, and for various reasons we don't live with our family and friends any more. And it's actually very painful, because the family is split, and scattered to the four winds…'

She is now dividing her time between Joburg and a village in the North West Province. 'It's near a village called Supingstad, and Lekgopung – two little villages near the Madikwe Game Reserve, very near the Botswana border,' where she is learning Setswana. Why Setswana? 'I like them. I walked with the Tswana people for two and a half months of the journey. Right the way through the Free State, the North West, and the whole of Botswana. And they're very rooted people.'

It is them she has to thank for the title of her book. 'Whenever I stopped in Botswana to chat to people, and we'd talk about the walk, they had this word "footing": "You are footing? To Zimbabwe? Hah!"' After this people usually had one of two questions: 'Where is your car?' or 'Where is your husband?'

She also loves the landscape in the area. 'Being in that vegetation of one's birth. As soon as I saw those thorn trees and felt that red sand under my feet then I thought, okay *here* we go – now the real journey can begin.' And then a thought occurs to her, that perhaps, the poverty notwithstanding, the locals feel the same way: 'The Batswana are proud and generous, and maybe that's partly because they don't have to battle like tenant farmers. In this village there's certainly no one starving, or anything like it. People look after each other. Some people have said to me – you're stupid, why don't you learn Zulu? But I just think they're fabulous people, so that's the language I wanted to learn.'

She is also highlighting the arbitrariness of borders – where South Africa, Botswana and Zimbabwe end and begin. They had an absurd experience of this on the walk, when one of her organisers remarked: 'Welcome to Hwange National Park.' His

GPS informed him that 'we're inside Zimbabwe right now and that The Old Hunters' Road weaves back and forth across the border all the way to Pandamatenga.' Further along, Patricia noted: 'I've just had a visit from a Botswana customs guy, who says we're camped on the wrong side of The Old Hunters' Road and that we're in fact inside Zimbabwe here. He reckons that we'd better move before we're arrested for entering the country illegally.' Botswana was three hundred metres away. There is a bizarre irony in the idea of a South African being arrested for entering Zimbabwe illegally.

Rather than sit in a classroom in the city learning the language, she opted for sitting in a classroom in the village. 'I sit at the back of a junior school class because I figure the children learn by rote, and they do – there are certain words and sentences that come up over and over again, and now I know those. But they're not the kind of things you use every day. You don't walk around telling people to shut up and open your book! So I can't use it practically yet. I'm thinking that maybe if I go and work with the women in the fields, with adults, maybe then I'll learn a lot more.'

As for the villagers' responses to her, 'I don't know if it's because there's a history of being with missionaries for ever and a day. The Batswana were colonised by missionaries, from David Livingstone on. Maybe they're used to the crazy attentions of these bizarre white people, but it's unremarkable to them. "You've come to learn Setswana? Oh." Moving right along.

'It's quite hard now. It's camping in very dry circumstances, with dust in every crack and every orifice. When the rains come, so do the snakes and the mozzies and the ticks. And it's hard to be isolated from your friends. But there's a grace with which they've welcomed me. And I can walk around the village at eleven o'clock at night without any fear.'

Her other project in the village is 'working with a group of 12-year-old girls, helping them collect and record old Setswana songs and stories from their *gogos*, because those are also disappearing fast.'

Since footing with Sir Richard she has struggled to raise funds for another expedition. The trip was partially funded by Discovery Health, but a large portion of the funds came from mortgaging her house. 'I just can't get sponsorship,' she says, and she puts it down to 'good old-fashioned sexism. Corporates sponsor soccer, rugby, cricket and golf, and they say, "We don't support individuals," but that's not true, there are male adventurers who get sponsorship.

'Guys want to do things as fast as possible. Deepest, fastest, highest, bestest... People have said to me, why didn't you do it faster? And I say, why would I want to? The slower I do it the more I'll absorb. You can't know a place if you're freaking yourself to death, trying to get through it as fast as you can, and cope with pain.' I'm reminded of the strange logic of *The Amazing Race*. 'But you can't know a place like that,' she says. 'Including your internal space.'

Men also tend to pride themselves on not needing help. Or if they do, preferably not from a person, as was humorously captured in a recent radio commercial: 'In 2002 Cape Union Mart sold its first Garmin GPS – to a man. Since then Cape Union Mart has provided thousands of male customers with Garmin technology, proving beyond doubt that real men do not ask for directions.'

'Perhaps I need to design an expedition that is solo, unsupported,' Patricia reflects, 'and that I don't have to spend any money on except my own. Again, mortgage the house and go and do it, don't let that stand in my way.

'Maybe Africa doesn't have a song of me, because of all the pain that still has to play itself out because of our history. But I do have song of Africa, and I'm going to sing it for as long as I'm able. And make my restitution and my peace in my own way.'

Two of the people who have most inspired her are French adventurers, Alexandre and Sonia Poussin. 'They walked from Cape Town to Israel, with just little daypacks. It was a wonderful journey. They relied on African people to feed them all the way, and it was all fantastic until they got to Sudan, and then it became dangerous. They were supported by the rest of the people on the continent.'

These days, Patricia says, she is obsessed with her death; or rather, with her mortality. 'Time is short. I don't know why people think they've got the luxury of time. We don't.'

From the Margins

I have been wondering where Lovey got her name. A nickname, I assume, from an English-speaking person; perhaps an employer of her mother's when she was a child. No, she enlightens me, it is short for her real name: Lovedalia. I hear 'Lovedahlia'. After a flower, I think. How beautiful. Again, I couldn't be further from the truth.

'My mum was at Lovedale College in the Eastern Cape,' she tells me. 'And then my father proposed to her. And she didn't want to get married because she wanted to study. She wanted to be a teacher. But in the old days, you know, if the man came and proposed marriage and went to your parents, you could never say no. And then she got married to my father, when she was in her second year of college. And then she was expecting a girl, me, and she called me Lovedalia.'

Lovedale has produced some famous names, including Thabo Mbeki and Chris Hani. Mbeki's father Govan was named after William Govan, the Scottish missionary who was the first headmaster of the Lovedale Institute, as it was originally called. 'But they would never allow you to study when you got married,' says Lovey. 'They would think that, when you married and then you study, you would be over your husband. Your knowledge... you would be brighter than your husband.' Consequently Lovey's mother never taught. She followed her husband to Cape Town, where he 'was working at Lever Brothers, in Salt River, who make the Sunlight soap. He worked there from 1944 and he retired in 1986; at the same firm all his life.' Lovey has been working as a domestic worker for forty-four years.

'I was born here in Cape Town, in Kensington,' in the northern suburbs, 'and we moved in 1958 to Guguletu' ('Our Pride'); 'it was called Nyanga West in those days.' What she doesn't say is that they were forced to move when Kensington was classified as a white area. 'I was doing Sub B when we left Kensington, and I finished Standard Six in 1964. I was going to do Standard Seven but my stepmother didn't want to let me. She said, "You must go and work." I thought I'll work for a year and then I'll go back to school, but then she said there's no money.'

'We moved to Khayelitsha' ('Our New Home') 'when I was already married. I stayed at my parents' house with my husband, and then they built the houses in Khayelitsha for the people who were living in the backyards. So we were moved there in 1985.'

'We were living in small houses. We used to call them the matchbox houses. There was only one bedroom and a small kitchen, and the bathroom, just a basin and a toilet, so if you wanted to add more you had to extend it yourself. And there was no electricity. We only got electricity in 1992.' Her children stayed behind in Guguletu to finish school, living with her brother and sister-in-law, and going to Khayelitsha over the weekends.

'Moving from Guguletu to Khayelitsha, the transport… it was far from where we work.' She says it in the past tense, but of course it is still as far. She says it like someone who has become reconciled to it.

'One of the most devastating and ineradicable traces of apartheid,' wrote architect Lindsay Bremner, 'will be its planning of the city. The marks apartheid left on human lives will fade in the course of time. But its special logic will continue to affect people's lives daily for generations to come.'

Just how far it is from where she works is almost beyond my

comprehension. On the day that we meet up, I have travelled by public transport from the southern suburbs to Kommetjie, where Lovey works one day a week, and it has taken me almost three hours (I had budgeted for two). Admittedly I timed it badly, and watched a train pulling out at just beyond sprinting distance – after my half-hour walk from my family's home in Kenwyn, between the suburban and Cape Flats train lines – as I approached Kenilworth station. (A timetable was last available for purchase in 2001.) That meant another half-hour wait.

When I arrived at Fish Hoek station, I had been warned that I would not find any taxis to Kommetjie; the last one is around 8 a.m. It meant getting a taxi to Ocean View coloured township (which of course does not have an Ocean View) and a half-hour walk to Kommetjie. Lovey seems astounded that I have made this walk. I am astounded that she travels out here to work once a week. But when her employer moved from Newlands to Kommetjie she weighed up the checks and balances and decided it was worth making the journey. 'I am happy with them,' she says.

Her day starts at 4.30 a.m, 'because I like to do my things in time, I don't like to rush. If I come by taxi, I have to take a taxi from where I live to the taxi rank at Site C,' the area of Khayelitsha closest to the city, 'so that I can get a taxi to Fish Hoek. And then I get a taxi from Fish Hoek to Kommetjie. I have to leave home about 5.50.'

While the birth of the minibus taxi industry provided a miracle to the previously immobilised – travelling to areas where municipal transport did not go, frequently, and stopping almost anywhere you ask them to along the route (to the frustration of other drivers) – compared to other modes of public transport taxis are expensive.

'When we were travelling from Guguletu,' Lovey recalls, 'there were more buses.' Since the bus service has been 'corporatised' in the new global economy, state subsidies have been cut, and there are fewer buses now than there were during the apartheid years.

When steps are taken by government to improve public transport, like the planned Bus Rapid Transit, there is often resistance (sometimes violent) from taxi drivers, who seem to believe they should be a protected industry, and other developments will kill their business.

'It's still better using the buses when you can, though,' says Lovey, 'because it's much cheaper than using the taxis. Because for the taxis you can't buy a weekly or a monthly ticket. If I take the taxi to Kommetjie then it costs me forty-two rands a day. When the taxis prices went up then I decided I rather take a bus to Wynberg, and from Wynberg a train to Fish Hoek. That saves me a lot.

'When I come here then my bus is at 5.30, sometimes it doesn't come and then you get the next one at 5.40. Sometimes it comes full, so you must be there before.'

Three days a week she works in Rondebosch, on the southern suburbs line. Though Wynberg is five stops further than she needs to go, 'When I go to Rondebosch I take a bus to Wynberg – then my bus is at 6.20' – and backtracking, 'then from Wynberg I take a train to Rondebosch.' Wynberg, like Claremont, is a hub of commuter and economic activity; a 'modal interchange' where taxis, buses and trains converge. They are also often sites of opportunistic crime.

The cheapest way would be to get the train from Khayelitsha into town and then change to the suburban line all the way to Fish Hoek, but apart from the time it would take, Lovey says this is not an option for her. 'The trains are so full, the people they hang over the door. And it's not safe, you get mugged on the trains. I don't like travelling by train.

'And on that side, from Khayelitsha to town, there's no security on the trains like these suburban lines. Even the security are afraid of those lines. With those trains, the Khayelitsha train, Langa train, Mitchell's Plain, even if the train is full, if the thugs want to target people they target them. They mug people, even if the train is full. You never think they are going to target you. People squash, and you can't even move.' Violence follows when people resist. What is certain is that many of the security personnel guarding the suburban trains live in Khayelitsha.

Lovey is no stranger to violence. In 1997 her youngest son, Lonwabo ('Happiness'), was killed in a gang shooting in Khayelitsha. 'He was eighteen. At that time there were gangsters in the township, and they were forcing the other boys to join. They were calling themselves after that man called Tupac,' the rap artist who was shot and killed in 1996. 'The Tupacs… He's not even a South African. They don't even know Tupac. They heard it over the radio and saw him on TV. And the other one, they called themselves the Dog Pound' – a gang taking it's name from the rap duo Tha Dogg Pound who, like Tupac, was signed to Death Row Records. 'They were forcing the schoolchildren to join them, and if you don't join there was a group who would inform. He didn't want to join, he didn't like it.'

'It's quiet now,' she says with sadness. 'Some of them were arrested, but there were a lot who died. They would go to schools and go straight to the classroom, and then they would shoot people in the class…'

'So, I don't like to travel by train,' she says finally. 'I rather use the bus.' It seems that travelling, for the poor, involves endlessly juggling time, money, and the lesser of evils. 'When I go to Rondebosch I don't get up early,' she tells me. 'Then I get up at five o'clock.'

For the domestic staff travelling to Kommetjie, there are no taxis all the way there from Fish Hoek after 8 a.m. 'That's why we leave early, otherwise if the last taxi's eight o'clock and there's no more people – maybe there's three or five people – they say we can't take five people to Kommetjie.' If there were taxis later, Lovey says, she would come in later, 'but now I go back early'. She is not asking for much. 'I think if we would have more taxis from Fish Hoek to Kommetjie, if they could have them hourly after eight o'clock, it would be better. Just to come back and check if there are no people.'

And she is not just thinking of herself. 'For the people who start work later. You know some people, they get up early, but first they have to take their kids to the crèche and things like that before they come to work so they can't come so early, and they have to be dropped at Ocean View and walk. And if you miss the seven o'clock bus, then there are no buses from Fish Hoek to Kommetjie until nine o'clock. And that's the last bus until the afternoon. And that nine o'clock bus doesn't come straight to Kommetjie, it goes from Fish Hoek to Long Beach, to Noordhoek, and then to Kommetjie. It gets here about 10.15.'

There is also the issue of Cape Town's 'big-clouded winters', with its months of rain. 'It's very difficult,' says Lovey. 'You get wet from sitting and sitting. By the time you get to work you are sopping wet. We put our clothes in the dryer, if there is a dryer. Otherwise we just hang them up and we must wear them again wet. When it's windy you can't use an umbrella because the wind turns it inside out. And the rain gets through to your clothes, through your raincoat. You just have to walk in wet shoes.'

In the afternoon it is the same dance. 'I finish here at three o'clock, and then I can be standing there for an hour and you don't get a taxi. Sometimes it comes, and sometimes it doesn't come. Sometimes the taxis that come are going to Site 5 – you pass Ocean View and then it's the next township, Masiphumelele' ('We Will Succeed') – 'they don't go to Fish Hoek. Sometimes the 3.20 doesn't turn up, or sometimes it comes later and has filled up with people on the other side. And then when it comes here it's full already, and it just goes straight to Fish Hoek. And it doesn't come back. The next one is 3.45. That's the last one.

'We have been asking the drivers, "You bring us here but you don't want to take us back?" They tell us they're busy with people going to Ocean View and Sun Valley, Long Beach Mall. They say the people are not going back at the same time, so it's of no use for them to come and collect three or four people.'

There are buses, but in this instance getting the bus is more expensive than the taxi because she doesn't have a season ticket. 'It's only good for people who come here every day. In the afternoon they run every half an hour. The last bus is 4.15. If you haven't got money then you walk to Ocean View.'

Lovey says she dislikes walking. 'I used to walk but now I've got diabetes and high blood pressure and I get pains. The walk is tiring. Especially if you are walking on your own. If you are two, three, then we chat, you don't feel it, and then we are there.'

It is also not safe. 'The people who work at the garage always warn us not to walk on your own. These young ones from Ocean View, they target you, grab your bag and attack you.'

On my way over, the road between Ocean View and Kommetjie was one of the few places I've walked in Cape Town where I've felt uneasy. It was broad daylight. In fact so much so that it was blinding – there was very little shade. And no pavements, just gravel paths on either side of the tarred road. There are lots of cars, I told myself, it isn't deserted, I shouldn't be afraid. But there was no pedestrian traffic. In half an hour I saw two other people on foot. A young boy ran up behind me shortly after I got out of the taxi, and asked me where I was going. After two muggings, my wary-pedestrian default setting kicked in. Rather safe than sorry, I greeted him but didn't engage – momentarily imagining two others hiding in the trees, about to circle me as soon as my guard was down – and pretty soon he ran off ahead of me. Later a young man passed me in the opposite direction and asked for a cigarette. (I don't smoke.)

It was a strange experience, because even in the pedestrian-unfriendly suburbs of Johannesburg there would be domestic workers in the streets. Here, obviously nobody is expected to be walking. The walking will be done on the beach once your car arrives.

I wonder, given her early start to the day, if Lovey gets to bed early. 'I go to bed at eight o'clock, past eight,' she says. 'I watch

Generations,' her TV soap, 'and then after *Generations* I just go straight to bed.'

Thelma ('Buyiswa, but everyone calls me Thelma') travels from Khayelitsha to work in Maitland four days a week, and has no option but to get the train. Her English is poor and my Xhosa in nonexistent, so our conversation is more difficult.

'I'm not safe,' she tells me, 'but... I can't do anything. I'm forced to take a train, I haven't got money for the bus. I haven't got money for the first class. You must hold your bag. Specially at this time, December time. It's very very very bad. The security stay there on the station, they don't get on the train. They just stand on the platform. They don't know what is happening on the train.'

I'm reminded of the growing trend of 'women-only' coaches on trains in many parts of the world – Mexico City, Rio de Janeiro, São Paulo, Tokyo, Moscow, Cairo – and wonder if that would work here. Or is it, as some argue, treating the symptom and not the problem?

Since Maitland is on a different line from Khayelitsha, Thelma goes to Ysterplaat, 'the closest station by my job', and has a twenty-minute walk to Maitland. 'They haven't got a straight bus from Khayelitsha to Maitland. That would be better. And no taxis from Khayelitsha to Maitland, it's only train.' Her other option would be to get the train all the way into town, two stops from Ysterplaat, and get a taxi back to Maitland, but she can't afford it. 'With the taxis you can't get monthly ticket, then you pay every time. I am walking because I must save money.'

She leaves home later than Lovey, but gets home much later at night. 'I am leaving home ten to seven. About quarter past or twenty past seven I am on the station – I am walking a distance. Late afternoon, five o'clock I go to station. From station to Khayelitsha,' though the journey itself takes about forty-five minutes – 'the trains, every day it is so full, there are a lot of people using the train to Khayelitsha, sometimes you have to wait for a train – it can be about seven o'clock. I get to home at half past seven.

'If you take a train from town, it's better, it's not full.' At Cape Town station you will most likely get a seat, but once the train has passed through Salt River, the industrial area just outside of the city, the third-class coaches have filled up and you're lucky to find standing room. If you don't get a seat you will be standing for forty-five minutes. 'They need to put in more trains,' she says.

All in all, Thelma walks close to two hours a day, on each side of her train journey at both ends of her working day, and it gives her no pleasure. 'It makes me tired. Specially in the afternoon after I have been working.'

Thelma is also from the Eastern Cape, from the former so-called homeland of the Transkei. A single mother of two, she came to Cape Town to find work in 1994 because 'there was no work in Transkei'. She and the father of her children, 'we have never been married. He is in Transkei, he married the other lady. He has never supported me. That's why I'm working for myself.' Her impressions of Cape Town are not positive. 'Cape Town is too hard, too hard,' she says. 'But I am still working.'

She has been with the same employers for fifteen years. When I ask her if she is happy with them, she hesitates, and a 'better the devil you know' expression crosses her face. 'I haven't got a choice,' she responds.

For Thelma, life has not improved since 1994. It has actually got worse. 'At least in the old days the youth had respect,' she says.

Over the holidays she is happy to go home to the Transkei for three weeks, 'my sister and brother are there'. Her return bus ticket, just for herself, costs her about half a month's salary.

In 2007 Metrorail introduced the Khayelitsha Express. For more than four times the price of a third-class ticket, you can sit back and enjoy a complimentary cappuccino and only three stops along the way, all the way into the city. For the poor, who can't even afford a first-class rail ticket, this 'premier class' train is in another world. According to the transport minister at the time, Jeff Radebe, it 'is aimed at a customer prepared to pay for a superior and exclusive service offering comfort, convenience and speed'. This starts with a separate ticket counter at Cape Town station so you don't have to stand in a queue. Both Lovey and Thelma tell me, independently, that it's good 'if you are in parliament'.

In *Planet of Slums*, Mike Davis's sobering examination of the growing divide between the rich and poor globally, he observes how 'the colonial template provided a basis for the almost total segregation of state officials and African professionals from their poorer compatriots.'

A passenger reports on the Khayelitsha Express: 'The stewards wait outside and welcome you in at every stop … Even before the train departs a stewardess comes along and gives out newspapers and takes everybody's order. You have a choice between: Cappuccino, Espresso, Mochaccino, Hot Chocolate, Black Coffee, Black Coffee with Milk, and Hot Water … The seats are made from a type of suede … At the one end of every coach there is a table with a few stools and power points that one can use to power a laptop, with double adapters and the lot. No wireless network/ internet connection yet, apparently there are negotiations with MTN to make the train into a wireless hotspot.' *Blits*, Metrorail's commuter newspaper, assures us that 'a total of 22 security guards and 16 waiters are employed on the train'. There are security guards on the train twenty-four hours a day to protect the interior from theft.

One thing is certain, neither Lovey nor Thelma will be on the Khayelitsha Express any time soon.

Looking for Markers

I haven't seen Marthinus in twenty-six years. Not since the days of experimental theatre at the Glass Theatre in Pepper Street. Getting to see him now requires some coordination, since neither of us drive. So I do something I've never done before – make the one-and-a-quarter-hour train journey from Cape Town to Stellenbosch, where he now lives. He is a little concerned about my safety, since he's been mugged a few times on the train. I decide to take my chances and the journey proves to be uneventful. I'm delighted to be accompanied by opera most of the way. At Blackheath, about twenty-five minutes before we arrive, Sarah Brightman disappears along the platform with the owner of the boom-box. Then ostriches appear, and we are in the countryside.

Marthinus Basson grew up in a farming family in Darling, which is said to be 'less than an hour's drive from Cape Town, but a million miles away'. 'Ja…,' he reflects, and his resonant voice brings back memories, it feels like I saw him just yesterday, 'walking in the city is one thing, but walking in the countryside, as a child… there are no boundaries or barriers, *nè*, so it's just a huge bloody fucking landscape that you get lost in.'

I recall Wordsworth's contemporary, 'Northamptonshire Pheasant' (as he referred to himself), John Clare's story of searching for the edge of his horizon: 'I lovd this solitary disposition from a boy and felt a curiosity to wander about spots where I had never been before   I remember one incident of this feeling when I was very young   it cost my parents some anxiety   it was in summer and I started off in the morning to get rotten sticks from the woods but I had a feeling to wander about the fields and I indulged it. I had often seen the large heath calld Emmonsales stretching its yellow furze from my eye into unknown solitudes when I went with the mere openers and my curiosity urgd me to steal an oppertunity to explore it that morning   I had imagind that the worlds end was at the edge of the orison and that a days journey was able to find it so I went on with my heart full of hopes pleasures and discoverys expecting when I got to the brink of the world that I coud look down like looking into a large pit and see into its secrets … so I eagerly wanderd on and rambled among the furze the whole day … I was finding new wonders every minute and was walking in a new world often wondering to my self that I had not found the end of the old one   the sky still touched the ground in the distance as usual and my childish wisdoms was puzzled in perplexitys   night crept on before I had time to fancy the morning was bye   the white moth had begun to flutter beneath the bushes the black snail was out upon the grass and the frog was leaping across the rabbit tracks on his evening journeys and the little mice was nimbling about and twittering their little ear piercing song with the hedge cricket whispering the hour of waking spirits was at hand when I knew not which way to turn but chance put me in the right track and when I got into my own fields I did not know them everything seemd so different   the church peeping over the woods coud hardly reconcile me.'

'The worst experience I ever had was in Namibia,' Marthinus recalls, 'with a German friend of mine. We went up and stayed in Lüderitz,' previously a diamond mining area, now known for its ghost towns buried under sand dunes. 'It was about one o'clock in the afternoon and he said he wanted to see the desert, so I said, "Okay, let's get in the car," and we drove off and we stopped and then you have to walk. And it's obviously also a *sperrgebiet*, prohibited area, so you're not actually allowed to go there because of the diamonds. And it was still slightly rocky and scrubby, and you walk and you walk and you walk, and five o'clock sharp, we hit the edge of the desert.

'And there was one of those old machines that they brought out around 1910 – one of those strange long scoops. And the thing was lying there, this wreck of a machine, all rusted away. So he started taking photographs, and I said to him, "We really have to turn back now because it's going to get dark soon, and if it's dark we are not going to get out of this desert." So I started to walk back, and he started following me very soon after that, so I started following the tracks. And again, when you're walking towards a desert, the desert is the way in which you perceive your aim and you somehow mark it in that way. But when you turn around there's a completely different landscape. You've walked through that landscape, but you have no idea of what it looks like when you flip it around. So I started following tracks, and as the sun went down, all shadows disappeared. So now you don't look at the horizon any more, you're sort of scrambling on the surface trying to find markers. And it went dark. And I said to him, "Now we're fucked" – because there was not a single marker to be seen. So we decided the best thing to do is sit. And about an hour and half later the lights in Lüderitz went on, and you could just see a small, tiny little variation in colour on the horizon. So we knew, Aha, Lüderitz, that's where we need to go.

'So now we're finding our way through this landscape in the dark and slipping and falling. And then it got brighter and brighter and brighter, and finally we reached the tarmac. And of course then we had no idea where the car was, whether it was left or right. And then we had to try and figure out where we were. It's quite incredible when you get that sense of your markers going. Peculiar. You float.'

As a child, 'I walked the whole farm,' he says. 'I knew the farm from back to front. I had a playmate very often with me. But a helluva lot of the time I was alone as well. And I loved wild flowers, so I gathered the plants and replanted them at home. I made myself a veld garden.

'What was traditional with Afrikaner farms in those days was that you always had a coloured boy assigned to you when you left home. My bother and sister were much older and they were at boarding school so I grew up like an only child. So you had a playmate who was usually four, five years older than you, and you got involved in that, and you literally set up a kind of parallel universe to the one you know. A new one is created between the two of you. And that's the way you get to know the workers as well.

'Most of the time growing up in the *platteland* your playmate would introduce you to sex, because parents never spoke of it. The word sex was never mentioned in our house, ever. We were extremely sexually active from a very early age, and I discovered the word gay around 1966. There was a huge party in Johannesburg, apparently, and they were raided by the police and a lot of people were arrested. It turned out to be doctors and lawyers and *dominees*, parliamentarians, rugby players, and it caused an enormous scandal, and the government at the time was quite panic-stricken about it.' This was the notorious party in January 1966 in Forest Town, a quiet leafy suburb of northern Johannesburg; '350 in mass sex orgy!' the headline in the *Rand Daily Mail* proclaimed.

'And then I realised I was different from the other boys I was having sex with. One day I realised they're all having relationships with girls as well. So I read about this and I realised that is the word I've been looking for. And then I was at Paarl Boys' High, and I knew I was gay so I told people that and of course that changes the whole dynamic of how they relate to you.'

Things changed for Marthinus during his time in the army, doing compulsory military service. 'I was in Pretoria, and that was the first time I bumped up against cruising, quite innocently. We had a pass. I was with a friend from Bloemfontein and we went skating, and we were going to stay over at the house of a friend of his. And when we arrived there the one boy said, "I'm terribly sorry there's no space for you here, you must go."

'So now it's like one o'clock in the morning, I have no fucking clue where I am in Pretoria. I could sort of see the centre, I could figure that out, so I started walking. I knocked on two doors and said, "Please, I'm lost, can you just tell me where the station is?" – because the buses for Valhalla, the army base, left from the station. So I finally end up at Church Square, and I need to pee, I'm about to die. And there are no toilets. And I'm too decent – can you believe it, the middle of the fucking night... So now I have to go to the station, so I walk up to the station and the toilet is closed, so I walk all the way back and I decide, now I've got to pee, so there were these little alcoves and staircases going down, so I just peed. And the next moment a voice said to me: "What are you doing?" And I yanked out my pass and said, "I'm on pass, I'm on pass!" and saluted.

'And that became my first pick-up, and my first experience of having sex with a grown-up. Because then he said, "Don't you want coffee?" And the hand on the knee, and you don't know how to deal with this. It was actually... I found it terribly traumatic. It was extremely unpleasant. But the funny thing is then you suddenly became aware that there are places where there are connection spots.

'So you started looking. And then the city... I was so terribly naïve. You didn't know, you knew nothing. You didn't know that there were other people like that. You didn't know where to find them. So then you start becoming extremely primal. Once you became aware that this was a possibility, you started looking. And suddenly you could read in people's eyes. It was very subtle, but if a look lingered too long... And then you had to go through a huge amount of checks and balances, because you never knew where this would lead. You would see if somebody follows. And then it would become a kind of a stalking game. You stop. They stop. Do they stop long enough? Do you still like them? When they come too close, do you sense that there might be something unsettling?

'And you knew then when to escape as well, because very often you could just sense, no no no, something's not right. Or there was just something in the person that unsettles you, and you left the option to flee. And then you get that secondary panic where you just want to get away, so that you end up... Instead of a dance, it becomes a dodge, and you try and lose people as well. Once you understood that, the whole of the city became a playground.

'And then obviously that leads you into... the best place to pick up somebody is in a public toilet, because at least an erection is some manifestation, or validation, that this is a possibility. Yes, the person is interested, and it's not a policeman. I had someone arrested right next to me, where police just walked in, in rush hour, the toilet was full, and just because of the way that he was looking around, the police obviously saw that, and they literally grabbed him from right next to me and dragged him outside. I mean then you go into a kind of stupor, and you just backpedal and you move your way away from that again.

'It very often took hours, and it meant you had to change your schedule. You have to be somewhere, but then this is more interesting. So a lot of issues get flicked up in that.'

Though he doesn't drive, Marthinus learned to drive at a very early age. 'I was taught to drive at about four, in a Willis jeep. We all drove. I sat on my dad's lap and he allowed you to steer. It was a US army issue jeep during World War II up in the Sahara, and those things were sold on auction after the war and my dad bought one. So I drove a military jeep on the farm. And then later on tractors. But then after I dropped out of university in Stellenbosch, and went to Cape Town, I had absolutely no money. I was supposed to become a teacher, and then I switched to drama without telling my parents, and they were terribly upset and that was it.'

In Cape Town he joined the Space Theatre company, along with Pieter-Dirk Uys, Bill Flynn, Grethe Fox and Vincent Ebrahim (now best known as the father in the British television comedy,

The Kumars), among others. This was the original Space in Bloem Street, before it moved to its famous venue at the old YMCA at 44 Long Street. The theatre was founded by photographer Brian Astbury and his wife, Yvonne Bryceland, who brought many of Athol Fugard's early characters to life.

'I worked there as an actor and stage manager and set builder. We earned next to nothing, and there was certainly no security, so buying a car was never an option. And of course you just walked wherever you needed to go. At first we lived in Prince Street, and then we lived in the second-last house on Kloof Nek, which was quite a walk. But ag, you didn't mind, it kept you fit and you didn't even think about it. We walked down to work in the morning, we never took buses.' Later, when he worked for Capab, the Cape Performing Arts Board, 'I would always walk to the SABC from the Nico,' he says, referring to the Nico Malan Theatre, now Artscape. 'I just find it incredibly relaxing.

'I hadn't been in Cape Town for a while, and then I did a show for Mandela's ninetieth birthday at Artscape. And the first day I thought, I must get a taxi, and then I decided to walk. And what is wonderful about it – and that's when the city becomes interesting – is that by the third day people start saying hello, because you bump up against the same people, and a little form of community starts developing.

'I've always used trains as well, because it gives you time to read and think and observe people. In a car you've got to concentrate all the time, and I'm extremely short-sighted in one eye and not in the other, so my three-dimensional sense is quite badly developed.

'At forty-nine I got my learner's licence. I was very tense because I thought my brain had seized up, so I was studying like a fury. And I arrived there and there was a girl in front of me in the line, and the examiner said to her, "Oh hello, this is your fifth time isn't it?" And she started weeping, and she said, "I'm not stupid, I can't understand this. Why can't I get it?" We were twenty-seven who wrote and I was one of four who passed.' Though I once had a learner's licence, I remember being baffled by the logic of the test. To the question of where you should not drive, an answer like 'In the middle of the road' seemed too obvious. I was expecting some subtlety.

'So anyway, I had my learner's,' says Marthinus, 'and I had a car that I inherited from my dad, and then it died in an accident. I've had three vehicles. I've bought two – all second-hand shit. The first one was stolen. A friend of mine borrowed it and left the keys in the boot. The second one, a friend was driving and drove straight into a donkey in Botswana. And the third one, the one I inherited from my dad, I loved that car, it had huge sentimental value for me. And a friend said, "Let's go for a drink," and I stopped at the robots and as we took off a car drove straight into us. So now I've given up.'

Having worked in Belgium for a while, he reflects, 'Europe functions because it's got a socialist structure. I got to know that system quite intimately, and you can get anywhere you want by public transport at any point in time. So you never need to own a car – they take that responsibility straight out of your hands.

'Ja,' he says, turning his thoughts back to cruising, 'I never did the promenade stuff, which was the great cruising spot. The seafront was really the walking, picking up, showing off, promenading thing. There is a long history there that seemed to stretch all the way from Sea Point round to Camps Bay. That stretch was, I think, for people who were confident in their sexuality and confident with how they looked, so preening became part of that walk.

'Unlike the promenade, with the train line thing, where you combine your cruising with moving around on the train, you could drop off. The biggest thing was that it gave you time to figure out what your options were, whether you could trust the person, is it police? One night I was staying with a friend in Rondebosch and I had to cross the station to get to the house, and a bakkie drove up, a tiny Mazda bakkie with four big men squashed together in the front, and they drove straight at me and they stopped with the bumper against my knees. I tend to get very calm in those situations. I go into a kind of neutral stupor. Obviously they thought I wasn't giving them any reason, I wasn't running away, so there was no point in arresting me. But they started arresting left and right around me.

'The violence... They dragged someone I had an affair with out of one of the doorways and they battered him as well. So there was that sense of danger...

'And it was also exciting, because it's hunting, and stalking, and displaying. That whole wonderful sense of, how big is the distance? And it opens up a whole lot of options.'

American author Edmund White reckons that 'to be gay and cruise is perhaps an extension of the *flâneur*'s very essence, or at least its most successful application. With one crucial difference: the *flâneur*'s promenades are meant to be useless, deprived of any goal beyond the pleasure of merely circulating.' Looking back, White reflects on the time that he lived in Paris: 'most people, straight and gay, think that cruising is pathetic or sordid – but for me, at least, some of my happiest moments have been spent making love to a stranger beside dark, swiftly moving water below a glowing city.'

'Buildings became a part of it as well,' Marthinus recalls, 'because in the Parkade they had that old movie house, the biocafé,' where you could eat and smoke and watch B-grade double features, 'and that was a huge pick-up joint. And then sometimes you don't want to be there, so the building itself becomes a sort of walkway, up and down the stairs and lifts and things. So it becomes a vertical chase, as well.'

In a humorous retrospective on 'cottaging' ('to use or frequent public toilets for homosexual sex') in Sixties and Seventies Cape Town, Michiel Heyns recalls Stuttafords, the genteel department store, where ladies lunched in between shopping. The public conveniences 'were located on the same floor as the books department, indeed adjacent to it, which provided a respectable and educational excuse for loitering … The first of the inner chambers contained the pissers, the centrepiece of any true cottage. These, though, after the magnificence of the handbasins, were a letdown … The rows were back to back, running counter to the very essence of cottaging, indeed of all cruising, which is eye contact; here the over-the-shoulder exchange of glances was likely to lead to nothing more exciting than a crick in the neck.'

He bumps into an old friend, years later, who informs him: 'The big trick was picking up someone on the escalator … You remember, going down you had a view of the people going up and vice versa. Well, the idea was to catch someone's eye going in the opposite direction; the excitement was to see which one would change direction. But it made more sense for the one going up to turn round and follow the other one down and out.'

'*Now* you tell me,' says Heyns. It's all irrelevant at this point because 'there can be few activities on earth, other than breakdancing, less congenial to the over-forty than cottaging.'

'I went into a long relationship in the late Seventies,' Marthinus says, 'and then that whole cruising thing fell away to a large extent. Our relationship ended at exactly the time that Aids became an issue, and then it just seized up, went into the fridge.

'I think the need for it to be under cover has gone, and I think that has changed the dynamic totally. The fact that liberation has happened and that people have rights now, has to a great extent taken away the need for it.'

In Stellenbosch, where he teaches, however, 'I think the gay issue is still an enormous one for the kids. There's a huge charismatic Christian presence at the university, and they refer to it as the gay *demoon*, so it's difficult for the children here. The gay students find it quite difficult to find their way around those issues. Even in the Drama Department. So I wouldn't like to think what it's like for people in the Engineering Department, for instance.'

Probably best known over the years as the director of bold, visual productions like *Titus Andronicus* and *Tall Horse*, Marthinus says, 'I prefer working with the students at the moment, because it opens up the possibility to look at work that you would never be able to touch commercially these days. We recently did a production of *Cabaret*, that nobody wants to do any more.'

Making a living exclusively in the theatre is impossible now. 'The students, the really talented ones, often the ones who are not going to end up in television, become extremely despondent. They try for a couple of years, and they can't pay their rent, and then they disappear.'

The relative worth of theatre in the new economy is considered insignificant. Apart from popular musicals, it rarely has monetary value. 'It's immediate. It's not like an artwork that you can pay R23 000 for, put it away, and in fifty years it might be worth millions. Theatre is a collective investment in the quality of your presence.' All that remains are your memories.

'I'm working with ten high school kids at the moment, two of them have history as a subject, and two others had history until about three years ago, and then the option got closed down because there was too little interest. Now how the fuck do you move yourself through life without a sense of history? That should be compulsory, not even something that is negotiable. But of course with history you can't make money. It's meaningless.'

In *Planet of Slums*, Mike Davis describes two kinds of cities – those like Johannesburg that resemble doughnuts, where the poor are squeezed into decaying inner cities; and those like Cape Town, where the inner cities have become increasingly commercialised and gentrified, and anyone but the rich is pushed further and further out. The student communes of the Eighties are now long gone.

'The older I become,' Marthinus tells me, 'all my family has died now, so you don't know what to attach yourself to. You don't know what you're hanging off from. The new relationships that you build are also transitory, because in theatre it's a few months at most. In university it's three years. But everybody comes and goes, they pass through, so you somehow train yourself not to attach yourself to any individual in a very deep sense. I sometimes miss the markers. In any landscape you guide your life from a marker so that you don't get lost. But the markers have faded radically.'

I go in search of 10 Pepper Street, near the top end of Long Street, with its ghosts of wayward productions of Shakespeare and Chekhov, and Freud and Jung slinging cream pies at one another. It is indeed the '*grillerige* two shades of sea green' that Marthinus has warned me about, but the façade of the church that it once was is still clearly recognisable.

A young woman standing on the pavement outside sees me quizzically looking up at the building. 'Can I help you?' she asks.

'Do you work here?'

'Yes,' she replies, 'I work for the firm of architects.'

'Did you know that this building used to be a church?' I ask her. 'And then a theatre for a year in 1982.'

'No,' she smiles, 'but I was very young then.'

Street names, said Michel de Certeau, 'these words ... slowly lose, like worn coins, the value engraved on them, but their ability to signify outlives its first definition'.

'I've always been a little disappointed,' Marthinus told me, 'not with art very often, but in terms of landscape, and especially buildings. They're very often better in photographs than they are in real life. And I've stood in historical spots, in places where momentous things have happened, and all you can imagine is, where's the blood? Or where did it go? Because it's all covered up. So being in a place doesn't necessarily have specific meaning very often. I find the secondary experience via a novel is very often far more potent than the real one.'

I chance on an inscription that my old friend and poet Phillippa Yaa de Villiers wrote to me in her anthology, *Taller than Buildings*: 'Remembering all those half-forgotten streets, we carry them with us.' And it occurs to me that the markers are the people with whom we share our memories.

These Feet

'Did you know,' Denys Finch Hatton asks Karen Blixen in *Out of Africa*, 'that in all of literature there's no poem celebrating the foot? There's lips, there's eyes, hands, face, hair, breasts, legs, arms, even the knees. But not one verse for the poor foot. Why do you think that is?'

'Priorities, I suppose,' she says.

When they do write about them, Jeffrey Robinson remarks, 'People observe their feet or write about them with a unique detachment. The foot is not quite a part of the rest of the body.' This was certainly true for Alice, when she grew so tall that 'they seemed to be almost out of sight'. And then she worried that now 'perhaps they won't walk the way I want to go!'

In the title poem of her first anthology, *These Hands*, Makhosazana (Khosi) Xaba wrote: 'These hands remember / the metallic feel / of numerous guns / when the telling click / was heard. / They recall / the rumbling palm embrace / over grenades, / ready for the release of destruction. … These hands / have felt pulsating hearts / over extended abdomens, / they know the depths of vaginas, / the open mouths of wombs, / they know the grasp / of minute, minute-old clenched fists.'

I ask her if she would consider writing a similar homage to her feet. She answers with a belly laugh, perhaps because her early experiences of walking were anything but poetic. 'When I was young we walked because there was no transport.' Growing up in Ndaleni, a rural area close to Richmond in what was then Natal, 'we walked everywhere, including town, which was over an hour. We used to be given pocket money so we could buy those ginger things, those flat, hard, sugary ginger biscuits, because we'd get hungry. We only got a bus in our area when I was thirteen. And that was a big thing, "Oh, a bus, there's a bus!" And if you missed the bus you walked, because it came once in the morning and once in the afternoon. So walking was a way of life, it wasn't a choice I took actively.'

But later, as an activist, 'I used to make it a habit when I moved into a new place to just walk around it so that I knew it fully. It became an issue of security. I needed to know my surroundings very well, so I knew if I needed to dash I would know every single corner. I used to walk my neighbourhood a lot when I was in my twenties.' At that time Khosi was training at Edendale College of Nursing, just outside Pietermaritzburg. Later, she worked in an old age hospital in Pinetown. 'So I would walk so that I knew what the area was about, knowing I could be safe. Because if I needed to do anything, if I needed to run away, if I needed to hide, I needed to know how to find my way out. And then with time, when I was out of here, it was just exploring the place I was in.'

In 1986 Khosi left South Africa and went into exile with MK, the military wing of the ANC, for almost five years, in 'Zambia, Mozambique, Angola, Germany and the Soviet Union. Then I needed to understand where I was and to know the place very well. But also, for me, because I've always been physically active, it was the only thing I didn't have to pay for. Because there was no money to pay for anything. So besides exploring where I was for sheer fun and interest, it was the only exercise I could afford.

'When I lived in Lusaka, in Zambia, I used to get up at four o'clock because it was very hot and the sun came up so early, and I would walk for two, three, four hours. I would think, So-and-so lives there, let me try and get there, and see how long it takes me.

And sometimes it would take me a whole week to really get to the place I thought I would be going to, because I'd think, I'm too tired, the sun's too hot, and I'd go back,' bearing in mind that she had to walk back the same distance that she'd come.

It was also a means of walking away, a way of creating space, away from people who you lived with, 'people who were not necessarily your friends. They were just your comrades. Some of them turned into friends. But I think, because in exile I was trying to get somewhere in order just to see it, I often took routes where there were a lot of people. That way I didn't get lost.'

As a child, her mother gave her some advice which she valued in exile: 'When I was being sent to town, she said, "If you're feeling lost and you're in trouble, take a deep breath in, stand, watch the crowds. Watch the movement of people. Follow the biggest groups of people, just walk in their direction if you feel you can't ask anybody, for whatever reason; if you feel unsafe. Walk with the crowds until you can see a sign, until you can ask someone, until you feel safe. Don't go on a tangent on your own."' This was particularly helpful when she couldn't speak the language. 'So I've always done that if I feel unsure.'

She hasn't developed a love for any particular place. 'I connect with wherever I am,' she says, 'because I believe that I can make a home wherever I go, but that's different from developing a love for a place. I just believe that, wherever I am, I can make myself safe. I *will* make myself safe, and I *will* make it home if I choose to. It can be home for a week if I'm there for a week. I know people who sleep in a foreign bed and they say they couldn't sleep. I sleep everywhere and anywhere. So whatever place I'm in I connect with.'

If she has a love for any place it's the coast, no coast in particular. 'I love walking on any coastline. I love the sea. I love walking on the sand. I love when my feet go in, and I love to be able to look at my tracks.

'It started when I'd just finished matric and I was training as a

233

nurse, and one of the things that we did as students was that we'd hike a ride to Durban. For a lot of them it would be a chance to see their boyfriends in Durban. And for me it was just, okay, we're all hiking to Durban, what's in Durban? The sea. And so I would just go there, stay till it was dark, and just enjoy the sea in the dark, and then hike back. Now, whatever coast I find myself on, when I'm travelling and I'm in a city that has a coast, I'll go there so I can walk.

'I've just come back from Dublin and, stupid as it might sound, I'd never checked it on the map. I knew Dublin was in Ireland, it's the capital, full stop. But when I knew I was going there, I looked at the map, and I was sooo excited: "Oh my gosh, there's a beach, I can walk!" And it so happened that a friend of mine picked me up with a friend of hers, and we were talking and she said, "What do you like to do?" And I said, "Ag, I just love bookstores, but let me do what you like to do. I've come here to experience your life." And she said, "I love walking, I'll take you along the beach." I said, "Cool!" So there I was taking a train to meet somebody so we could walk.'

Back in Joburg, in Yeoville where she lives, she has been put off walking in recent years. Not because of a lack of safety – quite the opposite. It's the suburban safety measures that get in her way. 'There is nothing that drives me so nuts, trying to walk here, as when they started putting up these boom gates. I started avoiding the ones that I knew were there. And then after a month or two I'd find, aaahh – now there's another one! I hate the fact that I have to stop and greet somebody, and I have to find out where the little gate is. And interestingly enough, I hate it more when I'm walking than when I'm in the car.'

Security guards usually seem very grateful to have a passing pedestrian to chat to. I recall a time when I walked from Norwood to Killarney every week for a course of acupuncture. Over a period of a few months the security guards outside business premises in Houghton along the way, who at first seemed a bit surprised by my presence, came to recognise me, saying hello on the way there and goodbye when I passed by a couple of hours later on the way back.

'When I walk I want to feel a sense of openness,' says Khosi, 'so I deliberately choose streets that I know are quiet. I go anywhere I want to go, because I feel that I should be able to – that's just the mental attitude I've developed over time. I refuse to be threatened by "this is unsafe, that's unsafe." If there's an alternative between two places, one that's going to be unsafe and one that's safe, and what I need can be found where it's safe, of course I'll go there. But I won't avoid places.'

Having a gun to her head on the 1st of January 2001 made her decide that keeping off the streets wasn't the solution. 'It was as I was leaving the house in the morning. And after that, for some time I didn't walk. And then I developed the attitude that… I knew the normal ways of checking the streets and making sure that if there's somebody following you, you cross over. I knew those kinds of security things. But what I realised when I was mugged was that I panicked when the person was next to me, and I didn't feel strong in my body. So what I've done since then is to make sure that I stay physically strong, and anybody who comes to face me, I look them straight in the eye, because they often want to catch you off-guard. So now I walk with an attitude.'

'Fear' comes for different reasons, and the nakedness of having a light shone on her poetry is one that makes her feel more vulnerable. In her latest volume, *Tongues of their Mothers*, she writes: 'The fear of being published / is not just fear of having / every inch of your skin / laid out for everyone to touch at will. / It's more than the fear / of having your gut / unravelled on a display table for the public to scrutinise at leisure.'

In 1993, when her daughter Nala was a year old, when Khosi was thirty-five, she got her driver's licence. She describes it as 'the hardest thing I have ever done. I started when I went back to work when my child was two and a half months old, and I was learning just during the lunch break. And my boobs were large, and with the seat belt and two pairs of breast pads, by the time that hour was over I would be sweating all over. So the experience was very hard.'

But it changed her life. 'It's terrible having a child in a pram in Joburg. It's too much of a hassle. Then you have to carry the child, the child doesn't always want to walk. It just felt to me like… I'm no longer on my own. I must just help this child. I mean, what do you do when your child is tired of walking? But it didn't happen immediately, because I got my driver's licence, but I couldn't buy a car until two years later.'

And then there was no stopping her. 'That first year I had a car, I used to drive everywhere just to see a place. And I think at the time I visited absolutely every single friend. I would look in the newspaper at what's on where, for what you can do with a small child. I wanted to know what Joburg was like. Because I knew the limited Joburg from my walking.' And then inevitably traffic began to take its toll, and the novelty wore off. 'Now it feels like I've always driven. I still love long-distance driving, though.' It gives her the same kind of headspace that walking does. 'A mental space that allows certain things to come out.'

When Nala was eleven, Khosi became very excited because it seemed that she, too, was a walker. 'We did a long walk from Yeoville to Killarney, just to see how long it would take us' (about an hour and a quarter), and Nala had a lot of fun.

'Ja, it was pretty cool,' Nala says. 'You saw the road differently. You take different routes 'cos there are one-way streets that you can't take in a car.' But, happy to be *flâneur*-for-a-day, it turned out to be a once-off adventure.

'Then what? – Been there, done that?' I ask Nala.

'Pretty much,' she says. Now she is a typical Joburg teenager: 'I exercise at school with my friends, we go to the gym, walk on the treadmill.' But she assures me that it is not fear keeping her off the streets, it just holds no interest for her. 'None whatsoever,' she says emphatically.

Khosi is also walking less these days but not, as so often happens, because she is driving. 'I used to run as well, and in 2006 I did a fifteen-kilometre run and I hurt my hip, so I thought – uuurrghh, I'm getting too old for this. And it took a long time to heal, so I replaced it with yoga, Bikram yoga.' The sweaty one, where the same twenty-six postures are repeated in a heated room, the idea being that the heat helps rid the body of toxins. 'Since doing that it makes me feel strong, it makes me healthy like no other exercise has ever done before. I get into a mental space that is extremely challenging. I've never done exercise that is so hard to do.

'So that mental space now is in yoga. The walking and the running and the yoga are a way of being alone while you're in the world. And I find that poetry comes to me a lot when I'm on my own. When I'm in my head, not necessarily on my own physically. So I could be in a public space, like a restaurant, but I'd be sitting alone.' There is no expectation to engage with anyone else.

And yet, as is so often the case, there is an ambivalence about the solitary walk, the solitary run. In 'Cotton Socks', she writes: 'I wished we'd run the Soweto marathon together / just as we did the 702 Walk. / Although I knew you wouldn't come / I still bought two pairs of cotton socks / just as you did last year. ... Afterwards I massaged my feet, / rubbing in the foot cream you helped buy. / Then I lay naked on my bed, / the second pair of cotton socks cuddling my feet.'

One thing she says she misses about running is the camaraderie. 'Not so much with walking, but with running. How friendly other runners are in the street. I didn't feel it the same way with walking. It was such a pleasant surprise, many people running by greeting you.'

After one of her coastal walks in Key West, she writes, in 'The Brown Pelican': 'It took the harbour walk, four days later, / to stop wishing you were here. ... as I sauntered up Simonton Street / back to my room at Pearlsrainbow, / the solemn night embracing my gait. / I savoured the moments / and thanked the brown pelican for delivering you to me.'

It is the sea that she loves, not the beach. From another hotel room window the narrator reflects: 'This beach haunts. / So pristine it will not let me forget it, … A runner outside is passing this way for the third time. … In my youth I outran even the boys. But I walked my path, / the path some believed was meant for my kind, in my times. … my loss will never touch the ears of these sun-tanners who populate this beach.'

And then sometimes you take a turn in the road, and: 'I am in Wintersrand in winter. / The road sign, *Igoda Mouth / Wintersrand*, led me off the main road to Port Alfred / and I landed in this paradise we could have shared / had you chosen differently. … I lift my eyes to the horizon and the clouds / so that I can massage my heart for warmth.'

It is the endlessness of the ocean, she says, that allows her to breathe out. 'Because I think, when I walk, the idea that there's this endless wave… particularly when I haven't decided where I'm going, I'm just going. It could not end if I wanted it not to, because there is no specific destination, so it's open. When I'm walking and I haven't chosen where to go. It's like I'm giving myself a gift of openness.'

And when spring comes around again: 'The sun that stayed unseen since morning / refuses to end this winter day in private. / From its hiding place, it has painted the clouds / that now glow pink above the sea.'

At present, Khosi is immersed in writing a biography of Noni Jabavu, of the famous intellectual family from the Eastern Cape. Though much has been written about her father, DDT, and grandfather John Tengo, virtually nothing has been written about Noni – despite the fact that she published two books, *Drawn in Colour* and *The Ochre People*. A contemporary of Es'kia Mphahlele, a Google search on his name yields more than eleven thousand results; hers, fewer than three thousand. In 1933, at the age of thirteen, she was adopted by a British family, 'which, I was to learn in years to come, was to be a practical demonstration of the generations of friendship between families'. Her parents thought she could return home, skilled, and help improve the lives of others in South Africa.

But when apartheid was implemented in 1948 it meant that Noni was never able to return to her 'mother country' permanently, and she spent her life moving from place to place, referring to 'the peripatetic print of my feet', always with one foot in Europe and one in Africa. She finally returned in 2002 and spent her final years at the Lynette Elliot Frail Care Home in East London in the Eastern Cape until her death in June 2008, shortly before her eighty-ninth birthday.

In 1977, while Donald Woods was editor of the *Daily Dispatch* in East London, prior to his banning after Steve Biko's death, he employed Noni to write a weekly column. In one of her columns she told the story of a small boy named 'Galaxy … A name I'll not exclude from my "Book of South African Babies' Names" … How poetic, how imaginative, I thought. The universe. The stars.

'But on hearing the explanation, I felt surprised, even let down: for his parents knew nothing about stars, Milky Way, Southern Cross. The splendid name had been bestowed upon him because the day he was born, his father had acquired a second-hand motorcar, *unomaxesha* of the trade name. I spoke of the stars, of galaxies, they stared at me as if I was crazy, and said: "Those are always there. Why for us to bother looking at them? But a material possession like a motor car, now that is an important event."'

Despite her extensive travels, Noni longed for home: 'Returning now two decades later, I confess I surreptitiously "sway" to the seductive sound of Tikki-draai on the Xhosa radio programme.' And in 'Travel only confuses the mind', she wrote: 'Travelling is in fact very upsetting for a woman. Women like to be in their permanent nest. Making homes across continents can be a marriage-breaker.' Finally back home at the end of her life, she felt out of place. A relative told Khosi: 'Although she is black she is very European, with a European way of life. If she had gone to Middledrift she would not even be able to eat the foods she is used to.' Lynette Elliot recounted how at breakfast during her early days at the home, she asked: 'Where's the cream, no cream here?'

Though Noni's death was always imminent, since she was already advanced in years when Khosi began the project, when it finally came it affected her profoundly. A few days later she observed: 'When I decided to write Noni Jabavu's biography, I was driven by intense curiosity and utter frustration at what seemed to me as a lack of recognition of her pioneering role as a writer … While interviewing Wally Serote, who was living in Botswana during the same time as Noni, I learned something that confirmed my initial thoughts on her. "We men," he said, "did not know how to relate to her. She was a woman living far ahead of our times."

'Women's lives provide a window to a nation's history,' says Khosi.

Two Tails

1.

Once, in a time before high walls, I lived opposite a park. The stoep of the house was a perfect place to sit and observe the antics across the street. Little did I realise I was also being watched.

When I moved in, there was no space inside for my little couch, so my housemates and I decided to leave it on the stoep. Someone who spent his days in the park decided this was an ideal place to sleep at night. It wasn't long before someone else walked off with the couch, but the gatecrasher remained.

'We must have a house meeting,' said Gary. 'This dog has been sleeping here for days now, so either we must take him to the SPCA, or someone needs to take responsibility for him.' With a greying beard, terrier-like, he was obviously quite old.

'If this dog was a person he'd have been a car thief,' said Guy.

Sarah laughed.

The idea of owning an animal had always seemed a bit strange to me, but this one appeared to be quite independent. Content to terrorise the other dogs in the park – big and small – all day long, he really just needed to be fed, I reasoned, and so agreed to adopt him.

I asked our domestic worker Lizzy to choose a name for him, imagining she'd decide on an African name, but she was insistent we should call him Sheba: 'It's a nice name to call – *Sheeeebaaaaaa*,' she explained.

It never occurred to me that I would need to walk this dog, tearing around the Yeoville park all day as he did. But he had other ideas. When I left the house he would follow at a distance. Sometimes it was too late before I realised, I'd arrived at my destination, and he'd get to stay. At other times, when I remembered, I'd spin around after a few metres, and there he'd hover. After a 'Go home!' he'd slink off, back to the park.

Soon he didn't need me to accompany him, and he'd go and see my friends on his own: 'Oh, Sheba came to visit today,' Soli in Berea, or Annie, about four kilometres away in Bertrams, would tell me. 'I saw Sheba crossing at the pedestrian crossing in Rockey Street today,' said my friend Graham. At first I was astounded, I thought the dog was watching the lights. Then I realised he was following the people. Despite my better judgement, I grew very fond and proud of him.

About a year later I went travelling for three months, leaving him in the company of the household. When I returned he had moved in with a neighbour who allowed him to sleep in her bed. He came back for a while, and then I moved three streets down, away from the park. I bought him a basket to sleep in but he kept wandering back to the neighbour, and finally he stayed there.

Perhaps we kid ourselves that they need us to walk them. Who's walking who? As Nigerian author Chris Abani, living in East LA, once put it: 'In my neighbourhood, if you're walking without a dog, you get arrested. Because you obviously plan to mug someone.'

According to Jeffrey Robinson, 'The dog is the perfect compromise between the severity of solitude and the clutter of companionship', and in a world afraid of strangers, babies and dogs provide points of contact and conversation. Diane tells the story of how she met her husband: 'Every Saturday when my housemate had finished work, we would walk our dogs down to the beach. One day she noticed a man throwing sticks in the sea for his dog to retrieve. After she had invited him back to our house for tea

I told her that she was being most irresponsible, since as far as we knew he could have been Jack the Ripper. The man duly invited us out, but she declined because of a previous date. He spent the rest of the day with me, and is still with me nearly thirty years later.'

Calling in to a talk show, Karen sums it up: 'There is no delight like the delight of a dog who knows it's going for a walk, and you have to share in that delight, you just don't have any choice. And even if you've been working all day and you're sitting in your chair thinking, oh I simply can't do anything else, then you think, well, maybe later I'll take the dog for a walk. And all of a sudden there's this face in front of you with these beaming eyes and this enormous grin and this tail switching back and forth saying: Did you just think the W word! So you have to go, you have no choice. It's not like, oh I don't want to go to the gym today. You GO ON THAT WALK. And all of a sudden you're having the best time, and you're thinking, this is as good as it gets. I've been known to walk five or six miles when I only planned to walk a few blocks because we were having such a good time.'

2.

In the days when gambling was outlawed in South Africa and casinos were exiled to the so-called independent homelands, Romano and Clarence lived in Sun City, in Bophuthatswana in the northwest. Romano, a theatre manager, and Clarence, a dancer, decided to add an Afghan to their family, and so they got Bushka.

'Clarence had an Afghan when he was young,' Romano explains, 'and when we met, Clarence said he wanted a dog. Then he found out about some Afghans that were bred in Rustenburg, just over the border from Sun City.' The idea of these stylish dogs, which often appear to be fashion accessories, being bred in Rustenburg, a hot, dusty, style-less town, seems quite incongruous. And yet, Romano informs me, they come from dusty beginnings. 'Coming from Afghanistan, and Egypt, that whole area, their roots... they were actually used as gift exchange between kings and pharaohs up in Cairo.'

'But those dogs had shorter hair, because of the rocks and things,' Clarence adds.

'When we got Bushka,' Romano recalls, 'he was this little bundle, with no hair. He looked like a Labrador when I first saw him; his nose was still quite short.'

Funnily enough, though they grow rather long noses, Afghans have a very poor sense of smell. 'Afghans are sight-hounds,' says Romano, 'they're not really good smellers or sniffers. They have very good eyesight.' Consequently, when they wander they don't always find their way home. 'What happens is that the Afghan will get out of the property and then you won't see him. That's why they have a big Afghan rescue unit.

'But Bushka was a people's dog. Because he was raised in Sun City he was very people-friendly. He went where the people were rather than anything else. So he used to go to a place and then get lost. And I think he just used to have an adventure. That was Bushka's nature.

'Everyone loved him at Sun City, someone even built him a little pen. But he just used to leap over it, because they've got those long legs. The Afghan's legs are built like they are for bounding over rocks. That's why they've got very strong hips, long legs, narrow waist, and this broad chest. We often used to get phone calls from the security: "Bushka's on the golf course."

'I remember we celebrated his first birthday, and all the dogs were invited,' he says. 'He was a bit of a celebrity. The chefs at the hotel made him a cake that looked like a bone.' This, of course, was for the people. 'We went to the Calabash and got the dogs a big thing of lamb, so all the dogs had meat and bones, and the humans had pizza and cake.

'And then it was some time after that, we got this phone call one evening: "Your dog was found at the stable." And the owners were very upset. I think it was the first time he had seen horses in his life. And I said, "What must we do?", because we didn't have a car then. And they said, "No, we'll bring him, meet us at the parking lot." It was the Sun City police, and we went there and we opened the door of the police van, and there he was sitting in the back, crouching like a criminal. I'll never forget the look on his face. He knew he was in trouble. I pulled him out of that van, and he didn't want to come. He knew he was in the dog box. That was the first real brush with the law that he had.

'Many times we had to fetch him from the golf course, chasing the flamingos. People enjoyed him, I think he was a bit of a novelty. The only thing was, he became a bit of a public nuisance when he started walking through the restaurants.'

'They get bored,' Clarence explains.

'They are wanderers,' says Romano. 'They're pack dogs. You'll see them as a group,' he says, gesturing to their three Afghans lying together in the garden. 'If they're sitting together they're very comfortable with one another. And if one reacts to something, they'll all react. If one gets up and moves they will all move.'

When Bushka was two years old they moved to the Wild Coast Sun in the Transkei. He may have been a walker, but he was not a happy flyer. In all fairness, most people become a little queasy in small planes. 'We went in one of those little Comair planes,' says Romano, 'they used to call them the vomit comet. We gave him half a tranquilliser, and he howled all the way.

'I tried to get him into the cabin, but they wouldn't, so he was put in the cargo hold. There were about fifteen or so of us on the plane, and the next thing we hear this, Owwwooooooo,' Romano laughs.

'We loved it at the Wild Coast. It was very basic, nothing was locked. It was a ten-minute walk to the ocean. We moved into a ground floor apartment with a big lawn at the back, and a normal fence about a metre and a half high. And we put chicken-net above the fence, which made it about three metres high, because he used to jump over the fence and harass the cows on the other side. And that still didn't stop him. He used to scale it. Jump right over that three metres and get out.

'He came home one day, and his paws, his pads, were cut to shreds. His feet were bleeding. We searched everywhere, rubbish dumps, to find maybe there were mounds of broken bottles or something, but we couldn't find anything. So we have no idea where he went. We had to bandage his feet. That walkabout was a total mystery to us.

'And then one day we had gone to work and we came home and he was gone. Then it was the usual search procedure, I walked to the beach, walked to the places that we knew he frequented. There was a little restaurant called Fathers, and he used to go there and raid the bins and eat crayfish, so that was always our first port of call. No luck. So I spent an evening walking up and down the beach, hanging around, starting to panic. Because normally somebody would have seen him, we'd say: "Have you seen a dog with long blonde hair?" And somebody would say: "Oh ja, I saw him going that way." So the next morning we started phoning around, the vet, the police station, put up posters as far as Port Alfred.

'And about three days later we got a phone call from the vet, the dog had been found. What had happened was, there was a group of German hikers, they were hiking along the coast and he joined them, and they left him at the vet.'

A year or so later, around the time that Sheba was King of the Yeoville park, Romano, Clarence and Bushka moved to Johannesburg, to a cottage in Berea.

'When we moved to Joburg we had what we thought was a high enough wall, but he still scaled the wall. And that's where he started his adventures to Hillbrow. He walked from there, across that big main road, Harrow Road,' now Joe Slovo Drive. 'It's bizarre when I think about it now. It was a real eye-opener for us, because we didn't have any other dogs at that stage, until eventually we got Thadu and she kept him company. And then he wandered less. I don't know where he learned his street-smartness from; that I found fascinating.

'We came home one day and Bushka was gone, and then a friend of ours phoned us, he was working at the Three Sisters, the Greek restaurant in Hillbrow.' Lonely at home all day, 'Bushka knew we used to go there, so he used to go there and sit down. I got this call from Muzzy: "I'm sure I've just seen Bushka walking through Hillbrow!"'

'We used to spend a lot of money,' Clarence recalls. 'People used to ask: "How much was your dog?" And then we say: "Oh, two thousand five hundred rand." And then they say: "Okay, then I want a hundred rand."'

'So thank goodness Muzzy saw him that day and he kept him there and we went and fetched him there with a lead,' says Romano. 'I don't know how many times we had to walk somewhere to go and pick him up.' At that stage neither Romano nor Clarence drove. 'And he used to have this look on his face like, Okay, I know, sorry.

'But then he also got lost. He was gone, totally, and we didn't know where he was. We put up notices on all the trees. We used to take him to the park between Hillbrow and Berea. They had a dog enclosure there, so we used to take him there to run. So that was always the first place we went, because we thought, you know, the average dog will sniff their way back to a place they're familiar with. But not an Afghan!

'The one time we went to look for him at that park, we put notices all over the park, in that whole vicinity, and we eventually got a phone call from a man who had him in his flat in Hillbrow. We paid him a hundred rand reward.'

'A day!' says Clarence. This would have been an expensive rate for board and lodging in Hillbrow, even in those days.

In 1996 they moved to the suburbs, with a big garden and a three-metre wall, and Bushka began to put on weight. 'He wasn't as active then,' says Romano, 'but he was also quite old. And then he developed lung cancer. We had no inkling of it. He used to walk a little slovenly and drag himself around, and we just thought it was the summer heat of Johannesburg. And then I remember one morning, I went to work quite late in the morning, about ten o'clock or so, and he was lying under that rose bush,' he points. 'And I came home about four o'clockish, and he was still there. And we took him to the vet, and they phoned me the next morning and said he's got lung cancer.'

Now together for twenty-two years, married and living in Greenside, Romano and Clarence have three Afghans, and a Dalmatian with one blue eye and one brown. 'The Dalmatian keeps them entertained,' Romano laughs. But they don't take any of the dogs for walks any more.

'We used to, but it's too much of a schlep. When we moved here, we used to take them to Emmarentia and Zoo Lake,' the two popular parks in the northern suburbs for dog walking. 'And people walk their dogs without the leads. And our dogs always got attacked, so we decided we wouldn't take them there any more.'

Dog owners are divided on this issue. There is an ongoing battle between some dog owners and Johannesburg City Parks, who want to enforce a law at Emmarentia that dogs must be on leads, and fence off a section as a dog run where they can roam freely; much like the case in New York's Central Park. Some people reckon this is to keep the dogs from destroying Emmarentia's beautiful rose garden. But, says one user who travels to the park: 'There is no point in going all the way to a park if your dog is not allowed to run free. It would be less trouble to walk them on a lead on pavements close to home.' And then she points out: 'The park would be very dangerous for other users if dog owners decided only to walk in the streets near their houses, as they make up the majority of users during the quiet times, and their presence makes it less likely that opportunistic crimes are perpetrated.'

'So anyway,' Romano continues, 'then we started walking them up the road here, but still people walked their dogs without leads. And then one time, this woman, she knows her dog's a vicious dog, and she opens her gate to reverse her car out and lets the dog out. And the dog attacked one of the domestic workers. It charged across the road and bit her hand.' As a friend of mine observed, so often in South Africa dogs are kept as security systems, rather than as pets.

'I dread to think where these dogs would go if they got out now,' Romano reflects. 'Once they get out of this road, no one would know them. But they run around here. It's a big space. They charge around the pool, they charge up and down the driveway. They keep very fit, and they keep each other fit.' This is not as true for their owners, who are both driving now. Clarence got his licence at thirty-six, and Romano at thirty-seven. 'I hated Johannesburg when we first moved here,' Romano says. 'I used to travel by bus or minibus taxi, or walk, and there was no sea or mountains. It was only through driving that I discovered the beauty of Johannesburg,' the driver's city, seen through the windows of cars.

Looking over the top of his wineglass out at the garden from the stoep where we've finished lunch, Romano recalls Bushka's last days: 'He was so beautiful under the rose bush. It was blooming. It was so sad.'

Foreign Streets

It is a Saturday afternoon, threatening rain, and I'm glad of the excuse of my raincoat covering my bag as I head up Cavendish Street to meet with Bienvenue ('Welcome'). It's been a long time since I've ventured this far into Yeoville, and I'm now in unfamiliar territory. As I walk the fifteen blocks from Louis Botha Avenue, across Rockey Street, I enter another world.

I'm struck immediately by how many people are out in the streets, going about their weekends; many, as in any other suburb, getting their hair done. There is no shortage of hair salons in these parts (plus a few saloons, and a *saloona*). Even on the Sabbath, in my predominantly Jewish neighbourhood ten minutes away by minibus taxi, there were relatively few people out on foot.

As I make my way up the hill, I steel myself against being saddened by the decay of the beautiful old buildings, and the accompanying sense of loss. I'm thinking of 'Yeoville Confidential', Achal Prabhala's essay in *Johannesburg: Elusive Metropolis*, in which he expresses his intolerance for the bewailing of 'the ghosts of cappuccinos past … frankly,' he wrote, 'the stories bore me … My own Yeoville memories are exactly one year old … and I like that just fine.' I found the essay fascinating and enjoyed it enormously, in an abstract way, like I would reading travel articles about faraway places I'm unlikely ever to visit and have no desire to live in.

Some of my friends, home owners still living in the suburb, also grow impatient with nostalgia for the bohemian Yeoville of the past. The difference between us is that they're car people, now driving to Norwood and Killarney to shop, bank, visit bookshops and meet for coffee. I need these things within walking distance of my home.

Earlier, Prabhala had written that, despite how comfortable he felt in Yeoville, 'I realise that I owe this happy existence to owning a car'. Then he came to the conclusion that 'civilians have done me no harm in Yeoville, or indeed, anywhere else in South Africa. I realise that I owe this happy existence – in different ways – to owning a car that isn't posh (in fact, a borrowed VW Beetle that doesn't lock), to living in a building that is strict about security, and to being a dark-skinned male. Friends in similar circumstances, but crucially lacking their own transport, have not had it quite so good … It's not a nice place for the walking classes,' possibly the majority of Yeoville residents, 'at any time of the day, especially after dark. Women fear they'll be parted from their cellphones, and grown men prefer to walk in groups.'

At Hillcrest Mansions, a shell of its former self, I cross the street to the corner of Cavendish and Webb, and pass through the security gate into Xanadu. The young guard informs me sternly: 'You can't sit on the wall.' There will be no loitering here. Bienvenue comes down to fetch me, and we make our way through surprisingly quiet corridors. A sign warns residents that *Braais are NOT allowed on the balconies*, and I notice they are using energy-efficient light bulbs in the passages. The globes are bare. I have interrupted Bienvenue and his friends watching a soccer match on TV.

Bienvenue came to South Africa from the Democratic Republic of Congo in 1994, when it seemed like South Africa was finally becoming hospitable to its African neighbours. 'When I came, the socio-political environment in DRC was bad. They closed down the university for two years in my last year. I was thinking, like everyone, I can find things better. Get my papers ready as early as possible. Comparing to what we hear from some friends overseas… I don't know about the realities there, but when you are talking to them on the phone, they were telling you, things are better, I'm doing my job, I've got my papers. Then I was thinking I would have the same treatment here. Unfortunately it didn't happen.

'In the beginning we really experienced that attitude from people, saying, "Now you can go back to your country." This kind of language. That's why you experienced these xenophobia stories, it started a long time ago.'

He has lived in Yeoville for fourteen years and witnessed it changing. 'When I came in Yeoville then, I didn't find a lot of foreigners. Especially the Congolese guys, most of them were staying in Ponte City. So when we were here we were small. In the beginning it was a bit stressful. I used to go to Berea to see friends, otherwise I must wait until Sunday until I can walk to Berea to go to the church to meet my friends there. It was not quite easy, until more people were coming.

'It is totally different now. First the majority was a white community, then it was black, now 70 per cent is a migrant community.' It is now a uniquely pan-African suburb. 'Sometimes you can feel at home now,' he says. 'If you need help. We experience most of the problems together.' After the xenophobic attacks in May 2008, 'Some of my people I know, we founded an organisation called African Diaspora Forum. When this situation came here, the xenophobia stories, we say, no man, we can be together, try to fight those spirits. And in that time we decided to go to the refugee camps, to see what is happening. We found our brothers and sisters there. Myself I found my friends there, some people I know from Yeoville, in the camps. So the experiences were shocking.

'At that stage, the police, they became a bit softer, because they got instructions: Please, they are being harassed now, don't give them more harassment. They became better. But now it's back to the same.' By far the biggest problem he and his friends experience

252

is harassment by the police. 'For me, I can say it's mostly during the day, because during the day most of the people are walking around. The problem we are facing here, even if officially they are saying they are checking people because they want to fight crime – yes, it is right – but you then realise that they are really not fighting crime, they are just checking for foreigners.

'Myself, I remember three months back, I was going to catch my taxi to work from Berea. I find a group of policemen, around half past seven, there were about fifteen policemen around one of those vans, and other cars there. I even recognised one face. They were stopping on the corner of Joe Slovo and Olivia.

'The taxi from Yeoville to Cresta,' where Bienvenue works, 'now they cancel it. You know those guys from the taxi associations, they didn't agree about something, so now I walk to Berea, corner Lily and Abel Road, for the taxi to Cresta. From there I can save some money, because it's going straight to Cresta Mall; instead of taking two taxis, from here to town, and from town to there.

'So when I was going there,' a block before his turnoff, 'I met those policemen and they shout at me: "HEY, DON'T MOVE, DON'T MOVE!" They tell me to put my hands up. And then I put, and they check for everything, knife, gun. They didn't find anything. I was carrying my papers, my status, and it was also certified by the police, the Yeoville police. And then when they ask me for those papers and I show them my status and the police stamp, one of them, he just take it and he say, "It is *fake!*" And I was shocked. I say, "No, man,"' he laughs incredulously, "'it's not fake, it is real. You can even see the police stamp. I went to the police to certify."'

'Then they started to harass me, and they take me and throw me in the van. I was shocked, why they can do it. I was so confused inside the van, I found three or four people, and I don't know what to say, why they can arrest me just like that. And I was really disappointed. Until later on, one of them told them, "No, just leave him." So they opened and they gave me that paper. But this is just my story. There are a lot of people, friends and family, they are experiencing harassment every day. Especially in Yeoville, because those people are making their business in Yeoville.'

Then there is the ongoing battle of dealing with the Department of Home Affairs. 'When you go now to Home Affairs – this is the main thing those policemen are taking advantage of, they are talking about illegal immigrants or undocumented migrants – when you come to renew your papers, they say, "No, go back home."

'When you apply, you are just an asylum seeker until they allow you to stay officially. Now you become a refugee, and you get an official letter from the director of Home Affairs and your permit to stay. Maybe two years, and then you have to go back and renew it. But meanwhile, before they give you refugee status, it can take maybe three years, four years to wait. You gonna go back there after two months, or three months, to renew your permit. But the problem now, when people are going to renew, they don't want to take you, so then you become illegal. So when you go back home the policemen in Yeoville arrest you. Or when you go there, there are a thousand people, and they're taking maybe two hundred. The eight hundred they are leaving for Monday, you go back home, on Tuesday another thousand they came, they took a few. So those ones, plus the eight hundred from yesterday, they become a problem. Like my nephew, now it's three weeks he is going there. I ask him, "How are you walking?" He says, "I am just taking a risk."'

If it's not harassment from the police, 'it is just those robbers when you are walking'. In fifteen years he has been mugged as many times, with both guns and knives, always in the Yeoville, Berea, Hillbrow area. 'They will say to you: "Give me my cellphone!" Give me *my* cellphone! And then you ask, "Please can you give me my SIM card?" If they are kind they will do that. But they don't. Then they can just *klap* you. It is only by God's grace that I am still here.

'We are a bit confused,' he says sadly. 'Now they are saying, the World Cup, African Cup, Confederations Cup… I don't know which image they are selling. Now they say, okay we are better now. I don't know,' he shrugs. 'Because now the thing that is affecting me a lot is the people sleeping outside the church, like animals.' He is referring to the more than two thousand Zimbabweans seeking refuge at the Central Methodist Church in the city centre.

After fifteen years he now finally has permanent residence, but he doesn't see himself being here forever. 'For now, yes, because I can find my people. I've got more friends, so it's not like before.' Two years ago he married a Congolese woman whom he has known virtually since childhood, and they have a 4-month-old daughter. 'I would like to go back home one day and do my own business. There are two things. I'm thinking, if I have to go back and work in Congo,' since he's trained as a mechanical engineer, completing his studies at Wits University, 'then I would like to find an opportunity with an international company. Then it will be better. Otherwise I can plan, having some money, so I can go there and open a business, and create some jobs for the people. But just going like this, and sitting at home, is gonna be much worse.

'In DRC it is also a bit confusing, because they say it's gonna be democracy, everything is gonna be nice, but in practice it is not what they're preaching. But now, when you go there, you also realise that, oh, there are poor people, there are rich people, so now if I go there I'm gonna take my path. I'm gonna know what I can do. But if you gonna wait for the environment to be fine, *aii…*'

André is an urban anthropologist, and has been living in Johannesburg for over a decade now. He has a great love for the city. In his work and his personal life, one of the things that preoccupies him is the challenge of getting around Joburg.

'I grew up in Toronto, which is a very mobile city. Not simply in terms of public transportation – trams, trolleys, buses, underground – but also an excellent road network. At the same time there is a very strong culture of walking in the city. The city is very accessible, particularly the downtown part, and it is very normal for people to walk. And in some cases to walk longer distances, because it's easy and safe to do so.'

His parents were Hungarian refugees, and he considers himself both Canadian and Hungarian: 'Canadian by birth and Hungarian by heritage.' From the age of five he spent the summers in Budapest, so he thinks of both cities as home. 'I grew up in a multicultural environment,' and moving between places was never an issue.

Arriving in Joburg 'was a culture shock in as much as other middle-class people don't walk. People that I might meet, particularly at the university, on a day-to-day basis. And they will instruct you not to walk. But that didn't change my attitude to the urban environment, I continued to walk. I think that being a part of the city is social interaction, and that is fundamentally for me about meeting people unencumbered by the technology of a vehicle.'

Since he's been here he has lived in various parts of the northern suburbs, well known for its high walls, and that has also been hard to get used to. 'A lot of my life here has been about... in some ways... breaking down the walls that are put in front of me. People say, don't do this, or you shouldn't do that. Or the city's built in certain ways. As someone who loves to walk and experience other areas of the city and other people in the city, I am constantly frustrated. The effect of walls that are meant for insulation is often one of isolation. I think that's a critical tension in South African society.'

A year ago, his Greek-Zimbabwean wife Julie gave birth to triplets, and pushing the triple pram through the streets near their Parkwood home has prompted many conversations. 'We get a lot of engagement from everyone,' he says. 'There was the person working on his house who nearly fell off his ladder when he saw the three of them; and people tell us stories about their own families, and the multiples that they have in their families or people who they know. And then many passers-by simply stop and wish us well, because they recognise that we're not going to be getting sleep for a long, long time! Often the babies deflect direct communication because the conversation happens through the children. People speak to them, when what they are saying is actually directed at us.' Getting the pram along the often poorly kept or overdeveloped pavements is one of the biggest challenges.

Though he has been warned against it, he frequently walks downtown during the day, and 'there have been a number of occasions when people have tried to mug me as a pedestrian. Twice in Braamfontein, once in Newtown, and once in the CBD. All areas I enjoy because in many ways I'm a big city boy. I love the urban environment, the intensity, the pace. There's a constant spectacle of enjoyment, and seeing people from different walks of life is fantastic. It's one of the reasons that I love Johannesburg.'

Unusually, the muggers were never armed. 'It was always two or three attackers.' Opportunistic rather than organised. 'Sometimes people tell me I'm lucky. Others have told me that I'm "asking for it."'

In each case he fought them off, but what he finds most troubling is that 'they never ran away. Because if any criminal doesn't seek to leave the scene of the crime quickly, it means they have a confidence that the state and the security forces, the police, are not around to intervene. And that's a very real testimony to the lack of public safety.

'Being a part of the public is so much a part of my identity, and I refuse to give it up to those experiences. I miss not being able to walk at night, though; not being able to feel a part of the city at all times. It is a great disappointment, and a great loss. It's such a basic thing, human locomotion. It's a very important thing that is missing in South African society.

'Many South Africans that I've spoken to, people's experiences of crime have in many cases led to emigration. These people have been black and white and young and old, but often they have been part of a young family, so they've had responsibilities to children, and they feel that they can no longer take the chances for their children that they've taken.'

As to whether he sees his family staying in Joburg, he says, 'That's a question that's up to my employers, the university, as much as to myself. I have a great love for and intellectual attachment and investment in this city.'

Wendel has been in Johannesburg for six years now. Originally from São Paulo, 'I left Brazil when I was nineteen and lived in Montreal, Mexico, and here, so in ten years I've lived in four different countries, so I'll probably move again one day. But for now I'm quite happy.'

For the first four years here he couldn't drive. 'I was dependent on lifts and taxis, and I walked where I could. But there's also the distance, it's a big city, so you can't easily walk where you have to go.

'It's totally different here. I came from a culture of walking, and public transport. Everybody's walking, from your 95-year-old to your 5-year-old, take a bus and you get out and walk a few blocks to get where you need to go. And you have street life, business in the streets, so you can stop more easily. It's almost twenty-four hours that you can walk in the streets and have business open, coffee shops, pharmacies, banks and all of that. And everybody has bags, carrying heavy stuff up and down. And here, because of the cars, you hardly see that. You just put stuff in your boot.' Of course he means the middle classes, working-class people are often carrying heavy bags in and out of taxis and buses.

Joburg was also a culture shock for him. 'Very much so. I lived in São Paulo and then Montreal, and there you can cycle and walk, and everybody does that. I didn't have any friends who had a car at that time. Everybody depended on public transport and bicycles. In Montreal the traffic is quite bad, but you have your cycling lanes and routes through parks. It was a way to save money as well. Even in the winter, when it was minus twenty in the snow, I used to cycle.'

Driving for the past couple of years has taken its toll on his body. 'I've become quite lazy, to tell you the truth. Now I've started cycling in the gym. I grew up playing sports, collective sports – soccer, volleyball, basketball. Here I played soccer for a while. I met a lot of different people. It was quite interesting to meet up with them.' But once he got a permanent job, as a photographer, his life changed.

'At the beginning of this year I went back to Brazil and I was very unfit to walk around. With my work I need to drive. I have equipment to carry, so it's impossible to do this on public transport. So here you drive, stop, get out, do what you need to do, then jump in the car again.

'I used to walk for hours. Now I was walking in the park with my father, who is sixty-five – him and my mum, they go for at least one hour every morning, it doesn't matter which weather, to walk on the beach – and it was quite funny. The park was amazing, a little park, about half the size of Zoo Lake, and you have people doing exercise from six o'clock in the morning until nine o'clock at night. I was very impressed to see that activity. Packed, like a thousand people in the park, and everybody's walking, running, doing Tai Chi.

'Here people have a garden life. You invite people to lunch at your house and you do everything behind your walls. I'm used to going to the park with friends to have picnics in summertime, but we don't do that here.' Does he miss the open public space in Joburg's wall-to-mall culture? 'I do, I do,' he says. 'Extremely. It means a lot to me. When you grow up doing something it's part of you. It's part of me. That was my issue with Johannesburg in the beginning. It took time for me to understand that. It's not because Johannesburg is a bad city, hard core and all of that. I have lived in much more extreme, aggressive cities – Mexico City, and São Paulo is quite extreme. You need to fight for your space. You take public transport and you have to push people to get inside.'

One of the biggest problems, Wendel thinks, is the separation of business and residential areas. Since most of big business has migrated to Sandton, those who still work in the city centre, 'they work there during the day and bugger off in the evenings. They just come, work in their office the whole day, come down for lunch quickly, if they do that, and that's it.' Despite extensive upgrading in parts of the inner city, many people still simply drive into their parking lots at work and out again at night, without ever venturing into the city. 'Everything's nice and clean, with security guards on corners, but if you don't have people living there, that's major.'

He and his wife Alex now live in suburban Richmond, but 'a few years ago, when we were looking to buy a place, we thought, what about something in town? Because we thought we could get a nice old apartment. We thought it was going to be cheap. And it was about one and a half million. And at that time you could buy a big house, a two-bedroomed house with a garden for that price. So who's going to invest that kind of money?

'It's a big mistake, because they could bring artists and students and alternative people to live there, but they can't afford those prices. And those are the kinds of people who are going to think, I'm going to go and eat in the restaurant downstairs, and that's what's necessary.'

In his book, *Taming the Disorderly City*, Martin J Murray places the blame at the feet of developers and the market-driven economy, concerned only with money and not with people. He points to the 'competing logics' that 'intersect, overlap' and inevitably 'clash'.

Returning to the suburbs, and the way that people shy away from public spaces, Wendel reflects: 'In Sandton, one block away from the Village Walk, there is a park just behind there and it's always empty, and it's a big park. Nobody goes there for their lunch. We need to make public spaces safe. I think it'll improve people's lives so much if we can have public parks and swimming pools really working. I don't think it's that difficult. Here all the parks have palisades, so you can control who's coming in and going out. I'd say put policemen in the park, walking around or on horses or bicycles. You only need two or three security people with radios.

It helps to see a policeman around.'

What I'm trying to understand is why São Paulo, also a notoriously unequal and violent city, with its own 'fortified enclaves' and 'edge cities' for the wealthy elite, remains pedestrian-friendly in a way that Johannesburg has not.

'The violence does exist,' says Wendel, 'they're going to come into your house with big machine guns and clean out your house, that kind of violence. But somebody's not going to come with a gun to steal your cellphone and kill you because of that. They're going to look for something bigger. You're not going to be killed in the street. They're just going to take your cellphone or your wallet and run away.'

He is highlighting the argument made by Alex Perry, *Time* magazine's Africa bureau chief and author of *Falling off the Edge*, about the peculiarly disproportionate levels of violence in South Africa associated with very small material rewards: that 'violence might be half the point … Any policeman will tell you,' Perry elaborates, 'that violence is not a smart thing to add to crime. A smart criminal will try and get in and get out as quietly as possible. If you add violence to it, it increases your sentence if you're caught, it increases your time at the scene, it's a distraction, it increases how hard the police look for you. You don't want to do it. The fact that violence so often accompanies crime in South Africa … It's not just me taking your stuff, it's me confronting you. It's me confronting you with my alienation and my frustration.'

I go looking for the park in Sandton that Wendel mentioned, and realise I've walked past it many times and never noticed it. When I walk through the gate, at half past one on a Tuesday afternoon, I feel immediately ill at ease, and I realise it's *because* of the palisades. It feels so different from the park on the border of Parktown and Hillbrow that I visited a few days earlier, with a low pole-fence and children walking through on their way home from school. This beautiful park feels caged off. Apart from half a dozen or so men lying on the lawn and a lone sketch artist, there is, as Wendel predicted, no one sitting on a bench eating their lunch, and I feel that I would be trapped if I needed to run. The sign outside notifies me that: 'This park will be locked from 6 p.m. to 6 a.m. – By Order', and I wonder if it would be so bad to have a few people sleeping here at night, in exchange for an inviting open space during the day. Nothing is encouraging me to spend any time in here, and I walk once warily around the pond and straight out again.

Shortly after, I receive the newsletter of the complex in which I live, which informs residents that 'the servitude land has been opened'. We now have our own private park. In addition: 'a computerized tag security system for entrance to and exit from our complex' is to be installed. 'The system will consist of double booms for the residents entrance, a new boom to regulate the visitors entrance, a single boom at the exit with a scanner for residents and a drop box for visitors, card access, cameras, special entrance for pedestrians, etc. The access will be monitored and photographs of entry and exit will be stored on a computer system … There will be the implementation shortly during the nightshift of a K9 that will assist the guards with patrolling. Please do not feed the dog.' Life in suburban Joburg begins to feel surreal to me.

'Johannesburg is not an easy city,' Wendel reckons. 'We complain about it, but Johannesburg is a very young city and the revolution's still happening here. If you go to Paris and these old cities, they've been there for hundreds of years and they've been through their revolutions, and now they have a decent city. Here we complain that the roads are bad and you get stuck everywhere, there's construction, construction, dust everywhere, but that's what happened in New York a hundred years ago.' I think of Martin Scorsese's *Gangs of New York*, about the battle for territory in Manhattan in the mid-nineteenth century between the 'natives', born in the United States, and the recently arrived Irish immigrants. 'Johannesburg,' Wendel concludes: 'everybody wants a little piece of it.'

At 9.30 a.m. on a sunny Monday morning I feel perfectly safe in Rockey Street (I'm still wearing the raincoat, just in case). Or to be accurate, it's actually Raleigh Street, at the Joe Slovo end. Roses are blooming through the palisades at the Providence Healthcare Centre, and I'm struck by how clean the streets are. Either it was a low-key Human Rights Day weekend or the cleaners have already been.

I had come to meet Suzanne at her house a few blocks away. The gate and front door were wide open, but no one was in sight. When her friend answers the bell in traditional West African dress, he tells me she has gone to the market and will be back in about an hour. I ask him if there is anywhere in Rockey Street that I can get coffee. He looks doubtful. 'Nandos?' he suggests. I decide I don't need coffee that badly, and instead take a tour of the places where I once lived.

The synagogue next to the house in Hunter Street is now the Word of Faith Mission (*Eglise Parole De La Foi*), facing the M6 Restaurant & Bar opposite, already full – no food or women in sight. One corner down, that synagogue has become the Word of Life Assembly Church, and in the opposite direction is the United Church School.

Across from Olympia Mansions in Yeo Street, the houses have transformed into the Livewire Recording Studio, and Tafari's Hair Salon (*Braids Plats and More*). And what was once a yeshiva next door: www.churchofjoburg.co.za. I see my butterfly decals are still in the windows after a decade.

The house opposite the park is the most disappointing. The front wall is still relatively low by Joburg's standards, with razor wire on top, and one would still be able to see across the street from the raised stoep, if there was anything to see. This section of the park has been cordoned off and is filled with corrugated iron huts. The only activity in sight is construction.

Round the corner past the police station there is a crowd of people, mostly women and children, waiting outside the clinic. The newly renovated swimming pool is sparkling, and empty – a perfect place to swim laps right now. 'It is full when school is out,' the attendant assures me. As I head down Rockey Street – 'It's a one-way street, and it goes downhill,' actor Charles Comyn used to sing – at times I feel like I'm in Woodstock in Cape Town, or parts of London. Perhaps it's the Indian traders or the frequent *Wholesalers* signs. Things for sale now are mostly practical, and there is a refreshing lack of false advertising – what they say is what you get. Like the dedicated Nappy Shop, piled floor to ceiling with disposables. And the Mattress Store cc (*lay-bye accepted*), which also has a few fridges.

Very little is familiar to me, apart from Yeoville Hardware – everybody needs hardware – and the librarian, still at her post after twenty-two years. 'I still live in Yeoville,' she tells me. The chairs and tables are full of people reading books and newspapers.

When I reach the rasta shop it's the first place that draws me in, with a glimmer of the creativity of the Rockey Street I remember. 'I'm just looking,' I tell the rasta on duty.

'Yes, you must look, sister,' he says, 'seeing is believing.'

'What is the name of your shop?' I ask him.

'The Rasta Shop,' he says.

I laugh, and ask him if he is from Ethiopia.

'We are all from Ethiopia,' he says, with a red twinkle in his eyes: 'Ethiopia is the real name of this continent. Africa is just the name of the colonisers.'

I tell him that I may come back for one of his 'Legalise' backpacks (only R30), or the Obama T-shirt: 'Change We Can Believe In' (R120), and as I say it I realise, once I step outside, it's unlikely that I will be back.

The closer I get to Bezuidenhout Street, the more uncomfortable I begin to feel with the groups of men loitering in doorways. A tap on my shoulder startles me, and I decide to head back to Suzanne at her Ivorian restaurant.

Standing at the gate, her friend Marshall has changed, he is wearing a World Cup 2010 T-shirt. Suzanne is petite and gorgeous, quite different from the image her deep voice conjured up. She leads me through the front room, with empty beer bottles from last night on the dining and pool tables, and I have a feeling of *déjà vu*. Then I realise I'm not hallucinating. I have been here before, at a party in the mid-Nineties, when it was home to a group of young American volunteers with Visions in Action.

She takes me into a smaller room at the back of the house, with lacy pink curtains and tablecloths, and smart black place settings. 'This is my VIP room,' she tells me. 'You know those young ones, they like to make noise. Sometimes people want a quiet place where they can eat and talk.' She goes to the kitchen to get me a Coke, and her German shepherd puts his nose through the window to check if I'm kosher as a chicken walks past in the yard.

Suzanne arrived in South Africa from Côte d'Ivoire in 1997. 'The time the wars are starting. This time I was a student, and I marched there, and then people run after us and I run away.' English was a problem for her and so she has never finished her marketing degree.

'In the beginning, when I come, I know how to braid hair, so sometimes at home I got one or two customers in the day, and I do this to pay my rent. And thereafter, our Abidjan community needed somebody to cook for them, because our food, you can't get it here, so in 2002 I opened this business. Now sometimes I get South African people who come to eat. Before it was only our country people, but now it's better; Congolese people come, South African people also.

'In the first house, after two, three years, the owners come to chase me. After there, in the next house, after two, three years the owner chase me again. And now I am here. The problem here is the rent. I pay R10 500.' Though I haven't rented a house in many years, this sounds steep to me for this neighbourhood and the state of disrepair of the house.

'Now I've got the refugee paper,' she says. 'I went there last month and they gave me three months. I have to go back in June. Aaaahhh,' she shakes her head, 'nowadays it's very difficult. If you want to get the paper, the stamp, in that day, you must sleep there. You can go today, around five or six, and then early in the morning you can go in. Sometimes it's raining, then you must take the umbrella.' When you don't manage to have your papers renewed on the due date, 'If the police find you then you must pay them twenty rand, fifty rand. Sometimes we are scared to go out. So it's better to stay there until you get your stamp.

'Before I had problem from the police, because I was selling liquor and I didn't have a licence, but now I have licence. Before there was too much problems! Sometimes when I get a customer, he says, "My sister I need beer." Then after fifteen minutes the police are here.' There is a weird irony in this, given how long the police take to arrive when called for a serious problem. 'They ask, "Have you got a licence?" and you say "No", then they say, "Open the fridge," and then they take all the beer. Then sometimes they want to take me too, then I say leave me, and I can pay maybe five hundred rand. So now it's better, I've got licence.'

Her restaurant is closed on Mondays, and though she describes Mondays as her 'off day', this is not entirely true. It is her market day. 'I go to the market in town. I take a taxi. The butchery is by Mandela Bridge. Sometimes I take my stuff from Mandela Bridge, the meat, I put it here,' she pats her shoulder, 'then I'm walking to the Mozambique market for cassava, like big potatoes, yam. I make that with couscous. Sometimes I put one here, two here, two here, like this,' she says, demonstrating with her arms and shoulders, and the bags she has to carry. 'The Mozambique Market is not far from Noord Street,' she says, referring to the taxi rank from where she travels home. 'At the Yeoville market I can buy only tomatoes, because here it is expensive, and they haven't got some of my things.'

I wonder what she thinks of our public transport system,

compared to Abidjan. 'In Ivory Coast we have too much buses, big buses, not so much taxis like here,' she says. 'Also, the meter taxis are not too expensive like here.' I recall a traveller passing through who I waitressed with many years ago, making the observation: 'I can get a bus in Papua New Guinea, where people have bones through their noses, and I can't get a bus in Johannesburg!'

Suzanne is streetwise and has never been mugged. 'On the street,' she warns me, 'if you walk, and you see two or three person, men, you must be careful. You must be careful! If you see they are moving to you, my friend you must take your legs and run away,' she laughs. If she has to go out after dark – 'Sometimes I forget to get my stuff,' she says, 'and then I walk to the shop – then I take somebody with me.'

In her home she hasn't been as lucky. 'Two times they coming at home, around ten in the night. Two men, they say they are looking for Zambia people. I have about twenty customer inside. I say to them, "No, here is Ivorian house, not Zambian house". After one hour they are coming back, and they took everything – cellphones, money from the customer inside.' Now she has two dogs and she feels much safer.

She was not personally affected during the xenophobic attacks, when Yeoville was possibly the safest place to be, but like most African 'foreigners' she was on high alert. On the 18th of May, a week after the violence broke out in Alexandra, the headline in the *Mail & Guardian* warned: 'Violence Grips Johannesburg.' 'Eighteen May was birthday for my daughter,' nine years old, 'and there was too much people here. About four o'clock, this man from Zimbabwe came to tell me, my sister you must close everything because the people are coming from Hillbrow. But then nothing happened here.'

Suzanne has no desire to return to Côte d'Ivoire. One day, she says, she would like to be able to buy this house. 'I got no problem from South Africans. I like it here, I got my business. And in 2010 people they going to come. They going to need food.'

I visit an old friend, Jennifer, who has lived in Yeoville for over twenty years. At one time she and her husband were looking to move, and then they changed their minds. 'For one thing, we could never get the kind of house that we have here, elsewhere. But apart from that, we're happy here, so why move? We were also thinking of moving because we were thinking of downscaling, so we were fantasising about "lock up and go" – it was much less about moving out of Yeoville than about not having to think about the gate, the pool, dogs, having to get someone to look after the place when we go away.

'And then we also have an absolute attachment to the energy of the place. We stayed because we didn't want to abandon it and follow the trend of everybody getting out. Although I think that many people got out not because they saw the place changing, but because they saw their investments plummet, which they did, and now it's built up again. But even to find a lock up and go kind of place elsewhere is very expensive.

'We go up and down between being feeling tired of the mass of people around – because month-end in Yeoville... there's just a sudden wooooosssshhh. People either going out or coming in. And sometimes that sort of chaos gets to be a bit much. But on the other hand, I also love it.' Today is the first of the month, and I've noticed the little vans with their cardboard *Bakkie 4 Hire* signs out in the streets – obviously how poor people, with few possessions and no access to professional removal companies, get from one place to another.

'We've thought about venturing back into Rockey Street at night,' Jennifer says, 'to Tandoor,' the rooftop reggae club 'which is apparently still the place to go. But they say you must catch a taxi there, and you get seen in, and then once you're in it's fine.'

She still goes to Rockey Street during the day from time to time, if she needs the odd thing from the café. 'The other day I'd just been to Fruit and Veg City and done a three-hundred-rand shop, and I was just popping in for something and a guy stole it all out of the boot. What they did – they say this is happening now – the car guards distract you, and he opens the back door just as you're locking your car.' This is the first theft I've heard of, though, of a load of vegetables. 'So it's not really advisable to drive to Rockey Street, but I'm happy to walk to the café.'

The *spaza* shops in the neighbourhood, on every corner and in between, where you can buy virtually one of anything, also come in useful when she half-heartedly decides to give up smoking. 'First it's one, then it's two, and pretty soon I'm buying a packet again.

'When we had our kids here, my stepchildren, they did walk around. But as the years went on, by the late Nineties, we got a bit… looking out the door to check that they're all okay. And in the latter part of their school years they moved back to their mom in Highlands North, because I think they did feel a bit trapped here behind the wall. And all their friends were on that side.

'But there's something in our street… Ownership pride, I think. I have a sense of community here that is very rare in this city. I know all my neighbours.' For the past three years, she and her husband Nicky have been running a swimming group on Saturday mornings. 'From ten to twelve there's a group of kids from the area who come and swim. They arrived at our gate one day: "Please, please can we come and swim?" And I said to Nicky, "Oh lord, if we let this group come we're going to end up with thousands of children." And funnily enough, it hasn't become thousands of children, it's pretty much the same dozen or so children, but they obviously monitor it. They're about six to twelve or thirteen years old. And then somehow when they get to about thirteen… We had two teenage girls, but they don't come any more. There've been a few occasions when I've had to say, "Sorry guys it's full, you'll have to come next week," but otherwise it's been fine. And they draw and they paint and they play ball on the lawn and swim. We obviously have to be vigilant. There are many parents who don't know that their children are here, but we started sending a note for the parents to sign. And they know they must come at ten, not half past eight, and it's worked out well.

'So when Nicky and I go for a walk, we have "Jennifeeer, Uncle Nickeeeee...," even from children who don't come swimming, so people know us in the neighbourhood.'

The psychological effects of shrinking public spaces does concern her. 'I look at other suburbs... I really worry about the fact that our society's becoming so individualised in terms of people's needs. Everybody's really out there just doing and getting and going and moving for their own needs. And there's a kind of arrogance and an aggression that gets connected with that, and that upsets me.

'It has to have an effect, so that your spiritual, emotional, sociological connection with the world gets more and more closed in on itself, and more self-obsessed.' As Jeffrey Robinson put it: 'I realised that I had let the space around me ... become all angles and walls cutting me off not from the outside world of the city but from my continuity with the world.' Jennifer recalls: 'When I was very young and self-involved, a boyfriend I was walking with once said to me, "For heaven's sake, look up. Look up, look around you!" So now I make sure to look up.

'I used to walk all over the place, to Hillbrow, Orange Grove, Rosebank – put my packet of Camel under my bra strap and go – and over the years I have gotten to walk less and less. And yet, us South Africans when we go overseas, we walk miles... We will pay twenty, thirty thousand rand, just to go and walk!

'Nicky and I still walk to Observatory, but we have been held up. Five guys and a gun. The security from the golf course saw it all happening, though, and then everybody clicked in, so they did catch the guys.

'It didn't affect me, that one, but after a second mugging in Cape Town it affected me. The first time I could see it for what it was, I was very lucky to get off, but the second time... I realised it was the undercutting of my essential sense of joy and trust that I have. Because it feels like the things that really matter in the world, like a child being able to play in a street, and what it means for a street to be able to exist so that it can, these are things that don't cost money, it just costs a kind of a morality that a society demands and fosters and everybody supports. And it is horrible, or painful, for the trusting, open, embracing type of people, who there are many of, that are not allowed to have that. It's very sad that there's a sense of feeling that that is lost.'

Recently, her 79-year-old mother moved from the small town of George midway between Cape Town and Port Elizabeth, where she'd been for forty-five years, to live with Jennifer in Yeoville. Every day Elaine takes her little dog Daisy, who she describes as 'a thoroughbred mongrel', for a walk through the neighbourhood.

'The first time I went out I was a bit wary,' she says, 'but I don't have any fear. I haven't had any bad experiences. I'm so amazed how frightened men, more than women, are of this little dog. She's in a brace, and she doesn't bark at them or anything, but I've had quite a few funny interludes going up and down, where a huge man will see the dog and go across to the other side of the street. Some of them will go like this,' she puts her hands out in front of her. 'I could understand it if I had a huge hound,' she laughs. 'When I said to one man as he passed: "She won't hurt you", he said, "But they bite my ankles." It is very strange to me that dogs here mean fights or bites or whatever. She's in her little harness, and I'm just an old aunty!

'I speak sometimes to the women who have these beautiful little babies on their backs. I think I'm slightly getting known now. The only thing that frightens me is that the dogs of some people further up want to come out and fight, they're very aggressive. And now she knows, she pulls me back to have a fight with them, and I say to her: "Do you know what's behind there?"

'I wouldn't go walking, I don't think, if I didn't have Daisy to inspire me to exercise. I can't stride out, but she pulls me, sniffing all along the pathway.'

Jennifer unlocks the gate to let us out and her neighbour is arriving home. 'I see Ma is taking a walk,' Sibusiso remarks, as Elaine and Daisy blur into the crowd along the street.

On Fairways and Bunkers

Three thousand one hundred and twenty-six steps from my front door, en route to Moses' office, I pass the Killarney Country Club. Though I pass by here often, it always makes me smile; the way that, in the act of naming, perhaps we hope it will make it so. But this is still traffic-choked Johannesburg, and the noise and exhaust fumes float up from the M1 highway below to greet me as I cross the bridge.

In her 1930 essay 'Street Haunting', Virginia Woolf wrote that 'the golfer plays in order that open spaces may be preserved from the builders'. While this may not quite be the *reason* that the golfer plays, even those who are not members of the club benefit from it being there, if only to rest the eyes for a few moments. And god knows, Joburgers need whatever respite they can find from the invasion of the developers and the builders.

On the second half of my walk, shoulders forward, I'm reminded that it is only when I'm in a car that I notice how uphill this road is.

'It's good to have these green lungs in residential areas,' Moses agrees, when I'm in his office, looking through the window onto a leafy Rosebank street. Rosebank, I've been told, 'is the new Sandton'. The five-star Crowne Plaza Hotel, recently renovated at a cost of R315 million, is just a block from here. Rosebank is a more pedestrian-friendly suburb than Sandton, and the Gautrain will be passing through here. It is also on the bus route, though it's

273

unlikely that the business travellers staying at the Crowne Plaza – their 'brand's core market ... who need an environment where they can be productive and work effectively' – will be needing a bus.

'Open space, nice open fresh air.' Moses returns my attention to the golf course. 'When we started playing golf,' he and his friends, 'there used to be lots of public courses.' But in the age of privatisation, 'there are no more public courses any more. We started playing at the public courses because there still used to be white enclaves at the private clubs, but then more and more people could afford the membership fees. There was a joke in the beginning that "the BEE guys have arrived."' Even within the black community black golfers are sometimes disparagingly referred to as *amaBEE*, the newly Black Economically Empowered. Moses' introduction to golf goes way back, though.

'I'll tell you a story. In the early Eighties, when I started working in my first job, I was working in the accounts department, and every Wednesday afternoon people all used to go. And I used to remain in the office answering telephones, running around like mad, wondering where these guys were, and I found out later that they were playing golf. I never knew what it was. Even then, when I discovered what it was, I thought it was the white man's territory. But eventually I thought, I also want to learn to play golf. And a few years later I was in sales and I would play golf with some of the customers, and then, as our country changed, people who had been deprived got more opportunities.'

Despite golf being the butt of many jokes (except when it comes to what Tiger Woods earns), he became hooked, and has been playing for the past decade. As many golfers attest, 'it is very addictive. People can be obsessive. There are some people who play about three times a week. There are some who even play once a day. I play once a week, on a Sunday. Occasionally there are invites for a golf day, or just a business meeting with someone.'

Once described as 'a kind of inspired inertia ... the slow

withdrawal of the club from the bag, the gazing at the horizon, the return of the club to the bag, the withdrawal of another club', according to Moses it is a popular misconception that there's not much exercise involved in playing golf. 'You can't really play golf if you're unfit. There's a way you've got to swing so that you don't strain your back or your knees. It can be quite heavy on your joints, twisting and turning and swinging, so you're using a lot of energy.' I've been told that many injuries result simply from bending to pick up the ball. 'And the other thing is, how often do you find people walking six kilometres?' My hour-long walk along Glenhove Avenue from Norwood to Rosebank was only five.

'The average distance for a round of golf is about six kilometres, from where you hit the ball to where the flag is. That doesn't include walking to the next spot where you're going to hit the ball from. Your regulation time is about four hours, but people walk that in about four and a half to five hours. So it's five hours out in the open air, and it's much more healthy than walking on the streets of Joburg, with cars and smog.'

I wonder how much walking actually happens, and how much riding around in the golf carts. 'At most courses you walk,' he says, 'but the courses also have carts available for those people who don't want to walk. You do find some courses where they just don't allow you to walk, like the Lost City at Sun City. Because of the terrain, it's got uphills and downhills, and it's difficult to walk, so it takes much longer to play a round of golf.' And since time is money, for the course as well as the players, they aim to get the players off the course as soon as possible.

Does the money spent really translate into concrete business deals? 'You know what they say,' Moses jokes: 'A bad round of golf is better than a good day in the office. I find it calms me down, you forget about work, you forget about the office. Some golf courses don't even allow you to use cellphones. Some people write "networking" in their diaries, rather than golf.

'But seriously, there's a fallacy about... People say megadeals are signed on the golf course. I don't know anyone who actually signed a deal on the golf course. The value that one gets is the networking, the introductions. You get to meet new people, different people, and get to understand what they do. Invariably you go to the golf course and meet somebody who knows another person, so it does expand your network and gives you more access to various people, so I think it's money well spent. Consultants will charge you for this service. And from there you've got leads to follow up. Some people will tell you that it's easier to get someone onto the golf course than it is to a get a thirty-minute appointment in his office.' At this point I realise how lucky I am that Moses has generously agreed to give me an hour of his time. 'Now once you know that somebody is a keen golfer,' he says, 'and you want to get to know them better, then how better to do that than on the golf course?

'Some people get involved in golf by mistake,' he reckons. 'They've heard that people make deals on the golf course and come there with a false notion, and then they get hooked.

'The whole idea is that you can play golf with a person, it's a competitive sport, and you get to see how they play. Does he lose his temper? and so on. So it does help, to get another insight into a person. You spend four and a half hours with this person and you're walking and talking. And it's not just serious, at times you joke and it's fun.'

I mention one of the quotes from the irreverent book about golf, *A Good Walk Spoiled!*, that it 'is played mainly on a five-and-a-half-inch course, the space between your ears'.

'Well, if you think about it,' he says, 'golf is not a team sport, it's an individual sport. And the whole thing is about hitting this ball over a given distance, with only a number of strokes. And if you can hit the ball with fewer strokes you are meeting your objective. It's a challenge between you and your skill. And if you make a mistake you can't point a finger at anyone else. So I think that's the value of it as well. It starts in your mind. You think, I'm given one in four chances, so how am I going to make it to there with the four chances that I have? So that's where the strategic part comes in, with my application of the plans. It involves a lot of decision making, so you learn a lot about yourself. And other people.

'And in business it's all about pitfalls, so the idea is to stay on the straight and narrow, and avoid the trees and the pond,' he laughs. 'You go through a process, a thought process. There's ambivalence, and you think about all the obstacles, how best to do things. That's my target, and how can I best reach my target? So it's not like you just hit it.'

I've made the assumption that Moses' golfing partners are all male, but I'm wrong. He also plays with women, and his conclusion is that they play differently. 'It's the same strategy, but the male ego definitely plays a part. Often men want to hit the ball harder, and with women, as long as it goes to where they want it to go that's fine. We want to hit it further. You look at this big guy next to you and think, I can outswing you, and completely miss the target,' he laughs. 'I think women are more relaxed. If they lose their tempers they don't always show it. Often you'll see the guys quarrelling amongst themselves because they don't agree about something.

'There's lots of stress about caddies as well. Some of the caddies coach the players, give them advice. Some players accept that and others get annoyed. They forget that many caddies spend most of their time on the golf course.' I was under the mistaken impression that most of the caddies would be young men. Moses clarifies: 'The majority of the caddies are quite old, they're people who have been around for years. So my view is, that's *his* office. For some of the caddies, this is the only job that they know, because the golf course is like their career. And you think about this person, he has to wake up in the morning and organise transport, he's got to pay for food, he's got children…

'Some of the caddies are quite chirpy, and some of the guys don't like that. Other players think it's a lot of fun. Like someone will say, "I've played such a bad shot." And the caddie will say, "But what's new? You've been playing bad shots since you started." And then the caddies also take bets. And then he expects you, because he's carrying your bag, that you're going to win. And then he loses his money. So they put pressure on you, because he's got money on you and you're playing badly, so they tell you how to play.' And the player becomes the caddie's racehorse.

I'm curious to know what Moses thinks about the opinion that golf is a Eurocentric sport. His answer is simple: 'It's all about affordability. If you can afford it, it's not an issue. In the old apartheid days, black people used to be caddies, they couldn't play. Now more and more people can afford to play. It's an expensive sport. Let's face it, you can easily spend five hundred rand on a round of golf: your green fees, paying your caddie, your lunch and buying drinks afterwards.' This is after the initial cost of clubs, clothes and membership fees.

'The equipment is expensive,' he nods, 'and being a member of the golf club. There are different prices. At Killarney the annual subscription is about ten thousand rand. At some clubs you can find that your joining fee's about fifteen thousand rand, and then when you come and play you still pay about a hundred rand.' And that is when you are a *member* of the club.

'I don't play at a specific golf course. I play at Johannesburg Country Club and Killarney, Waterkloof in Pretoria. I belong to the golf society, we have at least one game a month with the golf society, and the other three weekends I play with friends. As long as you're an affiliated member of a golf club you can play at any course, it's just that it gets a bit expensive if you're not a member. If you're a member, then because you're paying your annual membership fees there, when you come and play you just pay a nominal fee. But if you're a visitor who is an affiliated member at another golf club, then you pay much more. And then there are people who play and are not members at any golf club, and that's very expensive.' I'm told that the strategy of many players is to join an obscure club in a small town anywhere in South Africa, with a course that they never get to see, but this gives them their membership card to the golf society.

'At Killarney, as a visitor my green fees are R250. If you go to Johannesburg Country Club the green fees are more than that. And if you go to Sun City it's R685 per person – that includes the golf cart and lunch, but doesn't include a caddie. So you can imagine, if you're playing three, four times a month, it costs you at least two thousand rand a month.' Discovery, the medical aid scheme, 'they now have a programme where, if you play golf, when you swipe your card at one of the registered golf courses you get points, so you get discounts on your credit card.'

So it helps to be a member of a club. 'One joins just to be affiliated, in most cases, but it's nice to play on different courses. It makes it more interesting, because golf's a game that tests your skills, and different courses have different layouts and levels of difficulty. If you only get to know one course, when you get to another course you'll struggle.

'But you do find that some clubs are still 90 per cent white,' he observes, 'and the way they keep it that way is with the green fees and membership fees that are much higher. I mean for me, I like golf, but I still watch my pocket. I wouldn't go and join a very expensive club. And even if I did I would find myself isolated. If you don't feel welcome there then you don't feel at home.'

What about the class divisions *within* the black community that are arising out of post-'94 affluence? 'Yes,' Moses agrees, 'it's creating a very big class division. I mean, you go to the golf course and you see the type of cars that people drive. The caddies will tell you, "Hey, these guys have got money!" They'll tell you who's who. Personally, I believe you'll never get rid of class distinction. We will never live in a classless society, let's face it. There will always be the haves and the have-nots. It's something that's inherent.'

What impresses me most about Moses is his complete lack of defensiveness. 'I worked my way up,' he tells me, when I ask about his personal history. 'Studied part time. I went to university, there was unrest, and then my father died, so I had to work to pay for my studies.' Now he holds the livelihoods of the half-dozen people he employs in his small company in his hands, and he is obviously at peace with himself.

'It's like this,' he says, 'I grew up in the township, in Soweto, and this whole thing about collective decisions and all that, I mean that's a cultural thing. But when you look at how people grow in life, the more people get educated, the more they are enlightened, the more they want to get out of this collective decision making. Because people start realising that they're individuals in their own right.

'But things move so fast, this generation is the *now* generation, the instant generation. Put your coin in the vending machine and Bob's your uncle, everything is there. Expect it, and if you don't have it…'

He is concerned about young people's sense of entitlement, and their lack of understanding of how to work towards things. 'They've got brilliant ideas. We'll do this, and we'll do that, but then they just sit there and don't make much effort. And how do you expect this to happen if you're just sitting on your laurels? You've got to be out, doing research. But you think things are going to happen just because you wish them to happen.' I wonder if this is why there are so few young people on the golf course. On the other hand, according to *A Good Walk Spoiled!*: 'By the time you can afford to lose a ball, you can't hit it that far.'

At home in Sandton, Moses tells me, 'I like to go to gym in the mornings, and if I don't go to gym then I normally take a walk around the block, at around 6 a.m. It's that desire to have some physical activity. Rather than say, I can't go to gym this morning, I'm lazy, then I just go and walk. Like I said, if you're not fit, you're not going to be able to perform well on the golf course.'

For the past eleven years, Alec has worked as a caddie at the Killarney Country Club. 'Before I was working for a stationary company,' he explains, 'as assistant storeman. And then in the Nineties the company was liquidated, and I started to work in piece jobs, gardening and such. I was doing a gardening job here, just outside the gate.' This is one of those streets where the home owners maintain beautiful gardens, or employ people to maintain beautiful gardens, on the 'pavements' (no paving remains), and pedestrians step off to make their way along the street. 'And then one day,' says Alec, 'they ran short of caddies, and they asked me if I wanted to come and help.'

At that stage he didn't know anything about golf. 'I saw some golf on TV. Before that I ran at school, athletics, and then when I came to Joburg I started to run marathons.

'I had no idea, if you are a caddie, what to do. The other caddies, they taught me. Like if you put the bag down you must know how to put it. You mustn't put it on the green. You must put it down flat, because sometimes the bag falls down. And then you're going to disturb the player! And that's another story,' he laughs. But it's obvious he takes his job seriously. He has come to our conversation prepared, with a list, to be sure that he tells me what I need to know.

'You greet your player, then you check the bags and the clubs; wet a towel and clean the clubs. Check your pitchfork, because you have to repair the pitch if necessary, and then give your player information – the course is bad on the left or the right. And you must know the rules, the local rules.' The Nyanza Club in Kenya has a rule that 'if a ball comes to rest in dangerous proximity to a hippopotamus or crocodile, another ball may be dropped at a safe distance, no nearer the hole, without penalty'. But since there are no such threats in suburban Joburg, Alec informs me: 'He must play it as it lies.'

Walking on the course is not easy going, 'because – you see this course, it's soft, like a sponge. When you walk, you can't walk properly. You're sinking, and you're carrying a load at the back. The golf shoes are very important, because they support you properly. But if you wear normal shoes, after a month your feet are starting to pain, because there is no balance. And because of the water, because in the wintertime we are standing on the dew early in the morning. For the shoulders, it's the balance of the back that's important. The second one, the bag for the afternoon game, then you're tired and it's hard to make it. You just do it because you need to earn money.

'The main thing is, you must make sure when the player hits the ball that you see where the ball is landing. You must watch.' I ask him if he has good eyesight. 'I try to eat carrots,' he chuckles. 'Otherwise you're going to be walking around all day, when the ball goes left and you go right!

'The direction is very important. You see, in golf, the hard job is on the green. If you approach the green, you must make sure you give the player the right club to reach the green. And then, the big job is, you must give the player the right line; how it's going to turn. If the ball is turning left, you call right. If it's going right, you call left.

'Some of the players, they come here without knowing how to hit, with no experience. When he's still starting to learn, he likes to get advice, but once he knows he doesn't like it. Sometimes when you start with him, he tells you, "I am a beginner." Then the important thing is you must look how he swings the club. The main thing is he must look down at the ball. If he doesn't look at the ball, the ball is going nowhere.' This may seem obvious, but I'm reminded of the joke about the man who wants to introduce his wife to the game. After a few swings and misses, she says to him: 'I can see that golf is a fine exercise. But what's the little ball for?'

'If he doesn't know,' says Alec, 'then you approach him, just do it like this. The main problem with the players is they want to reach the green. And then even if the tree is in front of him, he just wants to hit the ball! So then you've got to advise, "No, please, we are only second round or third round, come to the fairway, and then you can see where you are going. Hit the ball to the left, and then from there, once you can see the green you can hit the ball there." Some of them, they want to take that style of the driving range to use on the golf course. On the driving range you just hit straight – you are not under the trees, you are not in the flowers, there's no rules.

'Sometimes one, he will come with a mood from the house, and then once he arrives here you don't know, because you just take the bag, clean the bag. Then once you are in the middle of the course you can see, no… the ball's in the middle of the fairway, and you tell him, "Please, come to the right." And he says to you: "Thanks, I know."' With finality Alec puts his hand up. 'Then you know, I must be quiet today. When you tell him what to do is where you're going to clash.

'And then he goes to the left and the ball is far from where we like it. Then he takes it like it's *you* who is making the mistake. On those days, when you get to the eighteenth hole, it's like you played thirty-six. Then you are getting tired. Then you have to console him. You must approach him in the right way, then he's calming down. The main thing making him calm down is to score. And then relax.

'You see Andie,' he tells me, 'the thing with the players is that they are betting. Some players, they tell you when you're going to start, I'm playing for a lot of money. Sometimes it's ten thousand rand each, then they put it in the middle, that's forty thousand rand, and winner takes all. And they sweat. There's going to be a war. So when you pull out the club, you must know that is the right one. You're under pressure.'

He admits that he also bets on the players. 'Sometimes we caddies, we have a competition ourselves. We want to make the game to be hot. I say, "Today I am going to beat you! Because last time, your player he beat me." So we make a challenge. As far as twenty rand, forty rand.' There is cooperation between the caddies, he says. 'On the course we make a team. Once you take the bags and go to the tee, you must make sure you work together. But some of the young guys, they are not good caddies because they came later after the training was stopped.' Formal training ended a few years ago. 'And there's no discipline, they don't look after the golfers' property.

'On Mondays, when the club is closed, we caddies have a chance to play.'

Alec refers constantly to the players as 'he', and I wonder if he's ever caddied for women. 'I like to caddie for ladies,' he says, 'but here in Killarney are very few. The ladies I caddied for, now they're not playing any more. But I used to caddie for them. They play differently,' he confirms. 'The ladies don't miss the fairway, not like the men, because the men want to hit the ball very very far. The ladies hit to the fairway.

'After I was here one year, they used to bring me young children, to teach them how to play. From five to seven years of age. Hooo, that was a big job!' he recalls. 'The main problem is, you put them in line, and then one by one they hit the ball. But everybody wants to hit the front ball. So you must stop them and say, "No, your ball is there." You must relax and speak softly to them, quietly. But one, two, three, they want to hit the ball. Everybody wants to reach the green.'

He came to Joburg in 1981 from Sekhukhune in Mpumalanga, where his wife and son still live. 'And then I was trying to write matric. But the main problem, when I was working in stores, was no time to read. So I was getting one, one, one subject.' Now, at fifty-three, he is registered with Damelin College and trying again. 'I have finished my languages – English, and my mother tongue Sepedi, and Afrikaans. Now I am doing geography, maths, and biology. Maths is very difficult, because I need help. I need to go for lessons, but the main problem again is time, because if you are caddying you have to arrive here early in the morning. In summer at five o'clock, and winter half past five.' He wakes up at four o'clock to get a taxi from Berea where he lives.

When he had a permanent job, he says, he also used to play chess. 'In Joubert Park. Before '94, people touring South Africa used to come there. I met people from Australia, Italy, United States of America, Russia. But I left the chess when I started to work here in '98. Because Saturday and Sunday I am here. It's only Monday I have off.'

Does he ever plays chess at home with his friends? 'My friends, where I stay, it's mostly foreigners,' he says, 'they don't know about chess. One is Ndebele, from Zimbabwe, and Shonas, and one from Congo, and one from Malawi.' I wonder what his thoughts were about the xenophobic attacks last year. 'We heard about it a month before,' he says, 'that it's going to happen. Here, from the caddies. Because we come from different places. Some from Tembisa, Alex, Soweto. So I told my friends, "Next month, there are rumours, there's going to be this xenophobia."

'They said the people are going to attack the outside people. So we asked them, "Why?" They said, "No, the people is too much here in South Africa. They're taking the jobs. And some are taking the ladies. And some are stealing." So we are saying, "But it's unfair," because we know it is cheap labour. But attacking... You know, it's better to talk with them. Because we told them, "If you attack them... Some of them, the children are our sisters. Some of them are our friends. So how are we going to look at each other?" But it was coming little bit little bit little bit. We were talking about it, talking about it, until it erupted.

'Some of the caddies were happy about it, and others not. It was fifty-fifty. We had big arguments. In the end we said, we shall see. Some did not see the consequences of the thing. So we warned our friends, "If you visit that side, this is going to happen. They're going to treat you very badly."'

There are no foreign nationals working as caddies at Killarney. There are also no women. And no white caddies, seeming to illustrate Jeremy Cronin's observation that wealth has been deracialised but poverty has not. The caddie master selects the caddies, and 'most of the people who are caddying here, their mothers come from Limpopo,' says Alec. 'At Wanderers golf course most of the caddies come from Natal. The courses have got tribalism. It is not a good thing, we must know each other.

'If you have got tribalism, when you clash, it is not a good thing. Because when you are mixed, when you solve something, you can solve it easier. If you are from different tribes, another one is coming with a different idea. But if you are somebody's cousin, his uncle, it's too much. Then if you say, "You made a mistake", he can say, "Ah, you don't like me", or "You don't like my uncle." But if you're just together because of the job, then there's less problems.'

Though it takes up most of his time, caddying is not a reliable job. 'I'm just trying to make a budget to live, but you cannot. Because sometimes you can carry early in the morning and again in the afternoon, and you can make good money. And then the next day you expect to make the same money, and you're going down. Sometimes it rains. It's just like that, rough, going up and down.' He says he earns approximately three thousand rand per month.

'Some of the regulars, they phone. But most of the time we are just coming in the morning and hoping we are going to get a bag. Thursday is members' day, so then you know that you are going to get a bag. It's only members' day and the weekend when you can be sure you're going to carry.' There is a minimum fee of a hundred rand, but most members, he says, pay a little more. On average he earns around a hundred and twenty rand a game.

'The main problems we meet is with the guests, the people who just come here for the corporate days. The Chinese people do not want to pay. The Chinese and the Indians. But the black people who come from America is one of the best. When they come here they treat you well.'

And the racial make-up of the club? 'In about '98 and '99 there were a lot of black members here, but now they've run away, there's very few.'

Alec has a philosophy on this: 'I think it's still running in the heads of people, whites and blacks,' he says, 'we have to be trained to live a social life. Here in South Africa we still don't know about that, because if you come to play at the golf course, if you play together you make friends. If you come here and you are a black alone, you have to join the white men, and if you are white you join the black ones. And then you're going to talk about business, about life. But here they are still divided. You find that the blacks always play together, the whites play together.'

He says he's learned a lot on the golf course. 'I'm learning how business is run. The way the economic situation is going up and down. I know what is happening outside.'

For Life

'I've always walked, my whole life,' says Sandra. 'My father is eighty-seven, and he's a walker of note. Because he's old now, and he's alone, he'll get himself to a shopping mall and walk there. He couldn't walk in the streets now, he's afraid and quite frail. But I can remember when I was a child always running to keep up with him because he used to walk so fast. He had a little business in the centre of Joburg, in the city centre, and I used to walk from school, at End Street Convent, to his office.'

Accustomed to seeing her at the bookshop where she works, I was surprised to bump into her power walking through my neighbourhood one evening. No time to stop and chat then, when I catch up with her she tells me it's been eight years that she's been a member of Walk for Life.

'I joined when we were living in Bedfordview, and I absolutely loved it. I did it for about two and a half months, and then I said to my husband, "You've got to join me." And he said, "No, I'm not interested." And I said, "Well, come once or twice, and if you hate it I won't say another word." And he came and he loved it. Primarily because he walks with a whole group of ladies and all they do is chat about food!

'You get into groups with like-minded people. It also depends on how fit you are and how fast you walk. The fast walkers don't really have time for all this chattering and stuff. They get on and walk.

'When we moved from Bedfordview I joined the Norwood group, and they were sweet and all that, but a little too elderly and slow, and then I moved to the Melrose group just around the corner from where I live. And it's great, I love it.'

Her husband Jerry still walks in Bedfordview because he works close by. 'The little Bedfordview group is very friendly, they're mainly ladies, and they started having "come over for lunch on Sunday" every six months or so. And whenever they get together they always invite my husband, he's the only man from the group who gets invited. He's always giving them advice. A few of them live alone, and if something breaks he tells them how to fix it.'

Sociologist Maureen Stone, who grew up in Barbados and has lived in England for the past thirty years, describes the classic opening line in walking groups: 'Have you been walking long?' Her response: 'Ever since I stopped crawling!' She goes on to point out that 'walking away from war zones in Sudan, Zaire or Rwanda, or to the well to get water, is part of Africa's daily life'.

But in the suburbs, walking has become dissociated from life. 'I think particularly in a big city,' says Sandra, 'and particularly if you're a white South African, walking is almost an alien thing. I know that often when I used to walk on my own, people, particularly young black guys, would say "Marching along on your own" and things like that. And I never thought about it like that. I used to do it because I enjoyed it. I'd go walking early in the morning, or at dusk, it never worried me.'

I recall an incident when I was walking in Sandra's neighbourhood on a Sunday afternoon, a young black man walking behind me stepped off the very wide pavement on which we were the only pedestrians, to pass me. As though, fearing that I would fear him, he took steps to avoid that situation. It was a disturbing and saddening moment for me.

'When I first started bringing a bag and changing into my walking stuff at work,' Sandra picks up, 'my colleagues said, "What are you doing? Are you actually going to walk in the street for exercise? Why don't you just join a gym or something?" To walk on a treadmill. I find it fascinating.

'It wasn't about the environment changing, or becoming less safe, that made me join the group, because that's never worried me. A friend spurred me on and said, "Join with me." I used to go to a gym, but I hate gyms. I think gyms are quite unpleasant for a lot of people. It's sort of, "Look at me, here I am." The body-beautiful thing. For walking you throw on an old tracksuit top, a pair of decent walking shoes, and off you go. No one cares what you're wearing.' And at the gym there are the mirrors. 'I mean who wants to see all that?' Sandra laughs.

'I thought, if you join a group activity you're more likely to stick to it. Because the friend and I that used to walk together, we'd phone each other and say, "Listen, let's not walk, let's have a glass of wine instead." So joining a walking group was the solution to an arrangement that was going the way of many book clubs.

'Now, at Melrose, someone I walked with for years in Bedfordview has moved, and she's joined me. And we chat in such an undemanding way that it doesn't actually worry me. There's this understanding, I think it's a Walk for Life thing, that if you don't want to talk you just don't, and nobody pressurises you. There's a culture. They say, if you want to go ahead, just go. So you don't feel that inhibition and a need to socialise. Although there is a social element, and I think that's a positive thing because it makes you want to go.

'It's fascinating, people will tell you the most astonishing, intimate things. I'm interested in how these natural groups form. You have certain people who will always walk together. The speed of walking is definitely an element. You get the very serious walkers. And then you get the people who have come along just for the social element, and they don't usually last, because you've got to exercise as well as chat!

'In our Melrose group we've got the active walkers, and the runners, and then the old people who come along and just do two Ks and they get tired and they go home. But they come, you know. There's a couple, he's about seventy-eight and she's about seventy-six, and they walk and it's great. I think it gives them a bit of human contact as well.' I assume she's referring to a couple who are together, but 'No, they're not. We're eyeing them a little, because he fetches her now! The youngest in our group is around mid-twenties. For most people walking in a group is about safety.

'It's nice, you know,' she reflects, 'because if you think about it, the art of conversation, just chatting, is dwindling. People don't really do it any more.' These days we 'text' each other.

James Hillman, in his book *We've Had a Hundred Years of Psychotherapy and the World's Getting Worse*, points out that conversation and walking have a lot in common. 'The word means turning around with, going back, like reversing, and it comes supposedly from walking back and forth with someone or something, turning and going over the same ground from the reverse direction.'

'We go twice a week and walk about eight Ks an evening,' says Sandra. 'For me, I do it for the exercise. I could do without the social contact, but the people are nice. And I like exploring where I live as well. I like to see what's going on. There's a complete difference between driving through an area and walking through an area, you have such a different sense of it.'

Given the speed at which she walks, will she ever progress to running? She doesn't see it as progress, she says. 'I don't like running, I don't believe it's healthy – all that jolting of the skeleton. You use a totally different set of muscles, it's a different style.'

Passing a pavement book sale, I come across a copy of *Walking and Light Running*. 'Light running'? – it calls to mind 'light housework' – I imagine dusting, but no scrubbing. The back cover of the book tells me that I'll learn the difference between 'Nordic walking' – walking with poles: a 'summer variant' in Scandinavia of cross-country skiing – 'power walking' and 'light running'.

In the fast lane things get more serious. The challenges are less about predators you might run into on the street and more about the limits of your own body. Running is not for the fainthearted, or the weak-at-the-knees.

Russel was a Run for Life person. 'Unless you're an experienced runner,' he tells me, 'you've got to start off with walking. Part of that's indemnity – you've got to sign something. If you say, "No don't worry", and then you have a heart attack and die, they'll go: "What happened? Didn't you check him out"! You're meant to come with a doctor's certificate: cholesterol and heart. And then if you're not sure, they'll start you with walking. They put you on a field. And you start walking round the field, and you're not allowed to run until you've walked five kilometres in a certain time. You've got a clock so you can see how fast you're going at the end of every lap. They say, "Do it at your own pace." But some of those walkers walk faster than runners. You know, like the Olympics, where the heel's hardly lifted, like they're sliding along. They try and get you to walk a bit faster so you can get your heart rate up.

'And then I got a bit bored with the walkers, because they walk and they chat and they chat. Although I met some really interesting people – doctors and lawyers, people who I'd never get to meet otherwise.

'Then eventually you walk half a lap, run half a lap. And then when you can run five kilometres, they literally open the gates and release you onto the streets. When I was at my fittest I was running five kilometres in about twenty-three minutes. Road running. And I was doing the competition runs.' But he says he hates running. 'My knees are giving in. I picked up a little knee injury and it's never really gone away.

'I started off doing it because I was going through a midlife crisis, and I wanted to lose weight and get fit. That was pre-iPod days. When I run I do it with music, otherwise I start thinking about it too much. I have very obscure tastes – women vocal, jazz.' I hear Diana Krall in my head and can't imagine a running rhythm. 'No no, Diana Krall is too morbid!' he sets me straight.

'Ella Fitzgerald?' 'Noooo. Maybe jaz-zy is a better description. Missy Higgins, an Australian singer, absolutely wonderful.' I've never heard of her. 'Sara Bareilless. A woman called Adele, who I've discovered recently.'

His 14-year-old son has taught him the tricks of downloading music from the Internet. 'I'm on the iTunes store. I can buy stuff on iTunes – as opposed to stealing it off of some Russian site,' he makes sure I understand. 'These women are about nineteen or twenty and some of them write the most extraordinary lyrics. I'm very big on lyrics.' Rather than the chit-chat of the walkers, he prefers the young women's voices in his head. I think he'll like the deceptively sweet-voiced, irreverent Nellie McKay and her album *Get Away from Me* – an antidote to Norah Jones's *Come Away with Me*: 'I wanna get married / Yes I need a spouse / I wanna nice leave it to beaver-ish / golden retriever / and a little white house …'

'I bought a new pair of shoes,' Russel says. 'I'm thinking of starting again.'

293

Guiding Eyes

From time to time around my neighbourhood I see people in blindfolds being led by beautiful dogs. 'Norwood is a very nice training area,' Pieter explains. 'You've got pavements, but you've got lots of activity on your pavements, little cafés and coffee shops, and obstacles, moving obstacles.' Pieter works for the South African Guide-Dogs Association for the Blind, and has been blind since birth.

'I've been legally blind since birth, I met the definition, but I had a bit of sight as a child,' he elaborates, 'very partially, that started deteriorating at a very young age. I can still remember things like colours and basic outlines. The shape of a tree.' Blind poet Stephen Kuusisto describes this, when speaking of his own situation, 'like a person who looks through a kaleidoscope ... at once beautiful and largely useless.'

'Now I can distinguish between night and day,' says Pieter, 'but that's also going.'

As a child of the South African pre-television radio generation, I try and imagine life as a radio play. 'We're all blind on the radio,' said presenter Jean Feraca. But there are very real obstacles to navigate around out in the world.

Pieter was twenty-three when he got his first guide-dog. 'It didn't really occur to me to get a dog before that. I was a student, in the Eighties, studying Industrial Psychology at what is now the

University of Johannesburg. I'd heard about guide-dogs – I used a cane. It wasn't a friendly campus for a blind person to get around on. I was living about a kilometre away in a res in Auckland Park, and it wasn't the easiest route to get to campus, because you had to cross a very open area that used to be part of a golf course, which is difficult because you don't have any sound reflection, because it's a wide open space.'

Getting a dog changed his life. 'It increased my mobility vastly. Because I was withdrawn at the time. I wanted to be on my own, doing my own thing, wanted to be independent. I shied away from people. I didn't want to be part of big groups. And what I started realising is that, in general, there's a barrier between a disabled person and a more able-bodied person. In the sense that people are hesitant to make contact with the disabled person, because they don't want to offend, they don't want to say the wrong thing, they don't know what to do. Whether the person needs assistance, and to what degree they need assistance. So to avoid all of that a lot of people don't make contact. And the dog is an ice breaker. Because people can totally ignore the disability, and they say, "Oh, what a beautiful dog", and within no time you're having a conversation.'

The training process for and with a guide-dog is a rigorous one. 'First we do what we call puppy raising – basically a family will adopt a little puppy at about seven weeks, and raise it up till about a year. And the aim during that time is obviously socialising the pup, so it can have interaction with other people. The busier the family the better – if there's a mom and a dad and kids and pets and birds, it's actually better stimulation for the pup.

'Then the dogs come back to the training centre and they undergo about six months' intensive training, and it's at that stage that you'll see them here in Norwood. If you see someone wearing a blindfold it's usually an instructor doing the final testing of the dog. They need to be blind for that purpose. And then the dog gets allocated to a blind person, they get matched up. Is the person a fast walker or slow walker?, for example. And the personality of the dog – is it better for an introvert or an extrovert?

'Any person wanting a dog must have a certain level of independence, or mobility; preferably be able to use the long cane. And then you get matched tentatively with a dog. Then once they know who has been matched with who, the blind people go to live at the centre for about three weeks – there's a lot of walking during that time – and they get trained to become the trainer of their own dog. They're given the ropes.'

Kuusisto describes training with a guide-dog as 'boot camp' or 'canine kibbutz'. 'Ja,' Pieter laughs, 'it doesn't sound like a lot, but eight people and eight dogs on one bus and in one dining room… You can imagine, you have to be able to compromise.' He feels the rim of his cup as he pours milk into his coffee.

O'Reilly, a Golden Retriever, has been lying quite still between our feet under the table since we began talking, and – usually a little nervous of strange dogs – I'm astounded by his discipline and gentle nature. 'We have to make a very distinct difference between guiding and guarding,' says Pieter, 'because it will take just one guide-dog to bite somebody in a public situation, and that will be our reputation down the drain, so it's very important that the dogs are friendly and nonaggressive.'

A few years ago, as I was boarding a bus, a man sitting in front with a Labrador sensed my apprehension and he said, 'Don't worry, she won't hurt you.' Only as I got closer, and saw her harness, did I realise that he was blind. I sat with them and we chatted until they reached their stop. She was my first experience of a guide-dog. 'Golden Retrievers and Labradors are the predominant dogs that are used for guide-dogs,' Pieter confirms. 'They're very gentle souls.'

I had been under the impression that most guide-dogs were female. 'If you look at the ratio in the world, you apparently have more female guide-dogs than males. For a few good reasons. They're smaller, you can fit them in smaller places, especially when you're travelling. They're not inclined to be that boisterous and dominant, and also they have cleaner hygiene and habits.

'Lots of people will say, are they more intelligent? I suppose so,' he reflects, and then he adds: 'I always say, let's say females are more intelligent, but us as males know they train so well.' He laughs when I tell him maybe that's what women like men to believe, then they go ahead and do their own thing.

In his book *Eavesdropping*, Kuusisto recalls overhearing a conversation with some children. 'They were asking their father how the dog knows what I'm thinking.' They thought the dog was psychic. But in reality, the dog's behaviour is closer to what he describes as 'intelligent disobedience'.

'At a traffic intersection,' Pieter explains, 'you often have a lot of noise. And with newer cars, later model cars, it's hard to hear the engine above that noise. So the dog is taught that in a danger zone, if the owner makes a wrong decision about crossing the road, the dog will disobey the command and wait for the car to go past. It will just stay until the danger has passed.'

It strikes me that, drawing a distinction between guiding and guarding notwithstanding, the dog's natural instincts will probably kick in if Pieter is under threat from predators, and he is probably safer on the streets than a sighted person without a dog. 'That's possible,' he says, 'but I think the main thing is that the dog serves as a deterrent. The average person on the street doesn't realise we actually use very placid and docile dogs. To him it's a dog, it's got teeth, it can bite. So he's unlikely to try anything.' In twenty-two years of walking alone with a dog he has not had any experiences of violence.

Ironically, he probably walks more than the average middle-class Joburger. Apart from helping him get where he needs to go, as he says, 'You have to walk the dog. I walk an average of two to three kilometres a day. If I'm just taking the dog out for a walk I'll walk at least one or two kilometres; about forty-five minutes. In Alberton, where I live on the East Rand, and the older areas like Kensington, you still have paved pavements, so it's a lot easier there. In the newer and more modern suburbs you have grass verges and landscaped gardens, and lots of trees and rubble. It makes it difficult. Walking through grass verges is what we call country walks, where you have to walk in the road, on the shoulder of the road next to the pavement.' And, while modern suburbs aspire to aspects of being in the countryside, there is more traffic than on real country roads. 'A busy country road is quite a dangerous thing,' says Pieter.

'In our training with the Association, we go to different areas for different types of experiences: like Norwood, Parkview around the Zoo, and Louis Botha Avenue in Orange Grove. The Association bought a house in Norwood about ten years ago to take care of the instructors' needs. They use it as a halfway house, because it's much easier to drive from here to the different areas for training than to drive out all the way from Bryanston, where the offices are, and go back for lunch, and then drive out again.

Louis Botha Avenue, where a constant stream of minibuses zip along the narrow road between the inner city and Alexandra township all day long and late into the night, with its cacophony of hooters competing for customers, is considered by most drivers to be taxi hell, and is hair-raising even for pedestrians with all their senses available. There are frequent accidents. 'It's not easy,' Pieter agrees, 'but it's a wonderful area for training. You've got the taxis, vendors on the road, traffic noise, buses, lorries… We used to go into the inner city before, for that sort of training, but the inner city is just too dangerous now in certain parts. And then we moved to Braamfontein, but now Braamfontein has been dug up in many places because of all the Gautrain and BRT works.

'In Louis Botha you've also got lots of little shops. Usually about 90 per cent of what you take in from your environment you do by sight. But we make use of smells. You've got your pharmacy, that smells totally different from any other shop – clinical, a cleaning, medicinal smell. The hairdresser, another distinct smell. The grocery shop, a mixture of Cold Water Omo and all sorts of things that smell nice mixed with vegetable smells that's a little bit off. And meat, the butchery. The shoe shop, you distinctly smell leather. The hardware shop. The café on the corner, an old-oil chip smell. So you get a lot of information about exactly where you are. If you're unsure you'll go to a point of contact and start feeling your way around.

'And sound reflection, your hearing is vitally important. For instance when you walk across the opening of an arcade, you will most likely find a draught coming through that's carrying smells as well. Either a draught towards you, or a draught into the arcade. The sound from the traffic and the noises around you disappear into that opening. It doesn't reflect up against the wall and back at you. You will hear the opening.

'The same with trees, you hear the noises of the leaves blowing in the wind. And if you concentrate you can hear lamp posts when you're walking.' I struggle to imagine hearing a lamp post. 'Well, you'll hear that it's totally open next to you, and then you'll hear a break in the openness, and then it's open again. Especially when you're walking down a street with a lot of noise. You'll hear a car going past you with no interruption of the sound coming towards you, but if there's a lamp post between you and the car you'll hear a difference in the sound.'

He elaborates on his earlier experience of walking to university. 'When you walk across a field you don't have sound reflection, the wind doesn't whisper any sounds to you because there are no trees or anything, so you can easily lose your direction. This is when a dog is so helpful.

'The traffic has increased vastly in recent years, so you have to be much more careful than you had to be twenty years ago when I started with a guide-dog. Then, your bigger intersections, like around Kingsway in Auckland Park – with slipways and whatever – they weren't a problem. But nowadays, with the volume of traffic, it's creating quite a problem. You have to be on your guard all the time.

'You need to have confidence about what you're doing, your self-assertiveness, otherwise the dog will experience that you're unsure, you're uncertain, and that will have a negative effect on his work, his concentration, as well. You need to be in control at all times, and believe that you've made the right decision. Although the dog is there in the high-traffic-volume situation to warn you.

'You develop a very close relationship with the dog,' Pieter reflects. 'They have their status as a pet as well. When I get home in the afternoon and take off his harness, he's totally free. He's just another member of the family. He becomes a friend. He's your working companion, your confidant – because often you'll share your happiness and your sadness with your dog, you'll tell him about what's happened in your day. Or he'll know about it, he was there.'

But given the duration of dog years, seven to one human year, it is expected that an owner will outlive a dog, and a blind person is likely to have many guide-dogs in a lifetime. Unlike a child, who will more than likely love on after we are gone, dogs remind us of our own mortality. I imagine it must be very difficult knowing from the start of the relationship that your dog will almost certainly die before you do.

'Once it comes to the stage where he can't fill the role of a guide-dog any more,' says Pieter, 'that's a difficult decision to make. Ideally it's best when you can keep your dog as a pet. Some people don't always want to replace their dogs, for various reasons, for emotional reasons. In my case my mobility and independence are always of primary importance to me.'

O'Reilly is Pieter's fifth dog. 'We just recently finished our training together. He is slowly but surely starting to find a place in my heart, but my other one, Ronnie, is still very special.'

'A new dog never replaces an old dog,' Erica Jong wrote, 'it merely expands the heart.'

'Two years ago, before O'Reilly, I trained with Thornton,' says Pieter, 'a Labrador who unfortunately had to be withdrawn because of some aggression to little ones. But his predecessor, Ronnie, also a Golden Retriever, he retired early because of a little left-tendency that he developed, which became a bit worrying in a traffic situation, and he's still with us at home.

'In the beginning, when Ronnie was replaced, he went through quite a serious depression. In his mind he's still my guide-dog, because whenever we walk, my wife and I and our three dogs, Ronnie is happy when he's in front, because he's leading the way. To him it doesn't matter if he's guiding me, as long as he's leading the way. If he's walking behind he goes berserk. He pulls and pants and strangles himself on the lead.

'Since my wife started running her office from home he's in his element again, because he's got company during the daytime, there are people in and out. And he feels important in a different way. He's still not aggressive but he's now the leader of the house. When we're not there he'll run to the gate and start barking just to make it publicly known when there's somebody in the street. He makes sure that you know somebody is about to enter your space.'

Tracy, Pieter's 11-year-old daughter, 'has a real passion for her dog friends at home, that's what she calls them. When she was smaller, and Ronnie was my only dog – she was about four when I got him – she used to call him her brother. And then once Ronnie went into retirement he basically became her dog. She moved his mattress into her room.'

As a child, Pieter started school in Pretoria, at the Prinshof School, and then transferred to the Pioneer School in Worcester. Within the layers of marginalisation in South Africa, where literacy levels are generally low, among the blind they drop way down. 'Fewer than 2 per cent of the blind in South Africa are able to read Braille. Very few have the privilege to go to schools for the blind.' And while the unemployment rate in the country sits at around 40 per cent, about 95 per cent of the blind are unemployed. In the United States the figure is around 70 per cent.

'There are about four hundred working guide-dogs in the

country,' says Pieter, 'and over a million blind people in the country. Johannesburg used to have the only training centre until about two years ago, but recently a satellite training facility was opened in Cape Town, where they can accommodate three students at a time.'

I comment on O'Reilly, still lying absolutely still at our feet. 'You should see him at the end of the day, when I take off the harness,' Pieter laughs, 'he's a completely different dog!'

When we finish our conversation, Pieter is on his way to talk at a school nearby. One of the more interesting questions he's been asked by a small child, he says, was: 'How does the dog know how to drive the car?'

When the Meter is Off

Over the past few years a familiar sight to me has been Bongi parked opposite Obed's guard hut outside the entrance to the complex in which I live. As more and more middle-class Joburgers live in complexes, the term becomes a fitting metaphor for being in this city. These are two of the people with whom my life intersects who make it safer, but who live in and come from different worlds from mine.

At times when the minibus taxis don't take the route I need to travel, or they're on strike, or it's a ridiculous distance to walk, or after dark, I call Bongi and he is always reliable, always on time. At some point I moved from the backseat into the front, and we compare radio stations and talk about our lives.

Bongi came to Joburg from Geluksburg (Luck's Mountain), a rural village in the Drakensberg close to Ladysmith in KwaZulu-Natal, to find work in 1996. He was twenty-one years old. 'At first I was working in a warehouse for these big shops, supermarkets, in the south of Joburg, and Aaron,' his cousin, 'told me, "No man, there's not much money there, come this side." I was using his car for about one and a half years before I managed to accumulate money to buy my own car. It was good at that time, but now it is tough. When I arrived in this business we were busy, you didn't wait for a long time for customers, but now the price is going up and up and up, and it's becoming more difficult. Now we are

303

waiting a lot of hours. Out of eight hours of working it's about six hours of waiting. You just go out, you come back, you sit, talk with other drivers. The business is not good.

'Long time ago, I remember if you got someone who is going to Pretoria… Let's say you drop someone in Pretoria by eight o'clock, maybe you have to pick up that person around two or three o'clock, it was easy that time. You drop that person and you come back and you work here. But today, if you go to Pretoria there's no need to come back. Because you can come back and maybe you will have only one pick-up, sometimes nothing, and then you have to fetch that distant person in Pretoria again. So the best way is, when you get there in Pretoria, just to wait for the person.'

Widespread roadworks are also slowing things down. 'Jaaa,' Bongi nods. 'It was easy about four years back. It took just over thirty minutes, but now it's more than an hour. Even when there is no construction on the road, the traffic is growing very bad. In the pick-up hours, rush hour, it is much worse. If someone must be in Pretoria at nine we have to leave around six, when the traffic is less, if you want to be sure to be on time. Because if you leave around eight you are going to waste a lot of time in the traffic.'

The market for metered taxis has become saturated, there are too many cars and not enough passengers, and the situation is worsening as taxi companies keep pushing prices up to unaffordable levels, losing some of the business they do have, as fewer people are able to use them with any regularity. 'If someone is stuck,' says Bongi, 'or rushing to somewhere and they don't have a choice, then yes, but for someone who has the time and alternative…' Apart from tourists, those who might be able to afford to use taxis generally have their own cars. The only taxi drivers making any money now are the ones based around the exclusive hotels in Sandton, with prices to match the expensive cars they are required to have.

Though Bongi works for himself and not for an official taxi company, so he can adjust his prices as he chooses, he can only really do this with regular customers. When it comes to pick-ups he can't undercut the prices of his fellow drivers at the place where they park together, near the university in Braamfontein, without causing tensions.

Since he spends so many hours a day in the car, I ask Bongi if he ever walks. In Joburg, in Soweto where he lives, he says no, 'the problem is the time,' but when he goes home to his village he loves to walk. 'There's open space on the side because there's farms and mountains. And sometimes there is no alternative. I remember about three years back I had to walk from six to six, from the morning until the sun set, because in some places there is nowhere to drive, unless you can use a horse. I have an uncle there, and I had to visit him. And if you want to go there you can drive but sometimes the road is not good, it's a dust road and it's very shaky on the car. And to walk there is an easy thing. It is a bit far, but it was good for me because to walk is good exercise.

'Last time when I went to home I had to try to get the goats. The secret of the goats is that they move against the direction of the wind, so the wind is pushing them. And they can walk from morning until sunset, not getting anywhere. So you need to turn them around.

'I realised something, when I am at home now I am getting tired, because I'm not used to walking here. If I walk a lot today, then the following day I will get some cramps, that is what I notice. Because when I was looking for the goats I didn't even get them, I only got them after a whole day, they were so far away. We have to bring the cattle and horses and goats in around five o'clock, but when you realise there are no goats, then it means you'll only get them the following day. You try to find them but it's getting dark, so you have to leave the following day early in the morning and bring them down.'

I imagine long walks must have started for him when he had to get to school as a small boy. 'Because I was born on the farm,' he explains, 'and the school was far, you had to wait until you were a little bit older to go to school, maybe ten years old. So my mum decided to take me to live with Aaron's family, because the school was very close there, about a ten-minute walk. Then when I went to Standard Four I went to the school on the farm and we had to walk, and that was a bit far. If you left home about seven you reached school at nine.'

Though he got his driver's license at nineteen, he started driving when he was about twelve years old. 'We used to drive to fetch wood from the mountain, cut wood, bring it home. We learned to drive on the tractor.'

Geluksburg is described online as an 'isolated mountain getaway' with 'many paths for mountain walks'. Someone advises: 'Don't go there unless you have a 4x4' and tells us about '2 things in Geluksburg: no crime and no Internet'. It's easy to be romantic about the countryside – where poverty is escalating – when you have a job in the city to drive back to in the 4x4. Still, I find it hard to imagine leaving this peaceful place to drive all day and night in the streets of Joburg. Bongi is philosophical about it. 'I realised the people who are born in the rural areas, when they come to the city they are more successful than the people who are born in the city, because you can live a good life there. If you are coming from that side you have more advantages. You are more prepared for life.'

The youngest of four siblings, 'when we grew at home we used to play a lot. We were not used to sitting in front of the TV and those things, we used to swim in the river, ride horses. We used to ride the cows also,' he laughs, 'the baby cows. In Zulu we call it *amathole*. You know, when the cow is reaching the stage of being independent from mum. They are jumping, you can't even stay two minutes on top.'

These days, with end of year holidays and a few other visits during the year, Bongi spends about two months of the year at home. 'I miss it,' he says, 'especially in summer when it is raining. You can feel, even the clouds is very close, you can feel that fresh air. It's not like here in Joburg – Joburg is crazy. Sometimes there you see a car passing, and then you don't see another car for hours, it's very quiet. I can go to sleep at eight o'clock and wake up around six o'clock the following day. You hear nothing during the night, which is great because I don't like noise.

'If you grow up here in the urban areas, there's no work so much,' he says. I'm a bit confused, since he came to Joburg to find work, and then I realise what he's referring to is not employment but the need to work, understanding a work ethic. 'Like the kids who are growing up in Soweto, they don't do anything, they just go to school, come back, play ball, sleeping, eating… but if you are growing up in the rural areas there is a lot of work – girls work and boys work. You need to milk the cows in the morning, you need to fetch the cattle in the evening. If it is the time for cultivating, you need to drive the *span* with the cattle or the tractor to cultivate the land. My father liked to use oxes, and it's a bit of work to do, especially if the temperature is high. So you learn a lot of things there at home. Even my elder sister can drive the tractor.'

Returning to my original question, 'Walking is very good,' he says, 'because you have to use a different energy. When you reach a hill you must put more energy, the hard bit is going to increase. And when you reach the top of the hill it's great, because you have the view. You view things down. In summertime the mountains are looking nice, and in some places you have a lot of perfume. You can feel the breeze up there in the mountains, the sea breeze from Durban. I like to walk with the dogs also. I like animals. When I was staying at home fulltime I was not scared to hold the snake, but now I'm scared.'

He has not escaped being a crime statistic. The Joburg driver's reflex of locking the car's doors when you get into the vehicle has a twist as a taxi driver, when you have to weigh up whether you're more at risk from the people outside or inside the car. 'Because when you take people you don't know, you mustn't lock the door. They can put you in trouble.' For Bongi the trouble came on the 1st of May, Workers' Day, in 2006. He feels he needs to take some responsibility for it and has come to the conclusion that 'I made a blind choice that time, it was a bad day on my side. Because God can try to save you, but if you don't listen to your consciousness it can be a problem,' he says, echoing the Sufi proverb about the need to tie up your camel.

'It was a long weekend, and there was a music concert here at Johannesburg Stadium, near Bertrams. When I passed, there were plenty people, and the police they don't allow you to park. So I was driving down, and there was someone on the opposite side of the road waving for me, so I made a U-turn. Then he was trying to call other people, so in the meantime I made another pick-up, a guy just jumped in the car, I think he was a student from Wits and I took him to Yeoville. Then I came back, and there was that guy from before still standing there, and he asked me to take them to Houghton. But I made a stupid action, because there were other taxis around, so why was he still there? So I was a good target for him. He was a middle-aged man looking very smart. And then I picked him up with his colleagues, or whatever you can call them, and on the way they were using a cellphone, SMSing.

'We were driving along Central Street in Houghton, they asked me to turn on the third street, and then I realised there was something going on, but the place was very quiet so I didn't do anything about it. And then we drove, and when we reached the spot – it was a T-junction – this guy that was in front, he ordered the people who were at the back to hold me. The one who was at the back was having a gun, and then the one who was behind me, he held me like this,' he demonstrates, as though pulling his head against the headrest. 'But I think they made a mistake because the car was still moving, about forty kilometres per hour. And then I lost control, so when the car hit the pole, with that impact I managed to open the door and jump out.

'It was around 9 p.m. And when I went out of the car there was a guy who was standing in the trees and he just jumped out of the trees and into the car and they drove away. So this must be the guy they were SMSing.' Much like it is hard to remember life before cellphones, it's hard to imagine how criminals operated without them. Thankfully Bongi still had his phone so he could call his cousin to fetch him. 'It was a very sharp thing, the time, when they do this hijacking it takes less than ten seconds.'

Like most South Africans, who talk about crime as if it is normal, Bongi is pragmatic and still willing to see the best in people. 'Maybe it was not bad criminals,' he says, 'because I lost my ID, but when I checked everything, like Home Affairs and even the banks, they didn't do anything like fraud on my ID. I think they just threw it in the dustbin. But it was very difficult that time.'

Amazingly his car was found nine days later, in Alexandra, but he decided not to take a chance with it. 'It was working okay, but in the engine there was a lot of oil, and the inside of the car was very dirty. Then I sold it, because sometimes it's bringing the bad memory. Another thing, when these people steal the car they make high revving, and when you rev the engine too much it spins over, and it starts knocking after some time.'

Weighing up the economic situation with safety precautions, he says, 'Regular customers is what we have now, rather than to pick up anyone that you don't know, maybe you can get about two passengers like that during the day. In the day there is no problem, then we can pick up people. Another thing that is very important is to know where the people are going to. For instance, if you work at night it's not wise to take someone who is going to Vereeniging,' south of Joburg, 'it's more dangerous because it is far and the road is very quiet, because once you pass Southgate Shopping Centre the road is becoming small and it is very dark. The guys who are picking up people at night and taking them to Vereeniging, sometimes they are not coming back.

'Even here, the local fares to Yeoville and Bertrams, the streets are very quiet, so it's important to know exactly where the person is going to, which street, because sometimes these guys mention any street. For example in Melville, they use numbers instead of names for the streets, avenues. And if you get someone who is saying, "I'm going to Andries Street in Melville", you can see that person is taking chances. At night you can't take more than one man. Because the one who's going to give you trouble is the one in the back seat.

'In many cases they are using other cars. Let's say you are parking here, they will drive, and then they will pass and drop one person in front who will come and ask for the taxi. You can't see that because the town is busy. And then they will follow you until you reach that spot where they are doing the hijacking.'

Bongi is eager to move back home. 'I am interested in finding another business,' he says. 'I was trying to do the research. I tried to look around in Ladysmith, to see which business is required. I was willing to open a driving school, but when I got there I realised this business is overcrowded. But on cars, I realised that in Ladysmith if you are driving a car that is not a Toyota, if you've got a breakdown you are in trouble. You can't get the spares.

'The people who are running the business, because they want to make money, they don't want the stock to be on the shelf. They are running the spares like people who are in the food business, like if you order the food now then you need to finish it today. They don't want something that is going to stay on the shelf for a long time. So I said to myself, if I can be able to open a business that can specialise with three brands of cars, that can be good. I remember one year I was having a problem with the car, with a small thing, and then you can't move.'

With Rea Vaya – the Bus Rapid Transit system – and the Gautrain on the way, this is good news for commuters, but not for drivers of taxis of the minibus or metered variety. Business is bound to decrease even further for Bongi and his colleagues. 'It's better for me to find another business,' he says, 'because this one is sinking.'

Half a Continent,
Step by Step

On the 6th of April 1994 the genocide in Rwanda began. Three weeks later the world's attention turned elsewhere, to the 'miracle' happening in South Africa, with its first democratic election, but over a period of three months close to a million people were killed.

Innocent was visiting his aunt in Kigali on that day. He was thirteen years old at the time. He never returned home. They hid in the passage of her house for over a month before fleeing in their car. Eventually there was no space to drive, and his long walk began.

'I walked with my aunt for about a week, there were thousands of people walking, and then in the chaos I got lost and I was on my own, just walking with everybody, millions of people who were trying to leave the country. At one stage you walk in a group of so many people there is no space to walk. Everyone is pushing one another. Then people get tired and they just sit. And others get sick. So the crowd becomes smaller and smaller.'

Along the road he met a school friend who was also lost, and together they walked approximately three hundred kilometres from Kigali to Cyangugu on the border of the Democratic Republic of Congo (then Zaïre), where they stayed with his friend's aunt and uncle for eight months.

When the fighting stopped he decided to return to Kigali to look for his family, but a trader from DRC brought news that his mother was across the border in a refugee camp in Bukavu. He crossed the border by pretending to be the trader's son and was reunited with his mother and two of his brothers. Then he learned that his father had been killed on the first day of the genocide, and three of his six siblings were missing.

'We lived about two years in the camps, and then we were forced to move again. And then there was nowhere to run to.' In 1996 the revolution to remove dictator Mobutu Sésé Seko from power, which he had enjoyed since Patrice Lumumba's assassination three decades earlier, began in Zaïre. Kabila's rebel army attacked the camps, and about thirty-seven thousand refugees fled into the forests. 'So people who were walking away from the war in Rwanda, in the process they were getting killed in the DRC.

'Some people had cars, but a large portion of DRC is jungle, and the roads are not maintained, there's nothing, so those people who are driving are usually driving 4x4s. And because there are so many rivers, most people just drive up to that point and then leave their cars and walk. Whether you walk or you run, you just try to get as far away as possible.'

At fifteen his year-long mostly barefoot walk across the DRC began. 'From the border of Rwanda, from Lake Kivu in DRC, we walked to reach the border of Angola. It's maybe four thousand kilometres. The walk was sort of in a linear way, just walking in one line, following the people in front of you.' The images of refugees that we see on the news. 'Because left or right it's just the jungle, and if you get lost in there it's going to be very difficult to get back. So people stick together.

'The local guys, they've got homes in the jungle, they know short cuts to special places where they do their farming. And then they sell their products in the centres, and those centres are a distance away from one another. So you walk until you reach a commercial centre, if you've got money you've got food. If you don't have money you trade in something, shoes or clothes, a watch. Then that will be your provision for a week. Then you walk you walk you walk… Sometimes you walk for two weeks and there is no centre, the next centre is five hundred kilometres away. And you'll know because you'll meet guys who are coming from there, who went to sell their food there. You ask them, "Where is the next centre?" They tell you, "You're going to reach there by Monday." That's if you're walking fifty kilometres every day. You trade until you have nothing left to trade. By the time you've walked maybe three months you've got nothing.

'The only way to do it is just to survive the next step. If the troops find you they will kill you. So you have to walk. When we started walking it was a huge number of refugees from the camps. Walking, scattering in the bushes. People used to walk till their feet were so big. I saw women with feet as big as…,' he demonstrates the width of a soccer ball. 'Because of the nutrition, because people were eating a lot of bad meat in the jungle, baboons, rats... People got very sick. Even from fresh meat, like pork, maybe it's pigs that were sick, people died. So basically from that time I didn't eat meat, for five years. Just vegetables and fruits, and drink water.'

The water too could make you sick. 'And sometimes we couldn't find water to drink. I saw people drinking water that was like mud.' A bitter irony that some would survive the rebel soldiers and be killed by the water.

And then there were the rivers. 'If you come to a river and you can't cross it, then you have to stop. So the motivating factor was just to get as far away as you can.' This was how he was separated from his mother. 'When we arrived at the Congo River she had to walk back, she couldn't swim. I saw many people drowning. We could swim, but because the river was big there were only a few guys who could swim straight across. It took about two hours to cross.

'By the time we reached the border of Angola we were not more than fifty. When Kabila took power in DRC we were at the border of Angola. I got two kilometres from the border. Some people tried to go into Angola but they couldn't because there was still a war there. So people walked to the point where they couldn't walk any more. And then you decide that you're going to lie in the street. Wait for UN aid or somebody to assist you.'

I find it hard to comprehend walking from one war, through another war, and into another. But the borders become almost irrelevant as the wars bleed into each other. Conflict in the DRC was sparked by the influx of Rwandan refugees. The Rwandan Patriotic Front, which had liberated Rwanda from the genocide, assisted Laurent Kabila to oust Mobutu, who was accommodating many of the perpetrators of the genocide in the refugee camps, living side by side with survivors – the First Congo War. After relations between Kabila and the RPF soured, they supported his overthrow, fuelling the Second Congo War.

'By the time we reached that point, on the border of Angola,' says Innocent, 'I was the youngest, the smallest. It wasn't safe for us to go over the border because Savimbi,' the rebel leader, 'his men thought that the refugees were helping the Angolan government. There were lots of misconceptions. And then when we reached that point – me and two of my close friends, we met in the refugee camp, we walked together, then we separated, then we met again – we decided that we're just going to integrate into the community in Tshikapa. It's one of the richest places in the DRC, with lots of diamonds. And we stayed there for a year.

'When we arrived there, it's like you've got a mark. A refugee was a person who's known to be… He looks different, he's dirty, he's got thick hair, he doesn't have shoes, he steals… But that perception changed within a few months.'

Innocent remembers his first job. Unlike his friends, who were bigger and started earning their living producing charcoal, 'My first job was to sell cold water. That place is very hot. First you have to fetch the water from somewhere far, between a six- and ten-kilometre walk. This twenty-litre basin, you carry that to the village. When you get there you have to start looking for a fridge where you can put it for a while. Then you put the water in small plastic bags, one cup. Then you put the plastic bags in the basin and you walk through the village with the basin shouting *Mayi ya malili*, cold water. You go from A to Z, your customers are big guys who are standing on the street. You sell it for about fifty cents. And you do that for three months.'

He often speaks in the second person, as though remembering another time, another life, another person.

'When Kabila took over in 1997, he had been assisted by many of the troops from Rwanda, then he said all the troops must go back to their countries, and that fuelled the conflict again. Rwanda became the enemy of DRC, and people from Rwanda were considered enemies. And even though in that village people knew we were fleeing from the war, and by that time we could speak the local languages fluently, we just had to make the decision that we have to leave DRC. By that time we had a little bit of money, and we couldn't go through Angola, so we had to go to Zambia, which was a long distance. We took a train. It took about two months.

'Then I met a guy from DRC in Zambia and he was broke, not a cent, and he said, "You know, I've got a brother in South Africa, but I can't get to him, I don't even have money to give him a call." So I said to this guy, "You know what, I've got a little bit left, let's go." By the time we got to Joburg I didn't have one cent left. But this guy took me to his brother, a businessman in Alberton. We stayed there for about three weeks. And then I ended up in Ponte. I went to church and met some guys from Rwanda and they said, "There's this guy, maybe go speak to him", and I went there, and he gave me accommodation for about seven months. He had his wife and his kids, and he was helping a lot of people.' Ponte City, considered by many natives to be a druglords' haven, is also the first hope for thousands of displaced Africans arriving in Joburg.

Later, Innocent heard about Mercy House, a home for refugees started by Diana Beamish in 1996, not funded by any particular organisation but by a number of 'church persons' and groups. 'I met some other refugees and one guy recommended we should go there. "Teacher Di" is quite well known now amongst the refugees.'

Diana recalls what prompted her to start Mercy House. 'I was watching the footage of the genocide on TV and I was absolutely horrified, and I wanted to do something. I wanted to adopt a baby but that turned out to be impossible. In October 1994 a group of refugees arrived and I traced them to a disused mine. They had nowhere to go. I went there regularly, Woolworths gave me food for them. There were no windows, and rats were crawling over them where they slept. It was terrible.

'Then I went to the Comboni Fathers,' a Catholic missionary organisation, 'and they helped as much as they could, but their resources were limited. So I went to every organisation I could think of, and no one would help, not even the Red Cross, so eventually my aunt and I bought the house in Bez Valley.' Though Diana is Catholic, and most of the donations that keep Mercy House running are from the Catholic community, the home is nondenominational and takes in any refugee child who is in need. 'We simply take in orphans from the wars in Africa,' she says. 'We started with five Muslims and one Christian.'

Innocent considers himself nondenominational. 'I go to any church,' he says. 'You don't gain anything by limiting who you can be friends with.'

I am astounded, listening to his near-perfect English, to discover that he could not speak the language at all when he arrived here a decade ago. He puts it down to his primary education. 'At primary school I was educated in my mother tongue. If you need to learn French, English, you can do that from your first year of high school, but if you learn to think first in your mother tongue, to develop your cognitive skills, then learning another language is not a problem.'

Starting off at Task Academy, he moved to Highlands North Boys High, and finally to Sandringham High School because he wanted to do extra maths. Getting there was not easy. 'My first year at Sandringham was tough,' he says. 'I had to integrate, get involved in sport.' He did cross-country running. 'There were a lot of misconceptions about the kids coming from Highlands North – "they're rough, they smoke drugs, they steal". So I had to change all that.' At the age of twenty-two he matriculated with distinction, which earned him a scholarship for his first year at Wits University.

Now a big, tall man who works as an electrical engineer for a company in Pretoria, one of whose main clients is Eskom, South Africa's precarious electricity supplier, he reflects on living in South Africa as a 'foreigner'. He has driven from Pretoria to meet me, still using an international driver's licence, as getting a South African licence has proved to be hard. 'The South African licensing department is full of dramas,' he says. 'The last time I went to apply for a licence they said that I couldn't because I must produce a South African ID. So I went to get a driver's licence in DRC. I had to start working, so I had to drive.

'These xenophobic attacks,' he says, 'it shocked everybody. But most people actually saw it coming. The headlines were there, but people didn't pay attention. I think the fact that Zimbabwe went so bad, that there are so many Zimbaweans coming into the country, I think that's what triggered it. Because Zimbabweans are probably amongst the best-educated Africans. So these guys they just come, go into the townships, start a business, and before you know it he's bought himself a house.

'The thing that people fail to understand… I mean, they say that people are taking jobs from the locals. But which jobs? Speaking from experience, you're not going to get a decent job if you don't have a South African ID. You're not going to be promoted. The moment you don't have that you are excluded. If you do, it's an exception.

'The company that I'm working for, we are so overworked. They take on projects, but those projects are going to take so much time because there aren't graduates who have the skills available to employ.' As increasing numbers of South Africans are choosing to do business degrees, the sciences are being left behind.

'And many immigrants who can contribute to the country are not being given the chance, so they have to find a way of surviving. They have to start a business, and if the business doesn't survive they go into crime.' What he's pointing to is that skilled people are often forced to remain in the informal sector, competing for jobs with poor South Africans or deviating into criminal activity. So, while violence erupted amongst the poor on the ground, government and its immigration policies play a significant part in fuelling the conflict.

'My feeling is, I'm not a refugee any more. I said to myself, when I graduate I can no longer be considered a refugee. I'd love to stay in this country and contribute as much as I can. I'm not the type of person who says there's crime and what-what – I mean, crime is everywhere. You can't run.' He muses, though, on the irony of potentially becoming a statistic on a South African street. 'I've got friends who have been hijacked. I've got a friend who was walking in Yeoville, he got shot. The bullet went into his shoulder, missed his heart by about an inch. And that guy has survived bombs. They've gone through all that, and someone comes in Joburg and stabs you.

'My car was stolen last year, my first car. I was going to be in it about a minute later. I was walking towards it as the guys were driving off. I was mugged when I was a student, at knifepoint in Braamfontein.' A quick transaction, he says: '"Where's your phone?" "Here." You don't resist someone who's got a knife or a gun. If they want something, you just give it to them.'

But if anything forces him to move on, he says, it will be the ongoing battle to become a recognised citizen of the country, 'because I'm paying tax just like everybody else, and I'm working hard, and I can't benefit from the economy that I'm helping to build.

'You can live in this country for twenty years and not be allowed to become a citizen. That guy who gave me accommodation in Ponte, he's been here for sixteen years, he works as a fitter and turner, he's excellent at that job, and he doesn't yet have permanent residence. And because he still has refugee papers his boss is not going to promote him. He can't make him a manager or anything like that.' It's a frustrating subject. He becomes silent.

I imagine, after all the thousands of miles that he's walked, he wouldn't miss it now that he's driving. But he says he does. 'For the first two years when I got to South Africa I used to walk a lot. From Ponte, and then from Mercy House. I know town very well. For me walking is essential. You can't appreciate the car you're driving unless you've walked. You're not going to understand…

'I'm in the habit, if I'm driving from Mpumalanga for work and I see someone who's walking, I will be very careful, but if I know I'm not in any danger I will stop and give them a lift. Because I know, if someone's been walking for hours and nobody's stopping because they're scared this guy is a criminal, and the guy's just trying to get to work on time, I know what it's like, because I've been there.

'When I was doing vac work at varsity, we were doing some work in Vereeniging, at the power station. I used to knock off at four, but one day I finished at two, so I thought, let me just go, otherwise I've got to wait for two hours for these other guys to finish. So I started hitch-hiking. From that power station to the next town you walk about five hours. I walked for about two hours, nobody would stop, and then all of a sudden somebody stopped. And I couldn't believe it was a lady driving alone. This experience is something I will never forget. When you live in South Africa, it's crime, and you're just walking, and it's a lady by herself who stops.

'We were talking and she said she believes in helping out, and she thought I was coming from work, I had my hat. But I had been walking for long hours and people wouldn't stop.'

I suppose it is moments like these that restore one's faith in humanity. And yet, Innocent says, it's something he has never really doubted. 'Me, I've seen kindness everywhere I've been – from Rwanda, DRC, Zambia, South Africa. The guy who helped us get visas to Zambia, his life was in danger. He took a risk to help us. So I saw kindness all the way.'

What has surprised him more, he says, is his own survival instinct. Thinking of the war, he says: 'You walk past a lady, her husband has left her, she can't walk and some of her kids are missing, she's crying, and you look at your own life, and you can hear the bombs, and you get to a point where your emotions just run dry, you don't feel anything. Even if you're strong and you can help, you don't because your own life is at risk, so you just leave her.

'Many people lost their kids in the jungle. At some stage you're walking, and the fighting is so close that you just have to leave the road and go and hide in the bush in the hope that once everything is calm you can come back and start walking again.'

Miraculously, Innocent's mother made it back to Rwanda, and he has been back to see her. 'I was amazed. I couldn't imagine how she made it back.'

From March to Parade

'I am black and I am gay. I cannot separate the two parts of me into secondary or primary struggles. In South Africa I am oppressed because I am a black man, and I am oppressed because I am gay. So when I fight for my freedom I must fight against both oppressions.'

These were the words of the late Simon Nkoli before the first gay Pride march in 1990. Nkoli had been imprisoned for treason from 1984 to 1988. After being acquitted, he was forbidden from meeting with more than three people at a time, but he went ahead anyway and formed Glow, the Gay and Lesbian Organisation of the Witwatersrand, which organised the first Pride march.

Paul Mokgethi, now a researcher at Gala (Gay and Lesbian Memory in Action) was there at the start. He recalls his memories of that time: 'Some people were sceptical, saying, "Why do you guys want to have a march? It's not safe, it's not the right time." But we decided we were going to go for it, irrespective of whether people supported us or not. We expected maybe fifty or sixty people to attend, but surprisingly by the end of the march we had about eight hundred people.

'Luckily enough we also had the support of the police, the Metro Police and the City of Johannesburg.' All the more remarkable because this was the apartheid-era police force, perhaps caught up in the excitement of a moment of transformation. 'So we thought, as much as we might be in danger, we are also protected by the law.

'It was a great physical liberation, walking in the streets and chanting and seeing the response from people in the flats who were coming out in Hillbrow where we were walking. People were ululating. And for us, as we were walking, sweating,' he laughs, 'that energy, that power, it was a very exciting feeling.

'Journalists were asking pedestrians and people who were standing on the street, "How do you feel about this? How do you see this?" Some people were saying, "This is wonderful, the first time we see something like this, we are so happy." And others were saying it's total nonsense. I remember this one guy who said, "This is bullshit! Bullshit!" There were families as well, mothers and fathers with children. It was an amazing feeling.

'When we were planning the march, we came up with all kinds of ideas because some people were scared. "What if my colleagues at work see me? What if my mother sees me?" So we came up with the idea that those who wanted to should wear paper bags over their heads.' But the universe had other plans and the heavens opened up. The bags became soggy. 'Eventually people took off the paper bags, and we were marching and chanting the slogans.

'It also happened at the time when Nelson Mandela had recently been released, and the drafting of the new constitution, and we at Glow also wanted to make sure that the issue of sexual orientation was being entrenched in the constitution. Because there are all these perceptions that you can't be black and be gay. It's unAfrican, it's unchristian.

'So we also wanted to make a mark and to say that we as black people are also here: we are out, we are gay. We exist and we are not aliens. We are South Africans as well. And there were also quite a number of white gay and lesbian activists who were involved in organising the march, Donné Rundle, Graeme Reid, Edwin Cameron, Mark Gevisser...'

Many heterosexual people participated in the march as well. Conscientious objector David Bruce recalls his experience, a few months after being released from spending two years in jail: 'When

I took part in the gay Pride march later in the year I was still in that 1980s mode of showing solidarity with other causes. The march was a way for me to acknowledge the two gay lawyers who had defended me in the trial, Kathy Satchwell and Edwin Cameron.' Cameron is now a Constitutional Court judge. 'It was also a way for me to challenge my own discomfort – as a straight man – with "gayness".

'The year before I was sentenced I was massively depressed, and I felt a lot of anxiety about potential violence and sexual violence in jail. There were a few occasions of sexual menace in jail which I managed to sidestep. I also encountered the prison "moffies". There was a boy called Pieterjie, who wore these tight pants, and I remember being disturbed by these feelings of attraction to him at one point and being anxious that other people might observe this and label me a "moffie". While I was in prison a state-authored pamphlet also did the rounds alleging that the conscientious objector Charles Bester was refusing to do military service so that he could be in prison with me because we were lovers. Complete nonsense. These things added to the discomfort I had always felt with gayness.

'Some months after I was released from jail I read about the Pride march in *The Weekly Mail*, and then I started noticing posters up around town … My flatmate was also interested in going. The morning of the march we walked to where the march was to begin stopping along the way to have a drink at Florian's in Hillbrow.

'Once we reached the other marchers in Braamfontein my flatmate and I went in different directions, so it was quite a solitary event for me.'

Many strides have been made since then, and much has been achieved with regard to gay rights. Paul notes: 'As we look from that time until now, there are so many things – the Civil Union Act that was passed in November 2006; gay and lesbian people can now legally adopt kids; a spouse can put his partner on his medical aid and he can receive his pension. So we have seen a number of shifts, and things have changed dramatically within those years until now. We need to celebrate that.

'When we started Pride it was all about marching and making a statement, claiming space. But it has shifted from that time to now, being called the Pride Parade where people come and just walk for fun, making sure we don't lose that space, and putting that awareness in the community. Now it is a celebration, saying that we're here and we thank the constitution, we thank all the people who have liberated us. So it has shifted from being a political march to being a celebratory and entertainment day. Enjoying the freedom that has been achieved.'

Dennis recalls his training at Police College in 1988. 'The Police Commissioner came to the college and told us that there were no moffies in the police force, and people who were suspected of being gay were weeded out.' By 1996 they had formed the South African Gay and Lesbian Police Network, which had their first exhibition tent at the parade. 'Many straight policemen also came to support us,' says Dennis. 'We handed out keyrings, caps, balloons and whistles, and it was nice to see everyone walking around with those items.' Their presence had a powerful effect on a number of people. 'You could see the excitement in their faces when we told them who we were and why we were there.'

For Beryl, this was the highlight of sixteen years of Pride: 'I made a point of walking over to greet them. It was intensely emotional to see the policemen there in their uniforms. For my generation the police uniform is a sign of complete terror and disgust. If the uniform came near me I would get an anxiety attack. It was heart-wrenching for me to see these uniforms that had terrified me for so many years now being worn by men and women determined to establish their rights as gay people ... To find the tools of oppression now giving birth to liberated persons was overpowering ... I stood there crying and saying to a young policeman, "Thank you very much for being here. You don't know what this means. You're a very brave young man and don't think I don't appreciate that you are here.'"

Fundamentalist Christians have also had an ongoing voyeuristic presence at Pride over the years. One was reported to have remarked: 'I wouldn't miss it for the world.'

Paul was ordained as a minister in the Metropolitan Community Church eleven years ago, and he says, 'as a Christian and a religious leader, it gives me a platform to create a debate with these people. I'm able to have a conversation with them, we talk. That space creates a dialogue. So when they are quoting scripture I can say, "Yes, but what does it really mean?"'

In their book, *Pride: Protest and Celebration*, editors Shaun de Waal and Anthony Manion brought together many people's recollections of the first sixteen years of Pride. The stories reflect memories of exhilarating times, but they also reflect ongoing tensions as South Africa and the world have changed over the past two decades and many people have been remarginalised or simply left behind.

A growing fear of crime saw the parade move from the city centre to Rosebank in the suburbs in 2002. But it begs the question: is a crowd of several thousand really at risk from predators on the streets? Is this sort of en masse action not exactly what the city needs to reclaim its streets from criminals?

As Daniel Somerville, the 2001 coordinator of Pride, argued: 'All we were asking people to do was to take one day of the year to walk downtown together with twelve thousand other gay people – down the same streets that black lesbian and gay people walked every day. But they still complained that it was unsafe. I thought, well, it's unsafe to be a lesbian or gay person living in a township community yet they are expected to do it every day. You can't for one single day show solidarity?'

It must be acknowledged that there was an incident when the parade moved back to the city for a year in 2005. A bottle was thrown from a building above and a woman was injured. Understandably people were shaken. But could this not have been an isolated incident that could have happened anywhere? How much of the move back to the suburbs is really about the fear of crime and how much is the discomfort of the middle-classes having to face the poor at ground level, rather than moving through the leafy green of the suburbs?

'Every year it's the same story,' says Paul: '"Oh, we can't go into the city, it's dangerous." On the other hand, when we march in Rosebank on a Saturday afternoon, there are all these walls and nobody's there. Who are we parading for? For ourselves? It doesn't add any value as part of the broader community.' As De Waal and Manion point out, while resisting walking through inner-city ghettoes, Pride should guard against becoming an 'ambulatory ghetto' of its own.

'When we were marching downtown,' says Paul, 'even people who were not gay joined in. The street kids would come and dance and they were happy. Now it's a totally different thing. But this issue comes up every year. People were asking, "Why don't we take it to Soweto one year?" But it's all about money now.' There was also a suggestion of moving it further north, to Sandton, in order to attract the sponsorship of big business to the 'pink market'. There is talk of making it an international tourist attraction. It will be a sad irony if Joburg Pride becomes more accessible to international visitors, staying at hotels in the affluent suburbs, than to gay and lesbian people living in the townships.

Ten years ago De Waal noted 'the mainstreaming of gay pride', and observed that 'it makes perfect sense that in a globalised capitalist world the best hope for survival as a marginal group is to make yourself into a powerful consumer entity with something to sell and cash to spend.'

But what if you don't have anything to spend? In South Africa, with its particular history, it is black people who are remarginalised from the parade. For a number of reasons, including the ongoing legacy of apartheid architecture.

For those travelling from the townships, many without their own transport, it means catching two taxis to reach the suburbs. 'The people from Soweto,' says Paul, 'they have to get a taxi from Soweto to Bree Stree or Noord Street taxi rank, then a taxi from town to go to Rosebank. And again to return as well.' Taxis are less frequent on Saturdays, and people travelling home by public transport have to leave the city before dark in order to ensure their safety.

'They organise Pride now with these after-party events,' says Paul, 'where for example RuPaul will come and sing and the tickets are expensive. So at the end of the day, if you don't have money for RuPaul, if you don't have money for the after party, it's just for the rich and glamorous. And while a lot of people are still having fun and enjoying the concert, you have to ensure that by 5.30 p.m. you are heading back to the township. So the poor are always marginalised.

'Township gay and lesbian people are also put at risk, because now they are coming there, and they've been filmed by the SABC and people have seen the Pride Parade on the news, and then when they go back home at night people are waiting to harass them. So on the one hand we are saying to those people, come, celebrate, but at the same time we are putting them in danger.'

Bev Ditsie, one of the founding members of Glow, recalls her experience after the first Pride march: 'I was shown on TV that night taking part in Pride. It was a religious show and the priest was saying, "These people should be killed." All of a sudden I was getting funny looks from people in the street. I thought "Uh-oh, What have I done?" My grandmother got scared and thought I was going to be killed.

'Two days later I was sitting in my room when I heard voices outside calling my name. I ran into the lounge and my granny opened the door and told me to hide. About twenty angry men were surrounding our house demanding I come with them so that they could teach me a lesson. They wanted to rape me. The worst thing is that they threatened to take my grandma if I didn't come with them. My grandma stood at the door and said, "Come in, but one of you will die with me." The men mistook the iron rod she was carrying for a gun and left.'

While post-apartheid South Africa has led the way globally regarding legislation on sexual-orientation equality, rights are really only useful to those who have the power to exercise them. Many South Africans' attitudes have not changed. Black lesbians remain the most vulnerable targets of violence in the gay community and the practice of 'corrective rape' continues.

In 2006, Zoliswa Nkonyana, a 19-year-old woman, was brutally beaten and stabbed to death in Khayelitsha in Cape Town. The trial of the nine men accused has been postponed twenty times. The 7th of July, 2007 saw the murder of Sizakele Sigasa and her partner Salome Masooa. Their bodies were found by a jogger in a field in Meadowlands in Soweto. Their deaths prompted the formation of the 07-07-07 Campaign, which aims to create awareness about the ongoing violence committed against lesbian women. Last year Eudy Simelane, former Banyana Banyana soccer star from Kwa-Thema near Springs on the East Rand, was gang-raped and killed.

'The thing is,' says Bev, 'these cases are just seen as part of the regular South African violence, they are never logged as hate crimes, so there is no way of measuring the level of hate crimes that are happening. In Eudy's case, one of the guys turned state witness and said he was acting alone, but it was clear that she was raped by a number of people.' What is needed, Bev believes, is legislation that addresses the issue of hate crime. This would apply to xenophobia as well. 'If the legislation changes then at least that makes sure there's accountability. If these cases are logged as hate crimes we will get a clearer picture of how widespread they are.'

In the September 1999 issue of glossy magazine *Outright*, its readers were advised to ignore the direction that 'killjoy queer politicos' wanted to take Pride in. De Waal remarked that 'perhaps what *Outright* resents is the lingering sense that the march is about

more than getting drunk (as it recommends) and finding someone
to have sex with' and that 'the bulk of ever-so-white paraders …
need to be reminded that but for the efforts of those "killjoy queer
politicos", especially the late Simon Nkoli, there wouldn't be this
opportunity to cruise the streets at all.'

The tenth Pride Parade in 1999 was a tribute to Nkoli, who had
died of Aids the previous year. The mayor of Johannesburg at the
time, Isaac Mogasi, proposed that a corner of the city be named
after him 'as a tribute to one of its finest sons'. Glow chose the
corner of Twist and Pretoria Streets in Hillbrow.

Paul says it concerns him that there are so few activists in the
community now. 'The young gay and lesbian people who are coming
out now, most of them are going into marketing, advertising, that
sort of thing. Nowadays its all about money and image. But where
are the young gay people at the moment fighting to maintain our
rights?'

Much like the significance of June the 16th is often lost to the
youth today, many of whom see it simply as another holiday, a day
off, the origins of Pride are also forgotten. 'They feel that we've
got a new government, we've got a new president. Yes, it happened
and we are free, but people had to die for that freedom.'

Bev is now behind the camera as a documentary filmmaker.
'I'm an activist, I always will be, that will never change, the only
difference is that I'm no longer standing on a podium. Media has
become the major tool for me. I will always reflect my anger at
injustice. But through the media you can put it out there for a lot
more people to see.' She is at work on *Beyond Positive*, a ten-part
inspirational series on people living with HIV.

Paul recalls the friends he grew up with in Soweto in the
Eighties, his 'gay group', and how many of them have been lost to
Aids. 'Tshidi and Mpho and Zaza, some of the people who helped
start Glow and helped with the first march … Those three should
be here today.' They called themselves the Ted Dinards, after the
gay character in *Dynasty*. There were nine boys, and one girl – Bev.

'Now we are only left with four, all the other guys are gone because of Aids-related illnesses. Their lives could have been saved if they had had the courage to come out about being positive ...

'Tshidi's death in 2003 hit me the hardest ... I went to visit Tshidi after he fell ill, and tried to persuade him to see a doctor. But he was still in denial about being HIV-positive. By the time he did see a doctor it was too late, and he died a week later in hospital. His death made me so angry. If he had spoken to his friends we could have helped him to get treatment.' The death of Paul's friends has encouraged him to speak out on these issues and be open about his own HIV-positive status.

Remembering his teenage years, he says, 'We were young and crazy in the Eighties, walking in the streets of Soweto, putting ourselves in danger, people swearing or chasing us or beating us. But we were proud and for us it was exciting ... We never thought about it, but I suppose those were our first Pride marches – nine young gay guys and one lesbian marching through the streets of Soweto.

'You never know,' he tells me, 'when you do things you just do them, you don't think about what it will mean one day. That walk that we took on the 13th of October 1990, we didn't know how significant it would be. We were creating history.'

PS: Fast Forward

Gary Carter lives in Amsterdam, with Marius, his partner of twenty-five years, and their son Lucio. This interview took place via email in the air between London and Amsterdam during February 2005.

By way of introduction, how would you describe yourself and the work that you do?
Hmm. I'd describe myself as an artist, but that's not particularly helpful. It's important, though, because that's how I conceive of myself and my approach to everything I do, even the bits that aren't art.

I have two careers – the one is as a theatre practitioner and performer, making text-based multi-discipline performance pieces, and the other is as a media executive. The latter is where I earn my living, and the discrepancy between the two fields of operation is enormous.

As a media executive, I work on the continuum of idea development, acquisition and distribution. That is to say, I am involved on a day-to-day basis with the origination of patterned ideas for non-scripted entertainment television shows, and their related business and legal affairs. My career has been focused around the rise of Reality Television.

I currently work with FremantleMedia, the global production and distribution company which makes, amongst other things, *Pop*

Idol and *The Apprentice* worldwide.

What made you call your consultancy company 'Field'?
I chose the name Field because of its multiplicity of meanings: as a fertile space in which things can grow; a field of research; a field of expertise; as a defence (in the sense of 'to field a blow'). The latter because at the time, having come out of a brutal and punishing five years with Endemol, another production company, I felt the need for some protection ...

Where are you based now?
I live in Amsterdam, and work all over the world: however, I spend three days a week (mostly) in London, at the head office of FremantleMedia. Since January, I have been working exclusively with FremantleMedia, as Senior Executive Worldwide Television.

For some frequent flyers, the time in the air is some of the only time they have for themselves ... do you find this time relaxing, or do you find travelling tiring?
In a general physical sense, I find it debilitating physically, mentally and emotionally. By that I mean, I think air travel takes an enormous physical toll – the inactivity, the discomfort, the lack of air, the food – but also an emotional toll. I find it difficult to be passive, and air travel, particularly if you do it frequently, requires a degree of passivity because you are powerless to really impact what's happening to you (although it does help once you understand the routines, the excuses and the coding of signs around you). On the other hand, because my life is very public, and because I am exposed to almost 24-hour contact via a host of electronic devices, aeroplanes represent a kind of liberation, or privacy.

You once said you didn't think the body was designed to move at the speed of the frequent flyer's life ... Do you still

feel that? How do you manage it?

I believe that more and more. One of the primary things connects to the emotional toll I mentioned above: I think that the body and the mind require processing and transition times between events, and I think air travel is too fast for that to happen adequately. I manage it through the gathering of a long succession of tricks and tics which probably make me appear increasingly eccentric and irritating to my fellow travellers – but one of the ways I manage is to be less concerned about what my fellow travellers think. So I always travel long distances in a rather unbecoming cotton tracksuit. I drink vast amounts of water (which means I am forever in the toilet!). I pace up and down. I use eye drops. I cover my face in calendula oil. I don't eat aeroplane food (no! not even in First Class). I don't drink. I exercise before and after a flight, where possible. I meditate. I do ballet exercises. Oh yes. On the plane, I do them …

Do you prefer flying to driving or travelling in a car?

That's not a fair question. I dislike both. Driving myself makes me less irritated and keeps me active (as opposed to passive).

Any fears of flying? Any more since September 11?

I am very pragmatic about the chance of accident – it's part of the passivity I mentioned earlier. However, when I do take off, I always send a mental message to my partner that I love him, and always will, no matter what. He knows that too. When I land, I phone him and tell him I'm safe. That – the phoning – started after September 11, at his request. The impact on me has been that I keep my passport on my body in the air, along with a mobile phone – the phone in case I need to try to make contact, and the passport so that my body can be identified …

You lived in Los Angeles for a year, working for Disney. Did you drive then? Did you enjoy living in LA?
I drove then, yes, you can't not in LA really, unless you live in one suburb only. I drove an open coupé and wore a cowboy hat, and listened to Sheryl Crowe (this was 1996). LA is built to be seen from a car, to be experienced from a car, and Californian music really is the soundtrack to the city as experienced from a car, so it's somehow appropriate there. I still drive when I go to Los Angeles, there is a relief to arriving in a foreign city and knowing it well enough to do that. But it is a special experience in a car – try driving along the length of Mulholland Drive at sunset, listening to Sheryl Crowe, and you'll see what I mean! No, I didn't enjoy living there – it was the most unhappy period of my life, unquestionably. But I am fonder of it now.

What are your thoughts about LA these days?
It's not associated with my experience of living there, weirdly – I take it on face value, which is the way it wants to be taken, but it is surreal. I do have two very close friends who live there, both of whom work in television, and so going there is associated with seeing them regularly, a perk of my career. I have such a deep mistrust of America, and its epicentre is LA. I think it was one of the French post-structuralists who said that the US is significant because of the reality it constructs, and that reality is constructed in Los Angeles, which is why it is at once so fascinating and so scary. Los Angeles is a mono-cultural environment in which language has been disconnected from the meaning it has in the rest of the world, and where the image is constructed which 'real life' is based on.

Do you ever take leisurely walks? Do you try to make time for that in the places you visit?
Very seldom. Bike rides in Amsterdam. Every Monday I walk home with Lucio from his school, a long meandering walk which

he leads. Takes an hour. I very seldom have time to walk in the cities I visit: if I have time, I am usually desperate to sleep in order to minimise the impact of the travelling.

How have you found your brief experiences of walking in Johannesburg? Compared with other cities, what was your overriding feeling?
Walking in Johannesburg is so familiar, particularly in suburban Johannesburg. It reminds me of walking in the suburbs of my childhood in the Port Elizabeth of the Seventies – except for the walls. I am fascinated by the archaeology of Johannesburg walls, and have a habit of trying to date the additions to their height.

How do shifts in rhythm (jetting between places, to wandering around when you arrive) 'speak' to you as a dancer?
They are utterly disruptive and jagged – there is no transition, no flow – so there's a constant sense of 'wrench'. Everything I do in response to this 'wrench' is the equivalent of what a dancer would call 'release'.

Do you dance at all these days?
I dance on the inside.

Do you feel that time is a finite resource, or do you experience it as malleable?
I think time is an argument which one is constantly losing.

Do you move with ease between places, or do you ever have a sense of ambivalence about leaving?
I am paid to leave. I feel utterly without nationality, without affinity to location. I feel no ambivalence about leaving anywhere any more. I long for home constantly, but home is linked only to the important people in my life – Marius, Lucio.

Do you find it a strain that your friends are dotted all over the globe, or have you grown accustomed to it and feel the gains outweigh the losses?

A mixed blessing. On the one hand, I love the fact that I have friends in every port, that I have relationships with people of different cultures, professions, nationalities. But as the years have gone by, I find it harder and harder to keep abreast of these relationships.

Is there a danger of places becoming the same to you?

Places are the same because they are places: I do have different responses to all of them. I have favourites (Stockholm) and unfavourites (London and Paris) and even one place I hope never to go back to – Hong Kong. I have places I am afraid of (Moscow) and places where I feel like I am dying (Port Elizabeth). I have places I hope to go to yet, like Tokyo. I have been to places I never dreamt I would see (Spitsbergen) and seen things I will never forget (cod in a river in northern Norway at dawn).

You once said that you watch game shows in fast forward to get a sense of them, can you explain more what you mean by that and how it works?

Television programmes are extremely formulaic in their use of signs and tropes, signifiers for the audience. Like any temporal activity they have a rhythm. Most people pay conscious attention to the information and the action, and subconscious attention to the rhythm and the signs. I pay little attention to the former and all of it to the latter, because the former is usually in a language I don't understand, and it takes up too much time that way!

You don't have a TV in your home, do you?

No, we don't have a television in our house. People usually show surprise on the basis of my career – that because I make it, I should watch it (a lot). This is as logical as to say that if I was a doctor, you would expect me to have a sick person in the living room. I am proof that I don't need to watch television in my leisure time in order to make a career out of it – although you might argue that I could have had a better career in television had I done so. I would dispute that – television makers who derive all their knowledge and inspiration from television are extremely problematic and derivative, in my view.

It seems a strange irony that many South African men who left the country because they didn't support conscription, have actually done better for themselves in their respective fields than they'd have been able to do here. Any thoughts on that?
No. Never occurred to me.

The pace in your writing is very slow and spacious. Given your lifestyle, and the pace of your life, how does that shift happen?
I go into a trance when I write. At least part of me does, and it slows me down, it's not that I slow it down. The process slows me down. I suppose I should also add that the writing is really about structure, not about content, and the spaciousness comes from exploring the structure.

What is the thing you like most about your lifestyle, that gives you the most joy?
As a boy growing up in Port Elizabeth, I dreamed of getting away. And I succeeded. Every time I get on a plane, I am travelling further and further away from that starting point.

Anything you'd like to add?
Speed is the great lie we tell ourselves.

References

Preface: Who is Walking?

xvii Bradbury, Ray. (1951). 'The Pedestrian', in *S is for Space*. 1968, London: Rupeausterrt-Hart Davis.

xvii 'Just walking': Bradbury, Ray. (1953). '"Burning Bright": A Foreword', in *Fahrenheit 451*. 1993, New York: Simon & Schuster, pp. 13–14.

xvii 'criminal fact of having advanced by base pedestrian methods': De Quincey, Thomas. (1862). *Confessions of an English Opium-Eater*. 1978, London: JM Dent & Sons, p. 138.

xviii 'the future touches down': Iyer, Pico. (1995, August). 'Where worlds collide: In Los Angeles International Airport, the future touches down', *Harper's Magazine*.

xviii 'if a man found himself on a bus ': Worpole, Ken. (2001, November 8). 'How you travel is who you are', *openDemocracy*. <http://www.opendemocracy.net/ecology-climate_change_debate/article_458.jsp>

xviii 'I will build a motor car': Ford, Henry, in collaboration with Samuel Crowther. (1922). *My Life and Work*. 1925, London: Heinemann, p. 73.

xviii 'Of these, 949 required': Ibid, p. 108.

Conscientious Objections

1 Ngema, Mbongeni. (1988). Sarafina!, Cort Theatre, New York City, 28 January 1988 – 2 July 1989.
2 Kani, John. (2002). *Nothing But the Truth*, Market Theatre, Johannesburg, 17 September – 17 November 2002. Johannesburg: Wits University Press.
4 'the most notorious Quartz Street': Mpe, Phaswane. (2001). *Welcome to Our Hillbrow*. Pietermaritzburg: University of Natal Press, p. 6.
5 Kubrick, Stanley (dir). (1968). *2001: A Space Odyssey*. Warner Brothers.
5 Carpenter, John (dir). (1976). *Assault on Precinct 13*. New Line Studios.
6 'Then you shuddered into wakefulness': Mpe. *Welcome to Our Hillbrow*, p. 9.

Border Crossings

11 'conspiring to monopolize sales of buses': *Wikipedia*, 'General Motors streetcar conspiracy'. <http://en.wikipedia.org/wiki/General_Motors_streetcar_conspiracy>
11 National City Lines conspiracy: Klein, Jim and Olson, Martha (dirs). (1996). *Taken for a Ride*. New Day.
11 'I see a place': Zemeckis, Robert (dir). (1988). *Who Framed Roger Rabbit?* Touchstone.
12 'The pedestrian remains the largest single obstacle': Rudofsky, Bernard. (1969). *Streets for People*. New York: Anchor, p. 106, quoted in Solnit, Rebecca. (2001). *Wanderlust: A History of Walking*. London: Verso, p. 254.
12 'traffic interruption': Waldie, DJ. (2004). 'Metal and Flesh', in *Where We Are Now: Notes from Los Angeles*. Los Angeles: Angel City, p. 133.
12 Walk of the Stars: Solnit, Rebecca. (2001). *Wanderlust: A History of Walking*. London: Verso, p. 76.

12 Autopia: Banham, Reyner. (1971). *Los Angeles: The Architecture of Four Ecologies*. London: Allen Lane.

12 'animated scenes of cars discussing life's challenges': Hidden Mickeys of Disneyland. (2001). 'Fun Facts of Disneyland's Autopia.'
<http://www.hiddenmickeys.org/Disneyland/Secrets/Tomorrow/Autopia.html>

12 'There were things I said to my son': Dietz, Steven. (1989). *God's Country*. New York: Samuel French, pp. 101–102.

13 'if a neighborhood is to retain stability': Nicolaides, Becky M and Wiese, Andrew. (2006). *The Suburb Reader*. CRC, p. 253.

13 'places empty of anyone else's memories': Baxandall, Rosalyn and Ewen, Elizabeth. (2000). *Picture Windows: How the Suburbs Happened*. New York: Basic.

13 World War II poll on post-war ambitions: Coppola, Francis Ford (dir). (1988). *Tucker: The Man and His Dream*. Zoetrope.

13 Anita Bryant's visit to Flint: Moore, Michael (dir). (1989). *Roger and Me*. Warner Brothers.

14 'they put them great big windows on the sides of buses': Haggis, Paul (dir). (2004). *Crash*, Lion's Gate.

14 Davis, Mike. (1990). *City of Quartz: Excavating the Future of Los Angeles*. London: Verso.

14 Johnson, Don Hanlon. (2006). 'Speed Limits', in *Everyday Hopes, Utopian Dreams: A Reflection on American Ideals*. Berkeley, Calif: North Atlantic, pp. 33–46.

14 Out-take from the Emerald City: Lumet, Sidney (dir). (1978). *The Wiz*. Universal.

16 'invisible spectrums': Ridenour, Al, et al. (1998, December). 'LA to Z – Los Angeles California', *Los Angeles Magazine*.

17 'though I wanted to think I was different': Dietz, Steven. (1991). Unpublished essay.

17 'stood up by sitting down': Fowler, Bree. (2005, October 25).
    'A bus ride to freedom', *Star*.

17 'we don't ride on the back of the bus no more': Neville
    Brothers. (1989). 'Sister Rosa', *Yellow Moon*. A&M.

17 'an unstable, third world country on wheels': Waldie, 'On the
    Bus', in *Where We Are Now: Notes from Los Angeles*, pp. 136–
    145.

18 'brown city': Rodriguez, Richard. (2003). *Brown: The Last
    Discovery of America*. New York: Viking.

18 Getting lost in LA: Chris Abani in University of Southern
    California. (2004, May 17). *Writing L.A.: 'Reading L.A.'* .
    <http://www.researchchannel.org/prog/displayevent.
    aspx?rID=3362>

18 'It's the sense of touch': Haggis, *Crash*.

18 'The standard for the excellence of our stories': Waldie,
    'L.A. Literature', in *Where We Are Now: Notes from Los
    Angeles*, p. 123.

19 Holland, Heidi and Roberts, Adam (eds). (2002). *From
    Jo'burg to Jozi*. Johannesburg: Penguin.

19 Mpe, Phaswane. (2001). *Welcome to Our Hillbrow*.
    Pietermaritzburg: University of Natal Press.

19 'shows the complexity of blackness': Taitz, Laurice. (2001,
    September 16). 'Welcome to our literature', *Sunday Times*.

19 Minibus taxis: Fassie, Brenda. (1986). 'Zola Budd'. EMI.

19 Zola Budd and the Olympics: Henderson, Jon. (2000,
    November 5). 'The 10 worst mishaps in the history of
    sport', *Observer*.
    <http://observer.guardian.co.uk/osm/
    story/0,6903,391039,00.html>

19 Minibus taxi users in South Africa: Miller, Andie. (2002,
    July 3). 'Multiculturalism and Shades of Meaning in the
    New South Africa', *M/C Journal*, Vol. 5, No. 3.
    <http://journal.media-culture.org.au/0207/
    shadesofmeaning.php>

19 History of South African minibus taxi industry: Phakathi, Dumisani (dir). (1999). *Rough Ride.* e.tv.

Speeding towards Paris

20 'I apprehended for the first time': Didion, Joan. (1979). 'On the Road', in *The White Album*. New York: Noonday, p. 176.

21 'Speed is a drug': Bruns, Axel. (2000, May 8). 'Calls for Contributors: *M/C* "speed" issue', online posting. <http://groups.yahoo.com/group/media–culture/message/97>

21 Virilio, Paul. (1986). *Speed and Politics: An Essay on Dromology*, translated by Mark Polizzotti. New York: Semiotext(e).

21 Virilio, Paul. (1999). *The Information Bomb*, translated by Chris Turner. London: Verso.

21 Virilio, Paul. (1995, August). 'Speed and Information: Cyberspace Alarm!' *CTHEORY*, Vol. 18, No. 3. <http://www.ctheory.net/search.asp?searchvalue=Paul+Virilio&action=author&cmdSend=search>

21 'the social, political and military logic': Spoon Collective. (1996, June 4). 'New List: Dromology', online posting. <http://csf.colorado.edu/mail/psn/jun96/0025.html>

21 Tumbling down rabbit holes: Carroll, Lewis. (1865). *Alice's Adventures in Wonderland*. 1932, London: Macmillan.

21 'promenade without purpose': University of Manchester. 'The Flâneur', in *Visual Culture and the Contemporary City*. <http://www.sociology.mmu.ac.uk/vms/vccc/s1/s1_2/flanerie_3.php>

21 'botanising on the asphalt': Benjamin, Walter. (1938). *Charles Baudelaire: A Lyric Poet in the Era of High Capitalism*, translated by Harry Zohn. 1983, London: Verso, p. 36.

22 'a chance rhyme in every corner': Baudelaire, Charles. (1857). 'The Sun', in *The Flowers of Evil*. 1958, New York: New Directions, p. 106.

22 'by one of the most massive': White, Edmund. (2001). *The Flâneur: A Stroll through the Paradoxes of Paris*. London: Bloomsbury, p. 37.

22 'hopes to flush out the hidden haunts': Leslie, Esther. (1997). 'Spies and Art: In a State of Emergency', for the exhibition *Threats and Containments*. Byam Shaw School of Art, 12 March 1997.

22 'California has no past': Solnit, Rebecca. (2003). *Motion Studies: Time, Space and Eadweard Muybridge*. London: Bloomsbury, p. 6.

22 'penniless but driven': White, *The Flâneur*, p. 41.

22 Salon Indien: Erickson, Rick (ed). (1997, October 29). 'Looking Around for Nalpoléon III', *Metropole Paris*. <http://www.metropoleparis.com/1997/71103244/opera.html>

22 'an invention without any commercial future': Putnam, David, with Neil Watson. (1997). *Movies and Money*. New York: Alfred A Knopf.

23 'It showed a school-of-Monet style train': Glancey, Jonathan. (2005, April 14). 'Do the Locomotive', *Guardian*. <http://www.guardian.co.uk/arts/features/story/0,11710,1458978,00.html>

23 'at the sight of the train': Ibid.

23 'fled the café in terror': *The Internet Movie Database*, 'Trivia for L'arrivée d'un train à La Ciotat' (1895)'. <http://www.imdb.com/title/tt0000012/trivia>

23 'While capital ... must strive to tear down every barrier': Marx, Karl. (1861). *Grundrisse: Foundations of the Critique of Political Economy*. 1973, Harmondsworth: Penguin, pp. 538–539.

23 'A lot of people complain': Bosman, Herman Charles. (2003). 'Paris: Sidelights and Half-Laughs', in Stephen Gray (ed), *My Life and Opinions*. Cape Town: Human & Rousseau, pp. 97–99. Originally published in the *South African Opinion*, 31 October 1936.

25 'for businessmen the fantastic reality of life': Baudelaire, Charles. (1863). *The Painter of Modern Life and Other Essays*. 1986, New York and London: Da Capo.

Slow Walk to Freedom

29 Peck, Raoul (dir). (2000). *Lumumba*. Zeitgeist.

29 Altman, Robert (dir). (1993). *Short Cuts*. New Line.

30 Vladislavić, Ivan. (1989). 'The Box', in *Missing Persons*. Cape Town: David Philip, pp. 45–60.

30 'I was not emboldened': Theroux, Paul. (2002). *Dark Star Safari*. London: Penguin, p. 163.

31 'Maybe we should condemn a little more': Peck, Scott. (1994). 'The Tough Gospel of Scott Peck', *Pathways to Health*, Vol. 2, No. 3.

Finding the Balance

33 'You'd better slow down': Brand, Joshua and Falsey, John. (1990–1995). Northern Exposure. Universal.

33 'the body, step by step': Napier, John. (1967, April). 'The Antiquity of Human Walking', *Scientific American*, quoted in Solnit, Rebecca. (2001). *Wanderlust: A History of Walking*. London: Verso, p. 33.

34 'There is a secret bond': Kundera, Milan. (1996). *Slowness*. London: Faber & Faber, p. 34.

35 'Mobiles have no meaning': Sartre, Jean-Paul. (1946). 'The Mobiles of Calder', in *Essays in Aesthetics*. 1963, New York: Washington Square, p. 80.

36 Axel, Gabriel (dir). (1988). *Babette's Feast*. Orion.

37 Spicer, Stephen. (2003). *Striving for Imperfection*. The Unknown Gallery, Johannesburg, 29 October – 4 November 2003.

37 'the Free State's best-kept secret': Naidoo, Charmain. (2002, January 20). 'Liberating the Free State', *Sunday Times*.

39 'learned to live in the country' Pawley, Martin. (2002). 'The War against the Car', *openDemocracy*. <http://www.opendemocracy.net/ecology-climate_change_debate/article_481.jsp>

41 Bosman, Herman Charles. (1971). *Jurie Steyn's Post Office*, Lionel Abrahams (ed). 1991, Cape Town: Human & Rousseau.

41 'The difference between the city and the farm': Bosman, Herman Charles. (1986). 'Introduction', in Stephen Gray (ed.), *Bosman's Johannesburg*. Cape Town: Human & Rousseau, p. 8.

41 'flourished on vandalising and extinguishing its own past': Ibid, p. 11.

In the Footsteps of Bosman and Dickens, via Hillbrow

42 'Kaffirs? (said Oom Schalk Lourens)': Bosman, Herman Charles. (1998). 'Makapan's Caves', in Craig MacKenzie (ed), *Mafeking Road and Other Stories*. Cape Town: Human & Rousseau, pp. 53–57.

42 Mpe, Phaswane. (2001). *Welcome to Our Hillbrow*. Pietermaritzburg: University of Natal Press.

43 Bosman, Herman Charles. (2002). 'Unto Dust', in Craig MacKenzie (ed.), *Unto Dust and Other Stories*. Cape Town: Human & Rousseau, pp. 13–17.

43 Blyton, Enid. (1942–1963). *Famous Five Adventures Collection*. 2004, London: Hodder Children's Books.

43 Carroll, Lewis. (1865). *Alice's Adventures in Wonderland*. 1932, London: Macmillan.

43 'My father's family name being Pirrip': Dickens, Charles. (1867). *Great Expectations*. 1965, Harmondsworth: Penguin.

45 Mpe, Phaswane. (2001). 'Occasion for Brooding', in Allan Horwitz (ed), *Unity in Flight*, Johannesburg: Botsotso, pp. 161–171.

46 Bosman's essay on the word 'Kaffir': Bosman, Herman Charles. (2003). 'Aspects of South African Literature', in Stephen Gray (ed), *My Life and Opinions*. Cape Town: Human & Rousseau, pp. 168–170. Originally published in the *South African Opinion*, September 1948.

46 Linda, Bongani, et al. (2004). *Skin Deep*, Market Theatre, Johannesburg, 16 June – 22 August 2004.

47 Grass, Günter. (1959). *The Tin Drum*. 1998, Vintage. Originally published in German under the title *Die Blechtrommel*.

47 Mpe, Phaswane. (2002). 'Brooding Clouds', in Stephen Gray (ed), *Modern South African Short Stories*. Revised Edition. Johannesburg: Ad Donker, pp. 158–161.

48 'told me the funniest': Bosman, Herman Charles. (2003). 'So This is London', in *My Life and Opinions*, pp. 87–89. Originally published in the *South African Opinion*, 17 April 1936.

48 Duiker, K Sello. (2001). *The Quiet Violence of Dreams*. Cape Town: Kwela.

A Cappella

50 'No tits, no arse': Andrewpoulidies, Andrew (aka Graham Weir). (1996). 'Not the Midnight Mass: A History', *Mass Hysteria 2* liner notes.

50 The architecture of Long Street: Schonstein Pinnock, Patricia. (2000). *Skyline*. Cape Town: David Philip.

51 Walking as song: Chatwin, Bruce. (1987). *The Songlines*. 1998, London: Vintage.

52 'traffic safety trainers suggest': Waldie, DJ. (1997). 'Walking in L.A.', *Salon*. <http://www.salon.com/wlust/feature/1997/10/14auto.html>

56 'People are trying to invest the experience of shopping': Smith, Gail. (2004, May 21). 'Living outside of the category', *ThisDay*.

57 'What's up tonight on Channel 4': Bradbury, Ray. (1951). 'The Pedestrian', in *S is for Space*. 1968, London: Rupert-Hart Davis.

57 'We used to think nothing of walking three days': Scott-Clark, Cathy and Levy, Adrian. (2003, June 14). 'Fast forward into trouble', *Guardian*. <http://www.guardian.co.uk/weekend/story/0,3605,975769,00.html>

57 Road Runner sound effects (there is never any dialogue, except for 'beep-beep'): *Wikipedia*, 'Road Runner Cartoon'. <http://en.wikipedia.org/wiki/Wile_E._Coyote>

58 'in which a young executive conducts a business meeting': Rushkoff, Douglas. (1999, December). 'Remember the Sabbath', *New York Times*.

Moving Across the Page

61 'He preferred to be alone and in motion': Galgut, Damon (1982). *A Sinless Season*. Johannesburg: Jonathan Ball, p. 20.

61 'He is intensely happy': Galgut, Damon. (2010). 'The Follower', in *In a Strange Room*. Johannesburg: Penguin, p. 3.

62 'No one perhaps has ever felt passionately': Woolf, Virginia. (1930). 'Street Haunting', in *The Death of the Moth and Other Essays*. 1942, London: Hogarth, p. 19.

62 'one day walking round Tavistock Square': Woolf, Virginia.
(1976). 'A Sketch of the Past', in *Moments of Being:
Unpublished Autobiographical Writings*. Sussex University
Press, p. 81.

62 'Permit me to inform you': Walser, Robert. (2002). 'The
Walk', in *Selected Stories*. New York Review of Books, pp.
85–86.

63 'I have often wished': Solnit, Rebecca. (2001). *Wanderlust: A
History of Walking*. London: Verso, p. 72.

63 'by base pedestrian methods': De Quincey, Thomas. (1862).
Confessions of an English Opium-Eater. 1978, London: JM
Dent & Sons, p. 138.

63 'a strange coming and going of feet': Schreiner, Olive.
(1883). *The Story of an African Farm*. 2001, Johannesburg:
Ad Donker, p. 23.

63 'I'll have no tramps sleeping on my farm': Ibid, p. 44.

63 'Four wax-lights carried before me': De Quincey, *Confessions
of an English Opium-Eater*. pp. 150–151.

64 'the road unspooling': Galgut, Damon. (1995). *The Quarry*.
London: Viking, p.11.

64 'When he first started walking': Galgut, 'The Follower',
unpublished draft, p. 17.

65 'I must teach him': Galgut, Damon. (1988). *Small Circle of
Beings*. Johannesburg: Lowry, p. 77.

65 'I still think of him': Ibid, p. 108.

65 'he's learned to recognize other walkers': Galgut, 'The
Follower', unpublished draft, p. 18.

65 'As he comes to the crest of a hill': Galgut, 'The Follower',
in *In a Strange Room*, p. 3.

65 'with a curious formality': Ibid, p. 5.

65 'Then we can plan': Ibid, p. 22.

66 'Even here in South Africa': Ibid, p. 25.

66 'it turns out he hasn't found out': Ibid, p. 22.

67 'I could think of little other': Galgut, 'Lovers', in Small Circle of Beings, pp. 151–154.

67 'it seemed that, in my then peculiar mental state': Poe, Edgar Allan. (1840). 'The Man of the Crowd', in *Tales of Mystery and Imagination*. 1971, London: Minerva, p. 106.

67 'It was well said of a certain German book': Ibid, p. 103.

67 'how secure have I felt': Sebald, WG. (2001). *Austerlitz*. Penguin, pp. 172–176.

68 'I had a fancy in my head': Dickens, Charles. (1861). 'Night Walks', in *The Uncommercial Traveller*. 1901, London: Chapman and Hall.

69 'stranger, passing fearfully through the streets': Vladislavi , Ivan. (2006). *Portrait with Keys*. Johannesburg: Umuzi, pp. 54–55.

69 'A walking tour should be gone upon alone': Stevenson, Robert Louis. (1876). 'Walking Tours', in *Virginibus Puerisque*. London: T Nelson.

69 'Let her go at her own pace': Stevenson, Robert Louis. (1879). *Travels with a Donkey in the Cévennes*. London: T Nelson.

71 'That is our affliction': Galgut, *Small Circle of Beings*, p. 77.

73 'Let's go through Georgia fast': O'Connor, Flannery. (1955). 'A Good Man is Hard to Find', in *A Good Man is Hard to Find*. 1968, London: Faber and Faber, p. 11.

73 'I wonder that you do not': Thoreau, Henry David. (1854). *Walden*. 1971, Princeton: Princeton University Press, p. 53.

74 'the surprises, liberations, and clarifications of travel': Solnit, *Wanderlust: A History of Walking*, p. 6.

74 'your other talents are worthless': Ventura, Michael. (1993, May 21–27). 'The Talent of the Room', *LA Weekly*.

74 'It is comforting to feel the old possessions': Woolf, 'Street Haunting', p. 29.

Seeing by Ear

83 Nixon signed into law: Feraca, Jean. (2006, October 11).
Interview with Stephen Kuusisto, *Here on Earth*, Wisconsin
Public Radio.
<http://wpr.org/webcasting/audioarchives_display.
cfm?Code=hoe>

Stepping into the Future

96 '43 per cent of South Africans live on less than R250 a
month': (2007, June 21). Development Indicators Mid-Term
Review, South African Government Information.
<http://www.info.gov.za/otherdocs/2007/
developmentindicator/index.html>

96 '14 million South Africans': (2009, April 15). 'Banking on
Food Security for SA's Hungry', *Good News*.
<http://www.sagoodnews.co.za/general/banking_on_
food_security_for_sa_s_hungry.html>

96 'the planet's fourth': Bloom, Kevin. (2009). *Ways of Staying*.
Johannesburg: Picador Africa, p. 74.

Walking to a New Rhythm

98 'I am growing weary of life in this jungle': Levin, Adam.
(2003). *The Wonder Safaris*. Cape Town: Struik, p. 10.

98 'A terrified crawl from the door of death': Levin, Adam.
(2005). *Aidsafari*. Cape Town: Zebra, p. xii.

98 De Maistre, Xavier. (1795). *A Journey Around My Room*.
2004, London: Hesperus Classics.

99 'the sole cause of man's unhappiness': Pascal, Blaise and
Houston, James M. (2006). *The Mind on Fire*. David C
Cook, p. 95.

99 Chatwin, Bruce. (1987). *The Songlines*. London: Jonathan
Cape.

99 Chatwin, Bruce. (1989). *What am I Doing Here?* London:
Jonathan Cape.

99   Chatwin, Bruce. (1988). *Utz*. London: Jonathan Cape.

99   'The official reasons were': Koval, Ramona. (2001, February 25). 'The Truth of a Character: Shakespeare on Chatwin', *Perth Writers Festival.*
<http://www.abc.net.au/arts/books/stories/s424261.htm>

102 'a daily casualty toll higher than the killings in Iraq': Jasson da Costa, Wendy. (2006, May 31). 'SA roads a "war zone,"' *Daily News.*
<http://www.dailynews.co.za/index.php?fSectionId=499&fArticleId=3270757>

102 'After everything I've battled': Levin, *Aidsafari*. p. 108.

102 'diamond-shaped building of reflective glass': Honeyman, Janice. (1986). *Joburg Follies*, Market Theatre.

103 Matisyahu, (2005). 'Lord Raise Me Up', on *Live at Stubbs.* Sony.

103 Levin, Adam. (2005). *The Art of African Shopping*. Cape Town: Struik.

104 'grim concrete phallus of a tower downtown': Levin, 'La Zone Francophone', in *The Wonder Safaris*, p. 203.

105 'Only they don't walk': Ibid, p. 207.

105 'my father went to great lengths': Levin, *Aidsafari*, p.191.

105 'I think you should go and walk today': Levin, 'The Emperor and the Veils', in *The Wonder Safaris*, p. 89.

105 'I slipped quickly into the maze of streets': Ibid, p. 91.

105 'Not to find one's way in a city': Benjamin, Walter, quoted in Solnit, Rebecca. (2005). 'Open Door', in *A Field Guide to Getting Lost.* New York: Viking, p. 6.

105 'I walked alone as much as possible': Levin, 'The Emperor and the Veils', in *The Wonder Safaris*, pp. 92–93.

106 'own nothing and share everything': Levin, 'Hanging with the Hadzabe', in *The Wonder Safaris*, p. 34.

106 'We wake the clan': Ibid, p. 42.

Walking into Dance

109 'Our street was littered with broken bottles': Nicol, Mike. (2001). *Sea-Mountain, Fire City*. Cape Town: Kwela, p. 35.

110 'Something had come to an end': Ibid, p. 46.

111 'Most of the new inhabitants': Ibid, p. 43.

112 'they revved their cars': Ibid, p. 127.

114 'I no longer wanted to walk through the streets of Muizenberg': Ibid, p. 43.

114 'Graffiti defaced the coastal path': Ibid, p. 41.

114 'The southeaster is a phenomenon': Ibid, pp. 151–152.

115 'A heavy rain came on': Wordsworth, William and Dorothy. (1935). *The Early Letters of William and Dorothy Wordsworth (1787–1805)*, edited by Ernest de Selincourt. Oxford: Clarendon, p. 290.

117 'A discussion document from the City Council': 'Integrated Transport Plan 2006–2011', City of Cape Town. <http://www.capetown.gov.za/en/ITP/Documents/ITP_summary.pdf>

120 'Unless the past and the future': Le Guin, Ursula. (1974). *The Dispossessed*. London: Victor Gollancz, p. 153.

Grace Notes

127 'victims in possession of a firearm': Altbeker, Antony. (1998). 'Guns and Public Safety: Gun-Crime and Self-Defence in Alexandra and Bramley, January–April 1997'. Johannesburg: Gun Free South Africa.

Inside Out

133 Armah, Ayi Kwei (1969). *The Beautyful Ones Are Not Yet Born*. Collier.

134 'Africanized *Bladerunner* setting west of Grey Street': Reid, Donald. (2005). *The Rough Guide to South Africa*. London: Rough Guides.

135 'whose bodies follow the thicks and thins': De Certeau, Michel. (1984). 'Walking in the City', in *The Practice of Everyday Life*, translated by Stephen R Randall. Berkeley, Calif: University of California Press, p. 93.

137 'An architect built a cluster of office buildings': Roger von Oech's *Creative Whack Pack* – card 31.

138 'the thirst for lavish spectacle': Pather, Jay. (2004, April 23). 'Flexing imagination', *Mail & Guardian*.

139 'I wanted to capture the combination of dread': Robertson, Heather. (2002, April 14). 'Space Explorer', *Sunday Times*.

140 'On first visiting Hillbrow': Mpe, Phaswane (2005). 'On the Hillbrow Tower', in Terry Kurgan and Jo Ractliffe (eds), *Johannesburg Circa Now*. Johannesburg: Terry Kurgan and Jo Ractliffe, p. 54.

140 'The Dev': Pather, Jay. (2005). 'Hotel', in *Johannesburg Circa Now*, p. 56.

Mom's Taxi

148 'from safety to safety': Van Niekerk, Marlene. (1999). 'Take your body where it has never been before', in Ivan Vladislavi and Hilton Judin (eds), *Blank_ Architecture, Apartheid and After*. Rotterdam: NAi, (no page numbers).

Shabbat in Glenhazel

163 'The walking classes': Prabhala, Achal. (2008). 'Yeoville Confidential', in Sarah Nuttall and Achille Mbembe (eds), *Johannesburg: Elusive Metropolis*. Johannesburg: Wits University Press, pp. 309–310.

163 'the current escalation of violent predatory crime': Steinberg, Jonny. (2007, July 6). 'What murders mean for the street', *Business Day*.

165 'the seedbed': Mendelsohn, Richard and Shain, Milton. (2008). *The Jews in South Africa*. Johannesburg: Jonathan Ball, p. 32.

165 'I round the corner': Gerber, Chandrea. (2003). Unpublished essay. Travel Writing class, University of the Witwatersrand.

(in brackets)

167 *'saamgekoek'*: Van Niekerk, Marlene. (1994). *Triomf*, translated by Leon de Kock. 1999, Johannesburg: Jonathan Ball.

168 'a quick step pleasure': De Kock, Leon. (1997). 'Quick Remedy', in *Bloodsong*. Cape Town: Snailpress, p. 38.

169 'We streamed': De Kock, Leon. (1997). 'Nights I Remember', in *Bloodsong*, pp. 9–10.

169 'I am left with the unspeakable burden': De Kock, 'The Closing', in *Bloodsong*, p. 13.

169 'As I came to feel': Johnson, Don Hanlon. (1994). *Body, Spirit and Democracy*. Berkeley, Calif: North Atlantic, pp. 4–5.

170 Maturana, Humberto, with Gerda Verden-Zöller. (1996). *Origins of Humanness in the Biology of Love*, edited by Pille Bunnell. Exeter: Imprint.

171 'We have this growing phenomenon': Singiswa, Sipho. (2004). Unpublished interview.

173 'abandoned to the hungry but immobile petrol queues': De Kock, Leon. (2003, January 19). 'Bob's your uncle', *Sunday Times*.

174 'had no peace in all my bandit life': Sillitoe, Alan. (1959). *The Loneliness of the Long-Distance Runner*. 1966, London: Longman, p. 190.

174 'Operating never wearies him': McEwan, Ian (2005). *Saturday*. London: Vintage, p. 11.

175 'he is freed from thought': Ibid, p. 23.

175 'what we're really digging up': Cooke, Rachel. (2008, May 25). 'I used to feel like people were trampling over me to get to my husband. I had print marks on my body', *Guardian*.

175 'four thousand straight days in all kinds of weather': Auster, Paul and Wang, Wayne (dirs). (1995). *Smoke*. Miramax.

176 'I have gone to the edges': De Kock, Leon. (2006). *gone to the edges*. Pretoria: Protea, p. 9.

Metal and Flesh

193 'civilising influence': Kuusisto, Stephen. (1998). *Planet of the Blind*. New York: Dial, p. 150.

193 'Pedestrians are a problem': *Arrive Alive*.
<http://www.arrivealive.co.za/viewtopic.asp?topicid=392>

194 'a reckless pace': 'The history of road safety', *Cardiff Council Road Safety*.
<http://www.roadsafety.cardiff.gov.uk/about-us/history>

194 traffic accidents will become the third leading cause of death: Honoré, Carl. (2004). *In Praise of Slowness: Challenging the Cult of Speed*. 2005, New York: HarperSanFrancisco, p. 8.

194 33 513 fatal injuries registered: Donson, Hilton (ed). (2008, November). 'A Profile of Fatal Injuries in South Africa: Ninth Annual Report 2007 of the National Injury Mortality Surveillance System', MRC/Unisa Crime Violence and Injury Lead Programme.
<http://www.mrc.ac.za/crime/nimms_rpt_Nov08.pdf>

195 South Africa is number one in road deaths: Carte, David. (2008, October 15). 'SA's murder rate lags. Is this an error by the *Economist*?' Carte Blanche, *Moneyweb*.
<http://www.moneyweb.co.za/mw/view/mw/en/page663?oid=230480&sn=Detail>

195 Vanderbilt, Tom. (2008). *Traffic*. Toronto: Knopf.

Footing with the Ancestors

197 off to buy an electricity card: Glyn, Patricia. (2006). *Footing with Sir Richard's Ghost*. Johannesburg: Sharp Sharp, p. 86.

197 'told me their story': Ibid, p. 88.

197 'Several kilometres later it emerged': Ibid, p.144.

198 'It was clear within seconds that he was deranged': Ibid, p. 114.

198 'an emaciated brown puppy grubbing for scraps': Ibid, p. 26.

199 'At about the same time that Ffyona Campbell': Stone, Maureen. (2002). *Black Woman Walking*. Bournemouth: BeaGay, p. 3.

199 Campbell, Ffyona. (1995). *On Foot Through Africa*. London: Orion.

199 'wizened old men who gave me permission': Glyn, p. 159.

199 'For the two African women walking': Campbell, pp. 3–4.

201 'Karen Blixen put it so well': (2009, September 6). *Who Do You Think You Are?*, SABC2.

201 'a song of Africa': Blixen, Karen (Isak Dinesen). (1937). *Out of Africa*. 1954, London: Penguin, p. 75.

202 'clerical gentleman of my after acquaintance': Glyn, p. 169.

202 'Tim greeted me with bloodied hands': Ibid, p. 270

202 'we had come so many thousand miles to see': Ibid, p. 297.

203 'As we stood to admire': Ibid, p. 311.

203 'Crept up to the last bush': Ibid, p. 314.

203 'Elation and triumph': Ibid, p. 310.

203 'what I usually do when I'm sad': Ibid, p. 317.

205 'Welcome to Hwange National Park': Ibid, p. 266.

206 'I've just had a visit': Ibid, p. 287.

207 Poussin, Alexandre and Poussin, Sonia. (2009). *Africa Trek: In the Footsteps of Mankind – From the Cape of Good Hope to Mount Kilimanjaro*. Johannesburg: Jacana.

207 Poussin, Alexandre and Poussin, Sonia. (2008). *Africa Trek II: From Mount Kilimanjaro to the Sea of Galilee*. Portland: Inkwater.

From the Margins

210 'One of the most devastating': Bremner, Lindsay. (1999). 'Crime and the emerging landscape of post-apartheid Johannesburg', in Ivan Vladislavić and Hilton Judin (eds),

Blank_ Architecture, Apartheid and After. Rotterdam: NAi, (no page numbers).

214 'big-clouded winters': Watson, Stephen. (2000). 'Coda', in *The Other City: Selected Poems 1977–1999*. Cape Town: David Philip, p. 23.

217 'is aimed at a customer prepared to pay': Masango, David. (2007, October 31). 'Khayelitsha Express to reduce travelling time'. *BuaNews*.

218 'the colonial template provided a basis': Davis, Mike. (2006). *Planet of Slums*. New York: Verso, p. 96.

218 'The stewards wait outside': *Friends of the Rail Forum*. (2007, November 16). 'More about the Khayelitsha Express'. <http://www.friendsoftherail.com/phpBB2/viewtopic. php?f=144&t=967>

218 'A total of 22 security guards': Blits, *Media24*, quoted (2008, January 3) on *Friends of the Rail Forum*.

Looking for Markers

219 'I lovd this solitary disposition': Clare, John. (1983). *John Clare's Autobiographical Writings*. Oxford: Oxford University Press, pp. 33–34.

222 '350 in mass sex orgy!': quoted in Gevisser, Mark. (1994). 'A Different Fight for Freedom', in Mark Gevisser and Edwin Cameron (eds), *Defiant Desire*. Johannesburg: Ravan, p. 30.

227 'To be gay and cruise': White, Edmund. (2001). *The Flâneur*. London: Bloomsbury, p. 145.

227 'most people, straight and gay': Ibid, p. 147.

227 'were located on the same floor': Heyns, Michiel. (2006). 'On Graciousness and Convenience: Cape Cottaging 1960 to c1980', in Stephen Watson (ed.), *A City Imagined*. Johannesburg: Penguin, p. 33.

228 'The big trick was': Ibid, p. 39.

228 'there can be few activities on earth': Ibid, p. 37.

230 'these words': De Certeau, Michel. (1984). 'Walking in the City', in *The Practice of Everyday Life*, translated by Stephen R Randall. Berkeley, Calif: University of California Press, p. 104.

230 De Villiers, Phillippa Yaa. *Taller than Building*. (2006). Cape Town: Community Publishing Project.

These Feet

231 'Did you know': Pollack, Sydney (dir). (1985). *Out of Africa*. Universal.

231 'People observe their feet': Robinson, Jeffrey C. (1989). *The Walk*. Norman, Okla: University of Oklahoma Press, p. 8.

231 'they seemed to be almost out of sight': Carroll, Lewis. (1865). *Alice's Adventures in Wonderland*. 1932, London: Macmillan, p. 26.

231 'These hands remember': Xaba, Makhosazana. (2005). 'These Hands', in *These Hands*. Elim Hospital: Timbila Poetry Project, p. 10.

235 'The fear of being published': Xaba, Makhosazana. (2008). 'Fear', in *Tongues of their Mothers*. Scottsville: University of KwaZulu-Natal Press, p. 4.

237 'I wished we'd run the Soweto marathon together': Xaba, 'Cotton Socks', in *Tongues of their Mothers*, p. 34.

237 'It took the harbour walk': Xaba, 'The Brown Pelican', in *These Hands*, p. 22.

238 'This beach haunts': Xaba, 'This Beach', in *Tongues of their Mothers*, p. 7.

238 'I am in Wintersrand in winter': Xaba, 'Winter in Wintersrand', in *Tongues of their Mothers*, p. 46.

238 'The sun that stayed unseen since morning': Xaba, Send me a Sign', in *Tongues of their Mothers*, p. 30.

238 Jabavu, Noni. (1960). *Drawn in Colour*. London: Murray.

238 Jabavu, Noni. (1982). *The Ochre People*. Johannesburg: Ravan.

238 'which, I was to learn in years to come': Jabuva, Noni. (1977, February 9). 'Smuts and I', *Daily Dispatch*.

239 'the peripatetic print of my feet': Jabuva, Noni. (1962, March). 'From the Editor's Desk', *New Strand*, p. 323.

239 'Galaxy ... A name I'll not exclude': Jabavu, Noni. (1977, November 25). 'What's in a name?', *Daily Dispatch*.

239 'Returning now two decades later': Jabavu, Noni. (1977, June 1). 'Not the sound of music', *Daily Dispatch*.

239 'Travelling is in fact very upsetting for a woman': Jabavu, Noni. (1977, April 20). 'Travel confuses the mind', *Daily Dispatch*.

239 'Although she is black she is very European': Xaba, Makhosazana. (2006). Jabavu's Journey. Unpublished MA thesis, University of the Witwatersrand, p. 81.

240 'Where's the cream': Ibid.

240 'When I decided to write': Xaba, Makhosazana. (2008, July 4). 'A Paragraph on Noni Jabavu', *Book SA*.

240 'Women's lives provide a window': Xaba, Jabavu's Journey, p. 7.

Two Tails

242 'In my neighbourhood': University of Southern California. (2004, May 17). *Writing L.A.: 'Reading L.A.'*. <http://www.researchchannel.org/prog/displayevent.aspx?rID=3362>

242 'the dog is the perfect compromise': Robinson, Jeffrey C. (1989). *The Walk*. Norman, Okla: University of Oklahoma Press, p. 88.

243 'There is no delight like': Lydon, Christopher. (2000, July 10). *Why We Walk*, Interview with Rebecca Solnit, *WBUR: The Connection*.

248 'There is no point in going all the way': *EDGE (Environment and Dog Group of Emmarentia)*. <http://www.dogwalkers.co.za/>

Foreign Streets

250 'the ghosts of cappuccinos past': Prabhala, Achal. (2008). 'Yeoville Confidential', in Sarah Nuttall and Achille Mbembe (eds), *Johannesburg: Elusive Metropolis*. Johannesburg: Wits University Press, p. 307.

251 'I realise that I owe this happy existence': Prabhala, Achal. (2005, August 16). 'Ode to my Yeoville', *Mail & Guardian*.

251 'Civilians have done me no harm': Prabhala, *Elusive Metropolis*, pp. 308–309.

255 the challenge of getting around Joburg: Czeglédy, André P. (2004). 'Getting Around Town: Transportation and the Built Environment in Post-Apartheid South Africa', *City & Society*, Vol. 16, No. 2, pp. 63–92.

256 The effect of walls that are meant for insulation: Czeglédy, André P. (2003). 'Villas of the Highveld: A Cultural Perspective on Johannesburg and its "Northern Suburbs"', in Richard Tomlinson, Robert A Beauregard, Lindsay Bremner and Xolela Mangcu (eds), *Emerging Johannesburg*. New York: Routledge, pp. 21–42.

260 'competing logics': Murray, Martin J. (2008). *Taming the Disorderly City*. Cape Town: UCT Press, p. 126.

261 fortified enclaves and edge cities: Caldeira, Teresa PR. (2000). *City of Walls*. Berkeley, Calif: University of California Press, pp. 256–291.

261 Perry, Alex. (2008). *Falling off the Edge*. London: Macmillan.

261 'violence might be half the point': Crwys-Williams, Jenny. (2009, February 16). Interview with Alex Perry, on *The Book Show*, Radio 702.

262 Scorsese, Martin (dir). (2003). *Gangs of New York*. Miramax.

264 Obama, Barack. (2008). *Change We Can Believe In*. New York: Three Rivers.

267 Johnston, Nicole and Wolmarans, Riaan. (2008, May 18). 'Xenophobic violence grips Johannesburg', *Mail & Guardian Online*.

On Fairways and Bunkers

273 'the golfer plays': Woolf, Virginia. (1930). 'Street Haunting', in *The Death of the Moth and Other Essays*. 1942, London: Hogarth, p. 19.

274 'brand's core market': Jackson, David. (2009, June 3). 'Hotel opens doors', *Business Day*.

274 'a kind of inspired inertia': Nicol, Eric and More, Dave. (1983). *Golf: The Agony and the Ecstasy*. Robson, quoted in Exley, Helen. (1995). *A Good Walk Spoiled!* (no page numbers). Watford: Helen Exley Giftbooks.

276 'is played mainly': Bobby Jones, quoted in *A Good Walk Spoiled!*.

280 'By the time you can afford': Fredericks, Vic. *For Golfers Only*. New York: Frederick Fell, quoted in *A Good Walk Spoiled!*.

281 'if a ball comes to rest', quoted in *A Good Walk Spoiled!*.

282 'I can see that golf': Dunn, Seymour. (1953). *The Complete Golf Joke Book*. New York: Stravon, quoted in *A Good Walk Spoiled!*.

For Life

289 'Have you been walking long?' Stone, Maureen. (2002). *Black Woman Walking*. Bournemouth: BeaGay, p. 10.

289 'Walking away from war zones': Ibid, p. 26.

291 'The word means turning around with': Hillman, James and Ventura, Michael. (1992). *We've Had a Hundred Years of Psychotherapy and the World's Getting Worse*. New York: HarperCollins, p. 99.

291 Bös, Klaus. (2004). *Walking and Light Running*. Munich: Gräfe und Unzer.

293 'I wanna get married': McKay, Nellie. (2004). *Get Away from Me*. Columbia Records.

Guiding Eyes
294 'like a person who looks': Kuusisto, Stephen. (1998). *Planet of the Blind*. New York: Dial, p. 13.
296 'boot camp': Ibid, p. 151.
296 'canine kibbutz': Kuusisto, Stephen. (2006). *Eavesdropping*. New York: Norton, p. 155.
297 'They were asking their father': Ibid, p. 54.
297 'intelligent disobedience': Kuusisto, *Planet of the Blind*, p. 150.
300 dogs remind us: Junod, Tom. (2003). 'Dog Years', in Claudia Kawczynska and Cameron Woo (eds), *Dog is My Co-Pilot*. New York: Three Rivers, p. 273.
300 'A new dog': Jong, Erica. (2003). 'A Woman's Best Friend', in *Dog is My Co-Pilot*, p. 51.

When the Meter is Off
306 'isolated mountain getaway': *WhereToStay*. <http://www.wheretostay.co.za/kzn/mi/accommodation/geluksburg.php>
306 'many paths for mountain walks': *Accommodation direct*. <http://www.durban-direct.com/geluksburg/info'
306 '2 things in Geluksburg': *geckogo!* <http://www.geckogo.com/Travel-Tips/Africa/type/Local-Customs/>

From March to Parade
321 'I am black and I am gay': Nkoli, Simon, quoted in Ditsie, Beverly Palesa. (2006). 'Today we are making history', in Shaun de Waal and Anthony Manion (eds), *Pride: Protest and Celebration*. Johannesburg: Jacana, p. 19.

322 'When I took part': Bruce, David. 'It was a way for me to challenge my own discomfort', ibid, pp. 44–45.

324 'The Police Commissioner came': Adriao, Dennis. 'The Police Commissioner told us that there were no moffies in the police force', ibid, pp. 92–94.

324 'I made a point': 'Beryl'. 'A turning point in my life', ibid, p. 49.

325 'I wouldn't miss it': *Citizen* (1998, September 28), quoted in ibid, p. 107.

325 'All we were asking:' Somerville, Daniel. 'It's very easy to criticise the organisers of Pride, and very difficult to pull off the parade', ibid, p. 136.

326 'ambulatory ghetto': De Waal, Shaun and Manion, Anthony. 'Introduction', ibid, p. 8.

326 'the mainstreaming of gay pride': De Waal, Shaun. 'Let's have at least one revolution we can dance to', ibid, p. 118.

327 'I was shown on TV': Ditsie, Beverly Palesa. 'Today we are making history', ibid, pp. 19–20.

328 'killjoy queer politicos': De Waal, Shaun. 'Let's have at least one revolution we can dance to', ibid, p. 119.

329 'as a tribute to one of its finest sons': Sharp, Roderick. Excerpts from speech given at the dedication of the Simon Nkoli Corner, Pride 1999, ibid, p. 122.

329 'gay group': Mokgethi, Paul. 'Those were our first Pride marches', ibid, pp. 24–25.

About the author

Andie Miller started out professional life as an actress. From 1993 to 2007 she worked for the Centre for the Study of Violence and Reconciliation as resource centre manager and webmaster. In 2006 she received the Mondi Shanduka Newspaper Award for creative journalism, and in 2009 the Wits Ernst van Heerden Creative Writing Award for *Slow Motion*. She is a graduate of the Wits MA in writing programme.